Fiji Before the Storm

Fiji Before the Storm

elections and the politics of
development

Brij V. Lal

Australian
National
University

E PRESS

ANU
E PRESS

Published by ANU E Press
The Australian National University
Canberra ACT 0200, Australia
Email: anuepress@anu.edu.au
This title is also available online at http://epress.anu.edu.au

---

National Library of Australia Cataloguing-in-Publication entry

Title: Fiji before the storm : elections and the politics of development / Brij V. Lal, editor.

ISBN: 9781922144621 (pbk.) 9781922144638 (eBook)

Notes: Previously published: Canberra : Asia Pacific Press, 2000.
          Includes bibliographical references and index.

Subjects: Constitutional law--Fiji.
          Fiji--Politics and government--20th century.
          Fiji--Economic conditions.

Other Authors/Contributors:
          Lal, Brij V.

Dewey Number: 320.99611

Cover photo courtesy of AP Photo/Edward Wray.

First published by Asia Pacific Press, 2000
This edition © 2012 ANU E Press

Contents

Tables and figures

Tables

Symbols used in Tables

n.a.   not applicable
..   not available
-       zero
.   insignificant

Figures

Glossary

ACIAR	Australian Centre for International Agricultural Research
ACP	African, Caribbean and Pacific
ADB	Asian Development Bank
ALTA	Agricultural Landlord and Tenant Act
ALTO	Agricultural Landlord and Tenants Ordinance
ANC	All National Congress
ATA	Alternative Trade Arrangements
AV	Alternative Vote
BLV	Bose Levu Vakaturaga or Great Council of Chiefs
CAP	Common Agricultural Policy
CDF	Commodity Development Framework
CEDAW	Convention on the Elimination of Discimination Against Women
CGE	Central Government Expenditure
CLFS	Commercial Loans to Fijian Scheme
CDA	Christian Democratic Alliance
COIN	Coalition of Independent Nationals
CPO	Central Planning Office
CRC	Cooperative Resesarch Centre for Sustainable Sugar Production
CSIRO	The Commonwealth Scientific and Industrial Research Organisation
DMDP	Viti Levu Dynamic Multiracial Democratic Party
DP7	Seventh National Development Plan
DP8	Eighth National Development Plan
DP9	Ninth National Development Plan
EC	Earth Charter
EEC	European Economic Community
EEZ	Exclusive Economic Zone
EIMCOL	Equity Investment Management Company Limited
EU	European Union
FAB	Fijian Affairs Board
FAD	Fish Aggregation Device
FAO	Food and Agricultural Organisation of the United Nations
FAP	Fijian Association Party
FEA	Fiji Electricity Authority
FEMM	Forum Economic Ministers Meeting
FFA	Forum Fisheries Agency
FFI	Fiji Forest Industry
FHC	Fijian Holdings Company Limited
FIS	Fiji Intelligence Security Service
FLP	Fiji Labour Party
FNP	Fijian Nationalist Party
FNPF	Fiji National Provident Fund
FSC	Fiji Sugar Corporation
FSR	Farming Systems Research
FSRC	Fiji Sugar Research Centre
FTIB	Fiji Trade and Investment Board
GATT	General Agreement on Tariffs and Trade

GDP	gross domestic product
GIS	Government Information Service
GVP	General Voters Party
HART	Housing Assistance and Relief Trust
ICM	International Catchment Management
ILO	International Labour Organisation
IMF	International Monetary Fund
IRM	Integrated Resource Management
IWRAM	Intergrated Water Resource Assessment and Management
JPSC	Joint Parliamentary Select Committee
LMC	Landell Mills Commodity
LUC	Land Use Commission
MAFF	Ministry of Agriculture, Forestry and Fisheries
MPI	Ministry of Primary Industry
NATCO	National Trading Corporation
NFP	National Federation Party
NLC	Native Land Commission
NLTB	Native Land Trust Board
NMA	National Marketing Authority
NVTLP	Nationalist Vanua Tako Lavo Party
PAFCO	Pacific Fishing Company
PANU	Party of National Unity
POTT	Party of the Truth
PRB	Public Rental Board
PSA	Fiji Public Service Association
RFMF	Republic of the Fiji Islands Military Forces
RFTP	Rural Fisheries Training Programme
RRRT	Regional Human Rights Education Resource Team
SCOF	Sugar Commission of Fiji
SEAPAT	South East Asia and the Pacific Multidisciplinary Advisory Team
SPARTECA	South Pacific Regional Trade and Economic Cooperation Agreement
SPC	South Pacific Commission
SPS	Special Preferential Sugar Agreement
SRRA	Strategic Regional Resource Assessment
SVT	Soqosoqo ni Vakavulewa ni Taukei
UGP	United General Party
UN	United Nations
UNDP	United Nations Development Programme
UNESCO	United Nations Educational, Scientific and Cultural Organization
USAID	United States Agency for International Development
USP	University of the South Pacific
VAT	value-added tax
VKB	Vola ni Kawa Bula
VLV	Veitokani ni Lewenivanua Vakaristo, or Christian Democratic Alliance
WTO	World Trade Organization
WUF	Western United Front

Contributors

Alumita Durutalo teaches in the School of Social and Economic Development at the University of the South Pacific and is pursuing graduate research focusing on indigenous Fijian political developments.

Brij V. Lal is Professor of History and Director of the Centre for the Contemporary Pacific at The Australian National University.

Padma Lal is a resource economist and currently Director of the Environment Program in the National Centre for Development Studies at The Australian National University.

Robert Nortron is a political anthropologist with long term interest in Fiji politics at Macquarie University.

Biman Prasad is an economist at the Fiji Centre of the University of the South Pacific at the Laucala Campus.

Sitiveni Rabuka, executor of the 1987 coups, is a former Prime Minister of Fiji whose partnership with Indo-Fijian leader Jai Ram Reddy, secured the passage of Fiji's 1997 constitution.

Chandra Reddy is a political and social activist and community organiser with longterm interest in issues of gender and politics in Fiji.

Teresia Teaiwa is a creative artist and scholar teaching Pacific studies at Victoria University of Wellington.

Joeli Veitayaki is a marine resource economist and currently co-ordinator of the ocean studies program at the University of the South Pacific.

Acknowledgments

This volume had its genesis in a series of seminars and workshops held at The Australian National University under the auspices of the Centre for the Contemporary Pacific and the National Centre for Development Studies. Mr Rabuka's paper was delivered at the Centre for the Contemporary Pacific and sponsored by the Senior Pacific Islands Visitor Scheme funded by the Australian Department of Foreign Affairs and Trade's ASP 2000 Scheme. Papers by Brij V. Lal, Robert Norton, Padma Lal, Joeli Veitayaki and Biman Chand and Chandra Reddy were presented at the Fiji Update organised by the two centres in Brisbane and Canberra. Teresia Teiawa and Alumita Durutalo presented their papers at an election seminar at the School of Social and Economic Development of the University of the South Pacific, Suva, Fiji. I am grateful to the authors for their contributions and especially for revising their papers to meet the deadline.

I am once again in Maree Tait's debt for her encouragement and support. She and Debra Grogan organised the workshops with characteristic efficiency and effortless grace. Tracey Hansen's expert editorial advice was invaluable in the final stages of manuscript preparation. *Vinaka Vakalevu* and *Dhanyabad*.

Brij V. Lal
Canberra, October 2000.

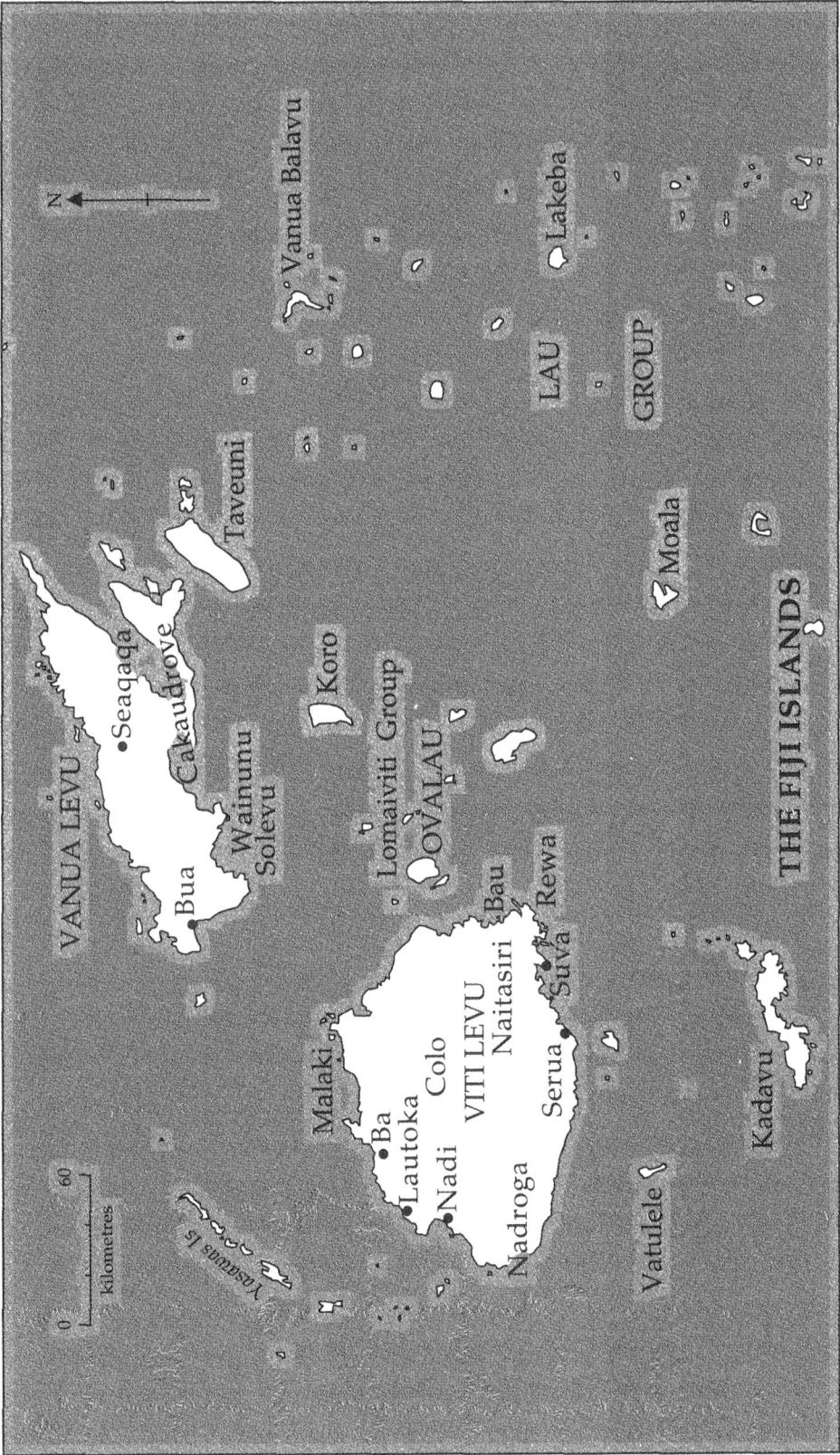

THE FIJI ISLANDS

VANUA LEVU

•Seaqaqa

Cakaudrove

Bua

Wainunu
Solevu

Taveuni

Koro

Lomaiviti Group

OVALAU

Bau

Rewa

Naitasiri

Suva

Serua

Vanua Balavu

Lakeba

LAU

GROUP

Moala

Malaki

Ba

Lautoka

Nadi

Colo

VITI LEVU

Nadroga

Vatulele

Kadavu

Yasawas Is

N

60

kilometres

0

chapter one

The future of our past

Brij V. Lal

January 1990. Fear and uncertainty stalk the country. The 1988 Sunday Observance Decree is in force, restricting recreational, sporting and nonessential activities. Public transport, shops, hotels, restaurants and cinemas operate on strict schedule. One can buy gas at gas stations, but not soft drink. Cremation requires a special police permit. Hindu and Muslim places of worship are torched and desecrated around the country, causing anguish and anger among citizens of all faiths opposed to the recent emergence of religious bigotry. The fragile fabric of multiculturalism is frayed at the edges. Cross-ethnic friendships formed over many years of working and living together are being tested. Divisions and suspicions run deep in a country already divided by culture, history, religion and language. Race as a 'fact' of life is on its way to becoming a 'way' of life.

The economy is teetering on the brink of collapse. Investor confidence has vanished, tourism is down, and capital is flying out of the country through dubious joint ventures and outright bribery. Fijian leaders, stunned by the strong condemnation of the coups by Australia and New Zealand, are exploring new trading and investment links in the Asian region. There is some success. Japanese companies are buying up big hotels and investing in resource-rich fisheries and timber industries. Malaysia has secured sole-source rights to supply Fiji's petroleum needs, and its Borneo Finance Group has begun a joint venture with the government-owned National Bank of Fiji. A Korean company is starting a citrus factory at Batiri in Vanua Levu. New tax-free zones have been established, giving companies exporting the bulk of their products lucrative long-term tax holidays and other preferential inducements.

There is no constitutional government in the country, which is run instead by an interim, unelected administration of former Alliance parliamentarians and other experienced technocrats. The 1970

(Independence) Constitution was overthrown in October 1987 when Sitiveni Rabuka declared Fiji a republic, severing the country's link to the Crown and the Commonwealth. Early efforts to restore Fiji to constitutional normalcy have come to nought, their stillborn reports gathering dust on the shelves. In September 1988, the interim cabinet set up a seventeen-member Constitution inquiry and advisory committee to recommend to the cabinet a Constitution which would 'provide adequate and full protection of the rights, interests and concerns of the indigenous Fijian people, and having regard to all the circumstances prevailing in Fiji.'

The committee consults the public in far from ideal circumstances. Freedom of movement and speech are restricted, symbolised powerfully by the presence of the security forces on the streets and roadblocks around the country. Its report recommends the political entrenchment of Fijian paramountcy through increased Fijian numbers in parliament, effective influence over recruitment and promotion in the public service and racially-weighted affirmative programs. Fijians will feel secure only if they dominate the parliament, the report argues. One side of the political and ethnic divide applauds the committee's vision for its cultural and political sensitivity to the aspirations of the indigenous community, while those on the other side reject it as myopic and counterproductive, an affront to values of human dignity and equality. Nonetheless, the committee's report forms the basis of the Constitution the president decrees on 25 July 1990. But the new Constitution is a deeply contested document. Its proponents want its permanent entrenchment while its opponents want it rejected outright. There is no middle ground. Fiji seems stranded in a cul-de-sac, a prisoner of its past. Emotions are high on both sides, the prospects of an amicable reconciliation bleak. No one knows when or if the country will be able to return to a semblance of its pre-coup normalcy.

January 1999. The East Asian boom, with all its promise of aid and investment, has gone bust and, with it, the ever implausible hope of an Asian-inspired economic miracle for Fiji. Traditional economic and diplomatic ties with neighbouring countries have been restored. Common sense and economic realities ensured that. The Sunday Decree now seems like a bad dream, as people laugh and play and work (and pray) freely on the day of the Sabbath. Freedom of movement and speech have returned. The much-predicted civil strife and upheaval, even a racial bloodbath, have mercifully not materialised. The 1990 Constitution, a source of much of the tension, has been replaced by another, more inclusive document, which itself is based substantially on the report of an independent, parliament-appointed Constitution review commission. Not perfect by any means—there is no such thing in existence anywhere—the new Constitution points Fiji to a new direction, toward inclusive, multiracial democracy which is respectful of international instruments on human, civil and political rights.

The journey has by no means been easy; there have been hiccups and detours along the way, and there are many pitfalls ahead. Still, Fiji has achieved an outcome few would have predicted in 1990.

Sitiveni Rabuka has been the man of the moment in Fijian politics over the last decade. In 1990, he was still in the army but his presence loomed menacingly on the national stage. He was slowly beginning to see himself as a man of destiny, a guardian of not only Fijian but of the national interest as well. In 1991, he left the army for a political career, and there was no turning back for him. The broadening experience of national public life was beginning to transform the once narrowly focused soldier into a leader with an awareness of wider obligations and responsibilities. In his contribution to this book, Rabuka tells his own story of growth and change. It is a partial account, to be sure, a glossy retrospective designed to accentuate his role and rationalise his actions; but it is no less valuable for that. Rabuka's recollections are also valuable for his account of his improbable but remarkably fruitful rapport with Jai Ram Reddy, the Indo-Fijian leader, who also deserves credit for his role in national reconciliation.

In May 1999, Fiji went to the polls under the new Constitution, producing a historic result. Four essays in this volume (Lal, Norton, Durutalo and Teaiwa) examine the election from a variety of perspectives. I emphasise 'variety' because an event such as an election in an ethnically divided society is always susceptible to multiple readings and conflicting interpretations. Nor, as editor, have I sought to impose any political or ideological 'spin' of my own. The pieces stand on their own, focused around the politics and the outcome of the elections, enabling the careful reader to make up her or his own mind. I provide a 'global' perspective on the issues and the politics of coalitions and of the campaigning which influenced the final outcome. Norton places the voting figures under microscopic scrutiny to read their implication for national political behaviour. He shows convincingly the increased Fijian support for the Fiji Labour Party in direct votes as well as through the preferences of its Fijian allies. But he also cautions that the 'interethnic convergence in shared material interests has ambiguous political implications. It brings the possibility of intensified ethnic conflict no less than a prospect for unity' (Norton Chapter 4:50).

Alumita Durutalo and Teresia Teaiwa alert the reader to issues which have not always received the attention they deserve. Durutalo provides, from a particular angle, an insight into the inner dynamics and subterranean undercurrents of indigenous Fijian politics. Class considerations and regional interests feature more prominently in Fijian political calculations than most outsiders often realise, issues which the colonially created myth of Fijian cultural unity strove to hide, she argues. Teaiwa's contribution on the politics of ambivalence on Rabi shows from close range how a small minority, on the margins of the nation's political consciousness, apprehends an event over which it has little influence but whose outcome will nonetheless determine its future.

The next four contributions remind us of other challenges which lie ahead for Fiji. Padma Lal looks at the future of the sugar industry, which contributes about F$230 million or about 43 per cent of the value of Fiji's agricultural production and around 40 per cent of the country's total export earnings. But the industry faces an uncertain future—preferential access under the Sugar Protocol of the Lomé Convention will have to be negotiated. The leases on which most of the sugar cane is grown are expiring and it is uncertain on what terms they will be renewed, if they are renewed at all. And then there are the problems of internal restructuring of the industry to reduce costs and increase productivity. Padma Lal identifies and discusses the policies needed to address these and other concerns, emphasising the importance of multidisciplinary research to underpin policy decisions. Joeli Veitayaki looks at the issues facing another major resource sector in Fiji: the inshore fisheries. He discusses the fate of previous government strategies to develop this sector and identifies the reasons for their failure. He is blunt in his prognosis. 'Government intervention' he says, 'should be selective and must recognise as its ultimate objective the handing over of all commercial functions to the private sector' (Veitayaki Chapter 8:148).

Chandra Reddy, herself a notable public figure in Fiji, alerts us to the challenges and adversities facing women in Fiji, and social attitudes and values which included 'very distinct and different social responsibilities assigned to men and women,' effects of the 'deeply rooted patriarchal systems in Fiji in which women are always relegated to the background,' and the 'result of religious and cultural attitudes that restricted and discouraged the potential contributions that women could make in positions of leadership' (Reddy Chapter 9:150). The situation has improved somewhat in recent years, and Reddy identifies the steps the Rabuka government planned to take to improve the lot of women. But there is still a long way to go, argues Reddy, in reforming attitudes and values that consign women to the subordinate sectors of Fiji society. In the final chapter, Biman Prasad identifies the economic challenges facing the new government. The new government has whetted the people's appetite for change, but its real challenge, Biman argues, will be to deliver on its state-backed social and economic promises within the context of increasing globalisation of the world economy.

The People's Coalition government was in power for a year when it was ousted in a coup by George Speight. Despite some notable achievements the government did not enjoy a smooth passage into office. It was beset with teething problems common to all new, inexperienced administrations. The problems were compounded for the Chaudhry cabinet which was not only new and inexperienced but also exceptionally weak. It was learning the responsibilities and challenges of government as it went along, on the job, with all the hiccups that the learning process involved. Its counterproductive tussle with the media was a case in point. The government saw the media as insensitive, arrogant and aiding the cause of its opponents (*Sunday Times* 28 August 1999). For its part, the media saw the government's attack as part of a strategy to divert attention away from the problems it was facing (*Fiji Times* 16 August 1999). Its handling of the issue of work permits for 'expatriate' workers in Fiji was another. Preference for locals is understandable, but as Mark Halabe, a garment manufacturer, put it, 'I don't enjoy financially hiring an expatriate manager but I would rather do that for the success of my business rather than hire somebody cheap who will destroy my company' (*Fiji Times* 22 July 1999).

The lack of political discipline among Labour's coalition partners was another problem for the government. The governing coalition comprised a number of parties with agendas and ambitions of their own, thrown together by a confluence of unlikely events rather than a deep sharing of a common platform. Some friction in the early stages was to be expected, but not active hostility. The Party of National Unity had two members in the cabinet, but the party leaders were among the government's strongest and most hostile critics and bitterly opposed to its policies, especially on land. Apisai Tora, multiracialist among other things, publicly opposed the idea of an Indo-Fijian as prime minister (*fijilive* 23 August 1999). Tora was subsequently removed as the head of the party, but he would re-emerge in another guise. Even some Fijian Association Party's members of parliament not in cabinet, spoke against the government. The effort to oust Adi Kuini Bavadra Speed as leader of the party was part of the strategy to destabilise the coalition and to harden Fijian feelings against it. The Veitokani Ni Lewenivanua Vakaristo (VLV) publicly rebuked the government over its handling of the expatriate work permit issue (*fijilive* 23 July 1999).

Saimone Kaitani's call for all Fijian parties in parliament to unite to oust the government, through protest marches and violence, suggested that he had not learnt the lessons of Fiji's recent political history. A spokesperson for the Soqosoqo ni Vakavuelewa ni Taukei (SVT) put it this way: 'It is important for the general public to know that the indigenous people are not happy with the present state of affairs. People don't really care that there was a democratically elected government under the 1997 Constitution that was duly formed after the May elections. The bottom line is that the bulk of the Fijians do not like being led by an Indian. If we are going to screw up then we'd rather screw up on our own, without another race's help. We're both capable of screwing up, but we think we'd rather do it on our own' (*fijilive* 3 October 1999).

'Screwing up' is what Fijian's opposed to the government began planning. Protest marches began in a small way, haphazard and disorganised until they came under the banner of a revived Taukei Movement led by Apisai Tora. Fijian civil servants and others grumbled about being marginalised; some feared exposure for incompetance or mismanagement; and some were worried their 'natural' right to accelerated promotion would be thwarted. They all joined the bandwagon opposed to the government. They achieved their goal of ousting the Chaudhry government on its first anniversary on 19 May 2000. The story of Fiji after that momentously tragic event will require another telling, although I have included an analysis of the Speight coups in this book with the knowledge that I do no more than scratch the surface. This book deals with events before the coup. Its principal significance is its historical value, a text which will have to be read to understand why things went wrong in Fiji, why yet another turning point was missed.

chapter two

The Fiji islands in transition
personal reflections

Sitiveni L. Rabuka

The years from 1987 to 1999 will no doubt be seen by historians writing about the Fiji Islands' political and social development as the Rabuka years. I am not vain enough, or naive enough, to expect that my story and interpretation of that period will prevail. Already a number of books and scholarly articles have been published about this crucial period in the Fiji Islands—some of them authored at the Australian National University. Naturally I don't agree with all the theories and conclusions.

As the person who was at centre stage from the coups through to the May elections, I welcome this opportunity to offer some personal observations and assessments. Let me take you back to my childhood and some of the people, events and circumstances that helped shape Rabuka the soldier, the military ruler, the politician, the practitioner of democracy and now Commonwealth mediator and peacemaker in ethnic conflict in the Solomon Islands.

I was born in a remote coastal village, Nakobo, in the province of Cakaudrove in Vanua Levu, the second largest island in Fiji. My parents were primary school teachers who in the 1950s and 1960s spent an average of two years on postings in village schools in the province. I am the eldest in my family and I have three sisters. Life for a Fijian boy in a Fijian village in the 1950s was simple and idyllic. I attended the village schools where my parents taught, helped grow vegetables, collect coconuts, cut firewood, weeded the lawn and did other daily chores. In my free time, there was a lot of playing on the beaches, swimming in the sea and the streams, spear fishing, wrestling, playing rugby football on the village green and cowboys and Indians in the bush. I was brought up as a Christian and my father was a lay preacher. In the village, after lunch on Sundays, bible school was compulsory for us children. I listened to my father's and uncles' sermons and decided I wanted to be a lay preacher, too.

A strong influence in my formative years was my uncle, Sakiusa, who bought me toy pistols, rifles and a mini soldier's uniform. He taught me the 'slope arms', 'order arms', and 'present arms' drill. At the age of ten, I told my teachers I wanted to be an army officer. My father did not agree with this ambition. At the age of nine, I left my parents and spent the next ten years in two boys' boarding schools. Life was strict and regimented in these institutions. At Queen Victoria School, we had military cadet training as part of our curriculum and this strengthened my desire to join the Fiji army.

I was head boy in my last year in school. The English principal of the school relied a lot on me to discipline the boys who were caught smoking, drinking or shirking garden work and classes. In my last year, I helped defuse a strike by senior students and was awarded the G.K Roth prize for leadership.[1] I was also a leading athlete and rugby player at school and when I left school, I represented Fiji in rugby in a tour of Wales and England in 1970, in athletics in the South Pacific Games in 1971 and as a decathlete at the Commonwealth Games in Christchurch in 1974.

Later in the army, physical fitness helped me set high standards for soldiers under my command and they respected me for that. I played sports with the soldiers and they often asked me for advice and help with their personal problems. I think I can truthfully state that I was a popular officer. I trained in New Zealand and Hong Kong on attachment with the 6th Gurkha rifles in 1974. In 1979 I attended the Indian Defence Staff College in Wellington in the state of Tamil Nadu and graduated with a masters degree in military studies from Madras University. In 1980, I was commanding officer of a Fiji peacekeeping force in South Lebanon and also Chief of Operational Plans for the UN interim force there. In 1983, after attending a course at the Australian Joint Services Staff College in Canberra, I was posted again as Chief of Military Personnel with the Multinational Force in Sinai.

My background—from isolated village to boarding school and thence to the military—was almost exclusively indigenous Fijian. I can see now how narrow and limiting this was. I do not denigrate my Fijian culture and origins. I love them dearly. But there is a larger world we must relate to. My experience overseas broadened my knowledge of life and other people. It sharpened my awareness of what could happen to countries or people of different religions, ethnic origins or cultures. When they are in conflict and unable to settle their differences peacefully, then a vicious circle of violence often erupts bringing untold suffering and tragedy to many ordinary people. In Lebanon and Sinai we were playing peacekeeping roles between nations and communities whose violent divisions seemed to have become unbridgeable. I learnt a lot not only about the role of the military in keeping the peace and law and order, but also about other people from different parts of the world and the complexity of the problems that they and their leaders faced. I became aware of the difficulties of building relationships of understanding and trust between people who have inflicted indiscriminate violence against each other. One lesson I learnt was that if you are in a position to influence the outcome of a situation of conflict that is likely to become violent, then you are obliged to do all you can to prevent violence.

That was the main reason I led the first bloodless coup in the Fiji islands on 14 May, 1987 to remove the coalition government led by Dr Timoci Bavadra's Fiji Labour Party from parliament. I had been privy to the plans of the nationalist Taukei movement that had formed after the victory of Dr Bavadra's party and I knew that the leaders of that movement were deadly serious about fomenting a violent campaign against the elected government. The indigenous Fijians are normally regarded as very friendly, accommodating and Christian in their attitudes. But I also knew what they are capable of when they feel threatened as a community and their emotions are aroused. And that was the situation after the defeat of the largely Fijian Alliance Party in April 1987. The Taukei movement was ready to violently oppose the Fiji military forces, whose then commander, Brigadier Ratu Epeli Nailatikau, had promised to the new government that it would not hesitate to use the military to put down any violent protest from the Taukei movement.

I did not agree with this decision because I believed if the mainly indigenous army was used against Fijians it would make matters worse. I came to the conclusion that it would be in the interest of national peace and security that the newly elected government (which I believe was not acceptable to the majority of indigenous Fijians), should be removed. I knew that a national Taukei plan for violent agitation in all the cities and towns was already in place and, having heard its leaders (some of whom were former military men with expertise in explosives and firearms), I knew that nothing was going to deter them from implementing their scheme to violently remove the government and stir up uncontrollable criminal violence. And so I acted. Many people today will still disagree with my judgement and the historic decision I took. But I am at peace with it. The history of Fiji would have been tragically different had I not lanced the boil.

The tension in the relationship between indigenous Fijians and our Indian population had been building up in the 1970s and 1980s. It was fanned by the racial nature of party political confrontation in parliament, and the preaching of the Fijian Nationalist Party. The Nationalists claimed that the Alliance government, led by Ratu Sir Kamisese Mara, had sold out indigenous Fijian interests at the 1970 constitutional talks on the eve of independence. There was a belief amongst indigenous Fijians that the Indian community, with their then majority in numbers and their dominance in the private sector, also wanted to politically control the nation. In 1982, a meeting of the Great Council of Chiefs in Bau had resolved that the 1970 Constitution be amended to increase the number of Fijian seats in parliament as a defence against the Indian 'threat.'

In the same year, Ratu Sir Kamisese Mara offered to discuss with the National Federation Party (NFP)—the main Indian political group—the idea of forming a government of national unity. But this was not accepted at the time by the leader of the opposition, Mr Jai Ram Reddy, because I think he felt the proposal was too vague. The emergence of the Fiji Labour Party (FLP) in 1985 with its multiracial platform did not dispel the Fijian belief in the Indian design for political domination, particularly when the FLP decided to form a coalition with the NFP to fight the 1987 general election.

At that time, I shared that belief. Although I understood that the Fiji Labour Party-National Federation Party coalition had won the 1987 general election fairly under the rules, that was not a matter that weighed much in the thinking of the leaders of the Taukei movement in 1987. They saw the new government as a vehicle for Indian domination. On the afternoon of 14 May 1987, I had a meeting with Fiji's media bosses to establish the new rules for the media after the coup, and this is part of what I said to them.

> It is your responsibility to pass on information, but be sure that none of the releases would inflame racial tension. As a Fijian, I am concerned about what the Fijian community can get up to. It would ruin the nation. What I have done this morning is a preemptive move to stop Fijian groups developing into terrorism or the Republic of Fiji Military Forces being used against the people.

I also said I would appoint a council of ministers drawn from the civilians, as a 'caretaker government', backed by the military, until a new Constitution was drawn up and a fresh election held under it. The Governor-General, Ratu Sir Penaia Ganilau, was to be re-appointed as Governor-General. I reassured the press that it would be free to publish the views of those who opposed the coup. The detained government leaders were to be released the next day and I added: 'They have done nothing wrong, and it is my responsibility to see they are comfortably looked after' (Thomson 1999:16).

The coup was seen in Fiji and overseas as not only a rape of democracy but also a racist anti-Indian act. For years after that, I was regarded as a 'racist', but this was what I said five days after the first coup in a radio broadcast

> To the Indian community I feel very deeply for your welfare. You belong here…You are part of our history and future. Please be assured that you have absolutely nothing to fear from this administration.

And this is what I said to the Indian soldiers under my command in September 1987

> To the Indian soldiers who are here, do not be alarmed or frightened about what I am saying. If you believe in me, work with me...We are fighting for the Fijians and not forgetting the welfare of other races in Fiji.

I was and I am still a Fijian nationalist in that I have a deep commitment to the welfare and interests of the indigenous Fijian people. I am also a firm believer in peaceful and harmonious co-existence between people of different cultures, religions and beliefs. My main concern from the beginning was—and still is—that in the Fiji Islands it is vitally important that the indigenous Fijians must feel politically secure. If indigenous Fijians do not feel secure, then it will be bad for ethnic relations and the government elected to power. If the Fijians feel secure, then other communities will also feel the same about their place and future in the Fiji Islands. In 1987, I saw these issues about security and identity predominantly from the indigenous Fijian standpoint. The Taukei movement in 1987 wanted to impose Fijian political power and preeminence regardless of what members of the deposed government and its supporters felt.

The Fijians had largely viewed the 1987 general elections result as a show of gross disrespect to them as the host community, because a Fijian-dominated Alliance government had been voted out of office by those who were regarded as *'vulagi'*, or guests. That was the political view of the situation from the Fijian cultural perspective and it does not sit well with the western democratic tradition that governments are elected and voted out of office by the will of the majority who, irrespective of their culture or history, are citizens with equal rights. In Fijian indigenous culture the concept of equal rights was foreign. It is the landowners and their chiefs who have predominant rights, which include the rights to assert what they believe belongs to them and to express that to others and the outside world. This belief also determines the attitude of most Fijians in the modern political arena. In other words, they believe the state should be under Fijian control, the national Constitution should express the values and symbols of Fijian culture and the citizens who are not of indigenous ancestry should understand and accept the Fijian attitude to legitimising institutions and social order in the nation. That may sound authoritarian and intolerant, but the indigenous Fijians also pride themselves on being accommodating, flexible and generous. If people who are not indigenous respect the Fijian view and develop a genuine sensitivity to the Fijian culture and the Fijian ways of accommodating the interests of others, then ethnic relations would have a very sound basis for development.

The victory of the FLP-NFP coalition in April 1987, with minority support of indigenous Fijians, was seen as not just a challenge but a threat to this Fijian belief. The extremists in the Taukei movement, as I have said earlier, were prepared to meet that threat with sustained and widespread violence. I conducted the coup to seal off that path and to move the country to a form of civilian constitutional rule that would be acceptable to the Fijians. The meeting of the Great Council of Chiefs five days after the first coup, on 20 May 1987, expressed the Fijian view and also endorsed the late Governor-General, Ratu Sir Penaia Ganilau's promise to move the nation cautiously towards a system of government that would be acceptable. At the time, it was hoped that what would be acceptable to the indigenous Fijian would be accepted by those who supported the deposed government. This was for the sake of returning Fiji to political stability, harmonious communal relationships and economic recovery. I subscribed to this view and maybe, in hindsight, I was very partisan and in a sense politically naive. However, in the circumstance of the time, no other view made sense to me. Acceptance of the view of members of the deposed government, that they had been unjustly deposed by a racist coup was out of the question and even the idea of accommodating them in the Governor-General's council of ministers was difficult for the Taukei movement to accept. Peter Thomson, the Secretary to the Governor-General described the situation after the coup very well.

> Spontaneous street violence spread to Nausori and Suva's surburbs, where mobs looted, assaulted and stoned people and property. That day's rioting was another confirmation that we were at the edge of a precipice of awful consequence. Up at Government House, the security briefing conveyed a message of incipient racial retribution and the reality of this threat and our duty to combat it underlaid all our efforts. For the duration of my time at Government House, the containment of the forces pushing Fiji towards that precipice assumed priority over all other issues and crises. I am happy for those who conclude the threat was over-stated. I don't believe it was, and it was the chief reason that, in spite of all he put awry in 1987, I recognised the willpower of Sitiveni Rabuka and the stop he put to overt communal violence in Fiji.

The objective of the 1987 coups as confirmed by the Great Council of Chiefs on 20 May 1987, was to change the Constitution in favour of the indigenous Fijians. It meant political control through an increase in the number of Fijian parliamentary seats, the protection of Fijian economic interests and provisions for affirmative action for indigenous Fijians to improve their position in education and commerce. The aim was to bring them on a par with other communities. It was also an assertion of the indigenous Fijian identity and the leadership role of the chiefs. Fijians, it was felt, held the key to political stability and economic development in the interest of all communities.

Ratu Sir Penaia Ganilau and Ratu Sir Kamisese Mara agreed with the Great Council of Chiefs' objectives in May 1987. But when the Deuba Accord was signed in September that year in a move to form a bi-partisan government there was no specific commitment, only a broad statement to review the 1970 Constitution. I learnt that deposed members of the Bavadra government were strongly opposed to the resolutions of the Great Council of Chiefs and my involvement in their discussions. If the deposed government had agreed that the Constitution would be reviewed and taken into account the resolutions of the Great Council of Chiefs, the Fiji military forces would have supported the government of national unity proposed under the Deuba Accord signed on September 24, 1987. That is why I took over the government again the next day. After a critical statement from the Queen, I received legal advice and decided to declare Fiji a Republic. It meant the end of the office of Governor-General and loss of membership of the Commonwealth. A new Interim Constitution was promulgated by decree on October 6.

In 1987, my view of politics and religion was simple. I believed then that if my Indian brothers and sisters could be converted to Christianity, then the relationship between the two main communities would be less tense, and we would have more in common. That is why I then favoured having Fiji declared a Christian state under the Constitution. My intention in 1987 was always to hand back political power to experienced civilian leaders, after ensuring that the objectives of the coups had been achieved. This I did after both coups—back to Ratu Sir Penaia Ganilau and Ratu Sir Kamisese Mara. I felt at ease after handing over the reins to those two chiefs in December 1987.

The 1990 Constitution

I supported the promulgation of the 1990 Constitution. I believed then that the Constitution had achieved the objectives of the coups as I contained all the measures that the Council of Chiefs and the great majority of Fijians wanted to be recognised and expressed. At the time I was not inclined to accept the criticism of the 1990 Constitution from outside Fiji, which seemed merely to mirror the Fiji Labour Party and National Federation Party positions. I felt that overseas critics, and especially the labour governments and trade unions in Australia and New Zealand, were interfering in Fiji's internal affairs and that they should exercise restraint in expressing views on a situation they did not understand very well. I believed the critics were trying to impose on the indigenous Fijian people western models and values of democratic government that were not acceptable to them and therefore inappropriate; but because of my growing belief that we had to find a way forward that would satisfy all the communities in Fiji, I came to regard the 1990 Constitution as an interim arrangement. It was to be a vehicle to get us back to parliamentary government, with the expected participation of the opposition parties. After the general election of 1992, we would then be in a position to review it. The 1990 Constitution had provisions at any rate requiring that it be reviewed within five years of the 1992 general election. I knew then that we would not be able to ignore the demands of the opposition parties once they were in the parliament.

Both NFP and Labour had participated in the 1992 general election for two reasons: to change the 1990 Constitution to make it acceptable to the Indian community, and to secure the renewal of the Indian tenants leases under the Agricultural Landlord and Tenants Act (ALTA) on satisfactory terms. The Fiji Labour Party, which had promised its supporters it would contest and win Indian communal seats and then boycott parliament, did an about-turn after the election and backed my appointment as prime minister by the first president of the Republic, the late Ratu Sir Penaia Ganilau.

I was by then the leader of the Soqosoqo ni Vakavulewa ni Taukei (SVT) Party founded by a resolution of the Great Council of Chiefs in June 1990, to be the main unifying political party for the indigenous Fijians. I had decided that if the gulf between the Fijian and Indian communities was to be closed and our differences reconciled, then I, as the person who had conducted the coups and widened that gap, should stay in the political arena and take a lead in the rebuilding of relationships. I had to take on the challenge of transforming attitudes and beliefs and accommodating interests on both sides, so we could arrive at a consensus. But after the 1992 general election, we had to tread cautiously because most of the members of the SVT were opposed to any significant changes to the 1990 Constitution. These people believed that the 1990 Constitution was the best for the indigenous Fijians and that it would be unwise to change it so soon after its promulgation. I had to proceed much more slowly than the impatient Fiji Labour Party wanted. That led to a rupture of the relationship between the SVT and the FLP which walked out of parliament in 1993, blaming me for breaking what they believed was an undertaking to immediately introduce the democratic Constitution they desired.

In the budget debate in 1992, I had proposed that my government and the opposition parties form a government of national unity. I felt changing the Constitution would be easier if the opposition came into the government. There was not much support for the idea from my caucus colleagues. The leaders of the Indian parties were also cautious, because there was a belief that government could use such a development as an excuse not to move on major changes to the Constitution. Nevertheless, I began informal meetings between myself, the leader of the opposition, Mr Jai Ram Reddy, and the Leader of the Fiji Labour Party, Mr Mahendra Chaudhry. This is how I recalled our first meeting on 24 December 1992, in my speech introducing the Constitution (Amendment) Bill about four and a half years later.

> We sat in my office and devoted our entire meeting to sharing our views and vision of the land that we share, the kind of country that we would like Fiji to be…We agreed that although as individuals, the people of Fiji belong to different ethnic groups, and whilst as communal groups we differed in our perception of the needs and interests of our communities, we believed nevertheless there was ample common ground to bind and unite everyone together. We all belong to this country, to this nation Fiji. We are one nation. We all want a better, secure future. We all want permanent peace for our country and its people. We all want to build a nation where each one of us, as individuals and a community, can freely develop and prosper, where we can all be happy and where there can be justice for all.

That informal meeting of the leaders evolved into a broader subcommittee of Cabinet, which agreed to terms of reference for the review of the 1990 Constitution. I want to digress a little here to say that at that time, a faction had developed in the SVT which was opposed to my leadership. It was led by the late Josevata Kamikamica, who I had defeated in the first caucus leadership vote after the 1992 general election. This group, in the presentation of the budget at the end of 1993, voted against it and forced us into another general election barely a year and a few months after the first one. This was the beginning of the break-up in the party I led. That group started the Fijian Association Party (FAP), now the largest Fijian party in parliament in seat numbers and in coalition with the Fiji Labour Party led by Prime Minister Mahendra Chaudhry.

To return to constitutional development, the Joint Committee of Cabinet, which included the opposition leaders, also agreed to the appointment of three members of the Constitution Review Commission and a constitutional adviser. And as you know, the Chairman was Sir Paul Reeves, former Governor-General of New Zealand; Tomasi Vakatora, an experienced former senior civil servant, senior minister and Speaker of the House under Ratu Sir Kamisese Mara's Alliance Government; and Professor Brij V. Lal, a Fiji-born academic. The constitutional adviser was Mrs Alison Quentin-Baxter, a very distinguished constitutional lawyer from New Zealand. We were fortunate to have such a good team who consulted widely in Fiji and overseas and produced a comprehensive and enlightening report with 694 recommendations.

The report was tabled in parliament in 1996 and a Joint Parliamentary Select Committee (JPSC) consisting of members from both sides of the house and the senate was appointed to study it and decide on the recommendations. I decided to be chairman of the committee at that stage of the negotiations because I believed I should steer the deliberations towards the consensus needed to take us to the drafting stage. There was strong dissent within my party to my involvement in the negotiations. It came from those who believed that accepting the changes recommended in the Reeves Commission report would mean political suicide for the SVT. They argued the Fijian people would not tolerate any drastic changes to the 1990 Constitution. I knew the risks, but I was convinced that what was more important was for us in the committee to provide collective leadership in steering the country toward a new constitutional settlement. I thought that if about half of Fiji's population (that is mainly the supporters of the opposition parties) did not regard the 1990 Constitution as their Constitution, then it could not be a sound basis for a democratic system of government to unite all the people of Fiji. My reading of the report of the Commission told me that not only had they done a thorough examination of all the relevant issues, but they had also provided very practical compromise recommendations for changes based on sound principles of law. All the interests of our different communities could be accommodated and expressed in the new vision of the Reeves report. I remember sharing with members of the Parliamentary Select Committee these words of Nobel Peace Prize winner, Archbishop Desmond Tutu

> Some people think reconciliation is a soft option, that it means papering over the cracks. But the biblical meaning means looking facts in the face and it can be very costly; it cost God the death of his own son.

Those words underscored what I felt about the reconciliation we had to go through. Our side had to be prepared to make sacrifices in negotiating a new Constitution which would meet the test of acceptability for all the communities in Fiji, and the international community, whilst strongly protecting the special position of the Fijians. I had to face the fact that many members of my party and even leading members of our side in the Joint Parliamentary Select Committee, did not fully share my view on the Reeves report. In meetings over a period of two months, we were able to agree to most of the recommendations of the report. We had with us then skilled Australian lawyer, Dennis O'Brien of Minter Ellison in Canberra, who drafted the new Constitution.

Whilst the Joint Parliamentary Committee sat, my caucus was also discussing the issues and I had to put my leadership on the line a number of times. Some of my Fijian members had taken the Reeves report to their local provincial councils and got them to pass resolutions either opposing or condemning it and favouring the retention of the 1990 Constitution without amendment. These developments were widely reported in the news media, creating the impression that the JPSC and Fijian politicians in favour of change were out of touch with grassroots feelings. There wasn't time to go to the people and fully explain the recommendations of the Reeves report or the work of the Commission. Because of the time limit placed on us by the 1990 Constitution, we had to complete the exercise, and get the Constitution Bill into parliament by June 1997.

The best way open to me for convincing my opponents in the party and the doubters in the Fijian community was to take the issue to the Bose Levu Vakaturaga, or Great Council of Chiefs, for the Chiefs' support. I thought there was no one better to put the case than the eloquent leader of the opposition, Mr Jai Ram Reddy. Inviting him to address the chiefs was in itself significant politically and was in keeping with the spirit of national togetherness we were trying to create. It was the first time an Indo-Fijian had made a speech to the Council. I quote part of what Mr Reddy said to the chiefs

> The Indians in Fiji, brought to these shores as labourers, did not come to conquer or colonise. We, their descendants, do not seek to usurp your ancient rights and responsibilities. We never have. We have no wish, no desire, to separate ourselves from you. Fiji is our home. Fiji is our only home. We have no other. We want no other. Our ancestors came to this land in search of a better life, in search of a future they dreamed of for their children and their children's children. Though they travelled to these islands long, long after your ancestors, surely the dreams and hopes of those who landed from the *Leonidas* were not that different from those who came ashore after the epic earlier voyages from the west. You are the chiefs of all the people of Fiji. The Indians of Fiji honour your place, and the place of your people, as the first inhabitants of Fiji. We seek not to threaten your security, but to protect it. We seek not domination; indeed, we cannot dominate: we are not the majority ethnic group in this multiracial nation—you are. What we seek is a partnership. We seek a country whose children of all races can grow up with deep understanding and respect for each other's cultures, languages and traditions. I am convinced the indigenous interests you have a solemn obligation to protect are in no way weakened under the arrangements we the members of the JPSC are proposing.

In an address to party supporters in Sydney on April 10 1999, Mr Reddy said this

> The memory of that meeting of the Great Council of Chiefs will remain with me to my dying day. All of us present had kept an appointment with history. The distance between us was closing and the future called.

Indeed, Mr Reddy's speech to the chiefs was a defining moment in our history and sealed the support of the Bose Levu Vakaturaga for the new Constitution. At the end of my speech in introducing the Constitution Amendment Bill on 23 June 1997, I said this

> Before concluding, Mr Speaker, I wish to particulary thank most sincerely, the members of my own party the Soqosoqo ni Vakaulewa ni Taukei, most of whom have had to shed our indigenous nationalism ideals and their separatism, and take on instead the most noble role of expanding our horizons to embrace the positive and all-embracing national patriotism for the good of this beloved country and all its people I will quote a verse from the Bible. As Paul wrote in his letter to the *Phillipians*, Chapter 3:13: 'Forgetting what is behind and straining toward what is ahead, I press on toward the goal for which God has called me heavenward in Christ Jesus'.

You know about the election results, how our SVT coalition with the NFP was decimated, and Labour and its partners won a landslide victory. The poetic irony is that Mr Reddy and I, the main architects of the 1997 Constitution, which was designed to bring about greater national unity, were essentially rejected by the voters. That was the price we had to pay for bringing in so much change in the process of Fiji's transition. Mr Reddy was probably punished by the Indians for getting too close to Rabuka, the coup-maker. My own SVT Party lost ground because it was seen as selling out the Fijians. But our multiracial vision for the country was right and I have no regrets about embracing it.

Labour Leader Mahendra Chaudhry was nominated as prime minister and duly appointed. That, of course, was another historic development. For the first time an Indo-Fijian had become head of government. Our new system of democracy was being tested to the full. Only a few years ago such an appointment would probably have taken us to the brink, and possibly beyond. Even now, there are those who are not comfortable with it—and indeed some who are vehemently opposed. We had some attempts to create civil unrest, but they came to nought. I understand there was an effort to persuade some army officers to intervene. The overtures were not well received. Within my own camp, defeated candidates started making nationalistic sounds similar to those of 1987.

But this time the circumstances were different. Many Fijian voters had deserted our party, so we could no longer claim to be the sole, authoritative voice of the indigenes. Other parties with significant Fijian backing had joined with Labour in government. To that extent the Constitution was successful in creating a viable multiracial administration. That was what it was designed to do. I had to explain that we would have been living a lie if we refused to accept the result of the election under the Constitution we had created and agreed to. We had declared that we were committed to its objectives. How could we turn around and reject it just because the elections had not gone in our favour?

The Constitution provides for winners and losers. We had lost and that was it. That was democracy and now it is at the centre of our arrangements for governance.

I vacated office and wished Mr Chaudhry and the new government well. Initially I had intended to be leader of the opposition. But following concern about my leadership, I decided to step aside. Then, surprisingly, I was appointed to the new post of chairman of the Great Council of Chiefs. This was a great honour, with heavy responsibilities. I tendered my resignation to parliament because I felt the Council chairman should be politically independent. Shortly afterwards, I was asked to become Commonwealth mediator to help restore peace and stability to the Solomon Islands, which have been gripped by ethnic tension and unrest. I am thankful to God that what I have learned about reconciliation and conflict resolution equipped me well for that task in the Solomons.

I want to end by briefly discussing my religion, for it has played a great part in whatever I have been able to achieve in bringing greater democracy and equality to Fiji. I am not—as some might think—a fundamentalist Bible basher. But I do have a deep belief in the teachings of Jesus Christ. He is my lord and my saviour and even though I fail Him often, I try hard to return to the fold and follow His way. My commitment to the Lord has strengthened me throughout my political life. I lean on Him to gain inspiration, to learn more about spreading goodwill, tolerance and understanding. There is a universal spirit of Christ which has a place and a voice in all religions. This is what I believe. I took great comfort during some of my most trying times in sharing with a multireligious, multiracial group of friends, brought together regularly in the name of Jesus. Among them I could express my innermost fears and thoughts away from the immediate pressures of politics. I went away from many of those gatherings with new resolve and with my spirits lifted. Those friends in Christ and many others from overseas continue to be a pillar of strength. When I was in the Solomons their thoughts and prayers were with me. I have no doubt whatsoever that this helped me achieve the first stage of my mission there. When I look back now to the defeat of the elections, and to what happened afterwards, I know that when you try to walk in faith you will be cared for and things will work out in the end, according to His will.

I hope this has widened your understanding of the Fiji Islands, their political and racial challenges and the significance of the Rabuka era.

Note

1   Roth, G.K. (1903–60) served as an Administrative Officer in Fiji in the 1920s, rising to become the Secretary for Fijian Affairs in 1954. He was the author of *Fijian Way of Life* (1953), Oxford University Press, Melbourne [Editor].

chapter three

A time to change
the Fiji general elections of 1999

Brij V. Lal

The 1990s has been a decade of unexpected political change in Fiji, confounding conventional wisdom and supposed understandings about power sharing arrangements in that troubled country. For the sheer momentum and unpredictability of events, it rivals the 1960s, Fiji's decade of decolonisation, a time of violence-threatening industrial strikes, keenly contested elections and by-elections, and tense conferences about constitutional systems suited to Fiji's multiethnic society. The 1990s too, Fiji's decade of progressive political democratisation, has had its tension and turbulence and false starts and extended detours as its people grappled with the unsettling aftermath of the coups and struggled to devise a constitutional order suited to its situation.[1]

The decade began on a divided note, as the architects of the coups of 1987 attempted to frame a Constitution to entrench Fijian political control within a nominally democratic framework. That goal was enshrined in an Interim Constitution promulgated on 25 July 1990. Contested and opposed by Indo-Fijians and others marginalised by it, and denounced by the international community affronted by its disregard for universal human rights conventions, the Constitution was reviewed by an independent commission five years later. The commission recommended a more inclusive, non-racial system of representation while protecting the legitimate interests and concerns of the different communities.[2] Two years later, most of the commission's recommendations, except for the reversal of the proportion of open and reserved seats, were incorporated in a new Constitution approved unanimously by parliament and, more significantly, blessed by the all-powerful Great Council of Chiefs. Within ten years, Fiji had traveled the gamut from coup to constitutionalism like few other countries.

In May 1999, Fiji went to the polls under the revised Constitution. 'Fiji's general elections now under way are expected to see the three-party coalition led by outgoing prime minister Sitiveni Rabuka emerge as the largest block in the new House of Representatives', wrote one respected observer after voting began, echoing virtually every observer of the Fijian scene. The report went on: 'The coalition conducted the most coherent campaign, making the most of the advantages of incumbency, and Rabuka was clearly the dominant figure in campaigning.'[3] The Fiji voters delivered a dramatically different verdict, electing by a landslide a newly formed, fractious 'People's Coalition' consisting of the Fiji Labour Party, the Party of National Unity (PANU) and the Fijian Association Party (FAP), with Labour winning 37 of the 71 seats in the House of Representatives, enough to govern alone. The other coalition of the Soqosoqo ni Vakavulewa ni Taukei (SVT), the National Federation Party (NFP) and the United General Party (UGP), suffered a massive defeat, with the NFP losing every seat, and the SVT winning only 8. The shock caused by this earthquake will be felt for a long time.

Ironies abound. Against all odds and all expectations, an Indo-Fijian, Mahendra Pal Chaudhry, was appointed prime minister—a prospect that would have appeared implausible just a few days earlier—and in coalition with a political party, the Fijian Association, whose overtures for political support to form a government in 1992 Chaudhry had rebuffed. Ratu Sir Kamisese Mara, whom Chaudhry had regarded as the evil genius behind the country's recent political troubles, was now hailed as an ally, a statesman providing sage advice to an inexperienced, hastily cobbled together administration representing divergent agendas and speaking with discordant voices. On the other side of the divide, NFP's Jai Ram Reddy had joined hands with SVT leader Rabuka whom he had refused to support—but whom Chaudhry had supported—for prime minister a few years back.

The two dominant figures of contemporary politics, widely praised for their leadership in the Constitution review, became generals without armies. Rabuka resigned from parliament to become (a commoner) chairman of the Great Council of Chiefs and the Commonwealth Secretary General's peace envoy to Solomon Islands. From coup-maker to international peace negotiator: it was a remarkable journey. For Reddy, also widely respected for his contribution to the country's healing, the results were a fateful replay of history. His party, under A.D. Patel, had played a leading role in Fiji's independence struggle but was consigned to the wilderness of the opposition benches for a generation. Now once again, he and his party were dealt a crushing blow and destined for a place on the political margins after helping deliver the best Constitution Fiji ever had and laying the foundations of a truly multiracial democracy. Parties which had played a marginal or negligible role in formulating the new Constitution were now poised to enjoy its benefits. The vanquished of 1987 had emerged victorious in 1999.

The conduct of the campaign and its outcome were determined by the provisions of the new Constitution. The first important feature was the provision for electing members of parliament, in particular the House of Representatives (the Senate being an appointed body). Of the 71 seats in the House, 46 are elected on a reserved, communal basis, with 23 contested by Fijian communal candidates, 19 by Indo-Fijians, 3 by General Electors and 1 by the Council of Rotuma. For these seats, the candidates as well as the voters belong to the same ethnic category. The remaining 25 are open (common roll) seats, with ethnic restriction for neither voters nor candidates. These open seats are an innovation for Fiji, designed to lead gradually but decisively away from communal to non-racial politics. Under the 1990 Constitution, all seats were communally reserved for the three ethnic communities (37 for Fijians, 27 for Indo-Fijians, and 5 for General Electors). The 1970 (independence) Constitution had a curious mixture of communal and cross-voting national seats where the ethnicity of the candidates was specified but all voted for them.[4] The way in which the open seats were contested proved crucial to the outcome in some constituencies and helped determine the overall result.

The 1997 Constitution also provided for a new alternative, or preferential, voting (AV) system, to replace the archaic first-past-the-post system inherited at independence. The AV was the system recommended by the Constitution Review Commission (Fiji Constitution Review Commission 1996:304–30). The ballot paper required voters to vote either above the line, accepting the party's allocation of preferences, or below the line, where they could rank the candidates themselves. Most voted above the line, and this had an important bearing on the outcome of the election.

The third feature of the Constitution which affected the outcome was the mandatory provision for power-sharing, entitling any political party with more than 10 per cent of seats in the lower house to a place in cabinet (in proportion with its percentage of seats). The party with the most number of seats provides the prime minister, who allocates portfolios in cabinet. Because of this provision for a multiparty cabinet, the parties in the winning People's Coalition formed only a loose coalition among themselves, leaving the details of power-sharing and leadership to be decided after the elections. This tactic gave them flexibility and internal leverage. The NFP, SVT and UGP, on the other hand, formed a binding pre-election coalition in a more conventional mould.

The campaign was the most relaxed in living memory. Trading preferences with other parties dampened what would have been a fiery campaign. For once, race was relegated to the background because both coalitions were multiracial. The constitutional provision for mandatory power-sharing also made political parties wary of being too aggressive towards each other because of the possibility of working together in cabinet.

The multi-party cabinet concept also erased the winner-take-all mentality. The long and difficult negotiations preceding the promulgation of the new Constitution had created goodwill and understanding and cross-cultural friendship among candidates facing each other in the election. The fact that the Constitution had been approved unanimously by the parliament, endorsed by the Great Council of Chiefs (also known as the Bose Levu Vakaturaga or BLV), and warmly welcomed by the international community, also had a calming effect.

The fear that the rights of indigenous Fijians could be eroded if a non-Fijian ruled, had often been used to mobilise opposition to that prospect, as had happened in 1987. People were generally ignorant of the way in which their rights and interests were protected in the Constitution. That was no longer true. The new Constitution was home-grown, devised in a transparent manner after wide consultation and in full glare of national publicity and international scrutiny. This was not the case with the 1970 Constitution which was negotiated in secrecy, approved in London and never subjected to a referendum. The 1990 Constitution was also promulgated by presidential decree with no popular participation.

For the first time, the legitimate needs and concerns of all communities were protected in a manner broadly acceptable them. The Great Council of Chiefs, whose constitutional role was recognised, could veto legislation that touched issues of concern to the Fijian people; it nominated both the president and the vice president; the ownership of Fijian land according to Fijian custom was recognised along with their and the Rotuman people's right to governance through separate administrative system. The Compact, a set of principles which all governments are enjoined to observe, provides that where the interests of the different communities were in conflict, 'the paramountcy of Fijian interests as a protective principle continues to apply, so as to ensure that the interests of the Fijian community are not subordinated to the interests of any other community'. And all communities were assured that affirmative action and social justice programs would be 'based on an allocation of resources broadly acceptable to all communities'. Clarifying the principles and procedures of governance helped greatly in allaying fears and doubts.

Political parties

Twenty-one political parties contested the election.[5] Many were obscure in origin and purpose and insignificant in their impact. If known at all, this reflected their entertainment value rather than their vision. Among these were the Natural Law Party, the Coalition of Independent Nationals (COIN) Party, the Viti Levu Dynamic Multiracial Democratic Party, the Tawavanua Party, the National Democratic Party, and the Farmers and General Workers

Coalition Party. The main actors were in the two coalitions, and in the Christian Democratic Alliance, which emerged on the eve of the campaign.

SVT/NFP/UGP coalition

This was a predictable coalition of three self-described mainstream parties representing the three main ethnic communities, standing on the basis of a firm pre-election agreement about power-sharing. The members of the coalition had worked together, and they promised to continue their dialogue and consensus. Sitiveni Rabuka and Jai Ram Reddy, leading the two main parties, had contributed significantly in securing the approval of the new Constitution in parliament. Rabuka had invited Reddy to address the Great Council of Chiefs to seek their blessing of the Constitution. The two had set up a joint parliamentary committee to resolve the complex issue of expiring leases under the *Agricultural Landlord and Tenant Act* (ALTA).[6] Rabuka and Reddy, so different from each other in training and temperament—one a soldier, open and intuitive; the other a lawyer, reserved and cautious—enjoyed a remarkable personal rapport, which they promised to translate into continuing cooperation.

Both leaders extolled the virtues of a pre-election coalition. Reddy said that

> a coalition that shares common goals, ideas and policies is more likely to succeed than a post-election multiparty government of hitherto mutually hostile forces. [Another] compelling case is the need to bring together the different racial groups as partners in the electoral process in order to reduce communal tensions that have historically characterised our elections of the past. We want to put an end to the long years of political rivalry between our different communities and usher in a new era of political cooperation—consistent with the aims and objectives of the Constitution. The valuable experience we have acquired during the making of the new Constitution and the immense goodwill that has been shown by the Fijian people can be made the basis for solving many of our difficult problems such as ALTA, crime, unemployment, health and education. They cannot be solved through confrontation but by working together (*Daily Post* 26 March 1999).

Each party had its own separate history. The SVT was formed in 1990, with the blessing of the Great Council of Chiefs, as the main Fijian party representing the Fijian community. However, the dream of Fijian political unity under the umbrella of a single party was short-lived (Lal 1998). The SVT was wrecked by internal dissension and rival ambitions among its leaders which brought about its downfall in 1993. Influential chiefs distanced themselves from the party they had blessed, Rabuka's leadership was questioned and ridiculed within his own party, and rival parties were formed to challenge the SVT's authority among Fijians—the Great Council of Chiefs' nominal sponsorship notwithstanding. Deserted by leading chiefs and former supporters, including members of the powerful Methodist Church, the SVT was not what it had been in the early 1990s, but it was still the largest party in parliament.

The SVT's main partner, the National Federation Party, was the oldest party in Fiji. Formed in 1963 to combat the Colonial Sugar Refining Company as well as the colonial raj, it had been in the vanguard of Fiji's decolonisation movement. After independence, the party was beset by bitter leadership battles and rampant factionalism. Jai Ram Reddy healed the wounds and restored some of its credibility, but its role as the sole voice of the Indo-Fijian community was effectively challenged by the Fiji Labour Party, formed in 1985 to combat the World Bank-inspired economic policies of the Alliance government. The two coalesced to win the 1987 election, but their month-long government was overthrown in a military coup.[7] They parted company over a range of essentially tactical issues in the early 1990s, and became bitter rivals as the election approached.

The third leg of the coalition was the United Generals Party (UGP), which emerged from factions within the small General Elector community of Europeans, Part-Europeans, Pacific Islanders and others of non-Fijian and non-Indian ancestry. The 'Generals' were once a powerful influence, always over-represented, but their parliamentary seats has been gradually shrunk over the years, from eight under the 1970 Constitution to five in 1990 and three in 1997. This shrinkage intensified competition among aspirants. Indeed, much of the dispute centered on the selection of candidates.[8]

The coalition agreement, signed by Rabuka, Reddy and UGP leader David Pickering, provided that the leader of the SVT, whoever it might be, would be the coalition's nominee for prime minister, while the NFP leader would become deputy prime minister, with the UGP being guaranteed a cabinet seat. Second, the parties agreed to share the 25 open seats, with SVT getting 14 and NFP 11. The two parties agreed to give their first preference to each other's designated candidates for the open seats, and not field parallel candidates or support independents or other candidates. The coalition would last until the next election, with the parties working together as coalition partners even if one party won enough seats to govern alone. Finally, the agreement provided for regular consultations to develop policy or resolve difficulties, but agreed to 'respect particular Party positions in agreed areas where special group interests may be affected'.

This escape clause was necessary because there were areas where the two parties had diametrically opposed positions. The privatisation of public assets was one, and it highlights the difficulty for the coalition in mounting an effective campaign as a unit. What one partner advertised as a major achievement, the other saw as a public policy disaster. The SVT government had sold 49 per cent of Amalgamated Telecom Holdings Limited for F$253 million to the Fiji National Provident Fund, and 51 per cent of the National Bank of Fiji to Colonial Mutual Insurance Company for F$9.5 million, ostensibly to promote competition in the private sector. It had also sold 17 per cent of Air Pacific for F$26.8 million to foreign airlines 'to strengthen the airline's international network and [increase] tourist arrivals', and 51 per cent of the Government Shipyard for F$3.2 million to improve its 'competitiveness and [win] international orders' (Ministry of National Planning Information Brochure 1998). These sales, the government argued, would free resources for growth in the private sector and enable it to 'focus more on improving the efficiency of its operations in the priority sectors, that is, core and essential services'. The NFP, on other hand, opposed privatisation of state enterprises which were yielding high returns or covered strategic resources, such as the international airport and shipping facilities, or those which were undertaken purely to fund recurrent fiscal deficits. It supported only those privatisation efforts in which the state had no legitimate economic interests or which were unprofitable or relied on permanent grants and subsidies. The People's Coalition was unambiguous in its opposition: 'strategic utilities such as water, electricity, telecommunication and civil aviation facilities must remain in public hands as viable units'.

Another issue dividing the parties was the status of state land. There are two types of state (formerly crown) land: Schedule A (52,513 ha) refers to land owned by landowning *mataqali* (clans) deemed to have become extinct by the time of Cession in 1874; and Schedule B (43,113 ha) refers to land which was unoccupied and had no claimants when the Native Lands Commission met. These lands were managed by the state. In the early 1990s, facing pressure from landless Fijians, the government devised a Bill to return these lands to Fijians and their management was transferred to the Native Land Trust Board, which also manages native land on behalf of Fijian landlords. The NFP criticised the government's proposal. It also opposed the policy of purchasing freehold land and giving it to the Fijians. It had been particularly vocal in denouncing the setting up of the Viti Corps, a government initiative to provide agricultural training to Fijian youth on a freehold property it had purchased for F$7 million. Other areas of disagreement included strategies for creating employment, strengthening economic growth and poverty alleviation.

The coalition agreement compromised both parties. The SVT could not highlight its pro-Fijian policies for fear of alienating supporters of its coalition partner, while the NFP had to soften its public opposition to the government. They were caught on the horns of a dilemma. As ethnic parties they were expected to champion the sectional interests of their communities. And yet, as parties which had worked together to fashion a new

Constitution and lay the foundations of a new multiracialism, they could not afford to adopt an 'ethnicist' position which might have sharpened their appeal among supporters, but in the process hurt the larger cause of reconciliation. The two parties were not standing on the joint record; they were standing on their promise to work together in future. It was a critical distinction which was lost on the electorate.

The People's Coalition

The People's Coalition was the other main multiracial coalition. Unlike the SVT/NFP/UGP Coalition, it was loosely structured, and details of the agreement and internal understandings about power sharing were never released to the public. The coalition consisted of the Fiji Labour Party, the Party of National Unity and the Fijian Association. Each had its own history and agenda, but they were united by one common, overriding ambition: to remove Rabuka from power and (for Labour) to remove Reddy and the National Federation Party as the party of the Indo-Fijians.

The Fiji Labour Party was formed in 1985 as a multiracial party backed by the powerful trade unions. Dr Timoci Bavadra, an indigenous Fijian medical doctor, was its founding president and leader, with the powerful Fiji Public Servants Association leader Mahendra Chaudhry as its mastermind and general secretary. Labour won the 1987 election in coalition with the NFP, only to be deposed in a coup a month later. The partnership did not last long, the rift erupting into a bitter disagreement over participation in the 1992 election. NFP participated, while Labour decided not to, until the last minute.[9] Labour's support for Sitiveni Rabuka as prime minister following the 1992 elections, drove the two parties further apart. Although they returned to make a joint submission to the Constitution Review Commission, the rift was widening. By the mid 1990s, Labour was a shadow of its earlier self, with most of its founding members having left for other parties, including many Fijians. By the time of the election, it had enticed some back. The FLP, although supported predominantly by Indo-Fijians, had continued to field Fijian candidates in previous elections, and kept nurturing its support base among workers and farmers and the trade unions.

The spectacularly misnamed western Viti Levu-based Party of National Unity (PANU) was the brainchild of Apisai Tora, the quintessential political chameleon. In a political career spanning nearly four decades, Tora had been a member of nearly every political party in Fiji, beginning with the Western Democratic Party in 1964, progressing to the National Democratic Party, the National Federation Party, the Alliance, the All National Congress, and the Fijian Association Party. He had been a founding member of the nationalist Taukei Movement, and an enthusiastic supporter of the coups. But throughout his tortuous—not to say tortured—career, he had been a fierce champion of western Fijian interests which, he argued, had been neglected in a government dominated by chiefs of the eastern establishment. PANU was Tora's latest vehicle to redress the longstanding grievance of the western Fijians and to gain for them an appropriate place in the Fijian sun. In the West were concentrated all the nation's wealth-generating industries: sugar, tourism, gold and pine as well as the international airport and the hydroelectric power stations, Tora argued, and he wanted a commensurate share of national power.

PANU had the blessing of prominent western chiefs, including the Tui Vuda—the paramount chief of western Fiji and vice president—Ratu Josefa Iloilo, Tui Nawaka Ratu Apisai Naevo, Tui Sabeto Ratu Kaliova Mataitoga, Tui Vitogo Ratu Josefa Sovasova, and Marama na Tui Ba Adi Sainimili Cagilaba. The list is impressive, but the chiefs' support did not carry as much influence as before (*The Review* May 1998). Tora first broached a coalition with the SVT, and wanted a seat-sharing arrangement which would recognise his influence in the west. He was rebuffed by western Fijian members of the SVT, especially Isimeli Bose and Ratu Etuate Tavai. Tora, they felt, was a spent force, his reputation for integrity and probity tainted by his impressive record of political bed-hopping. Moreover, the seat-sharing formula sought by Tora would have ended SVT's reign in western Viti Levu, a prospect no serious party could countenance. Tora then turned to Labour, which responded favourably. It was a coalition of convenience. Labour gave Tora a wider platform upon which, by relying on his cunning, he no doubt hoped to enlarge his own agenda. Tora promised Labour western Fijian support and assistance in resolving the issue of the expiring leases. The land issue was serious. On the eve of the election, Ba chiefs, who command the largest province, wanted 87 per cent of the leases not to be renewed (34,634 out of 39,725 ha) and in Sabeto, Nawaka, Nadi and Vuda, the chiefs wanted 92 per cent of the leases not to be renewed (12,728 out of 13,704 ha). Tora held—or seemed to hold—powerful cards.

The Fijian Association was the third member of the People's Coalition. It was formed in the early 1990s by Fijians opposed to Rabuka, ridiculing his leadership and attacking his moral character. Its founder was Josefata Kamikamica, an affable, mild-mannered but politically naive long-term head of the Native Land Trust Board and a member of the Mara-led post-coup Interim Administration (in which he had served as finance minister). He unsuccessfully challenged Rabuka for prime minister in 1992, but failed to get elected in 1994 and in later by-elections. After his death in 1998, the Fijian Association was led by Adi Kuini Bavadra Speed, the re-married widow of the founding Labour leader and herself onetime leader of the Fiji Labour Party and president of the All National Congress. The party's social philosophy was broadly similar to Labour's (*Daily Post* April 1999). In fact, nearly all its leading Fijian candidates were former members or friends of the Labour Party. But the party also contained a strange assortment of political refugees from other parties, with their own agendas and ambitions, united by the overriding desire to see Rabuka defeated. Sometimes the Fijian Association gave the impression of having a 'schizophrenic personality':[10] of saying one thing and doing another. One of its parliamentarians, Viliame Cavubati, was standing for the SVT while another, Dr Fereti Dewa, missed out on selection and launched a scathing attack on the party leaders. Its parliamentary leader, the ever unpredictable Ratu Finau Mara, had left politics for a diplomatic career.

The People's Coalition had few common understandings, which invited attacks from the rival coalition. Who would lead the coalition if it won? 'The party with the most seats', the Peoples' Coalition responded. Would that leader be a Fijian? The answer was the same. The coalition similarly had a flexible arrangement about allocating seats in the open constituencies. In some constituencies, it supported a common candidate, while elsewhere it fielded parallel candidates. Where it fielded parallel candidates, the coalition partners were given their second preference. This worked well for the most part, but created problems in some places. PANU, for example, expected to be allowed to field candidates in western constituencies with substantial Fijian population, but Labour disagreed and fielded its own, poaching some of Tora's own prominent supporters and potential candidates, among them Ratu Tevita Momoedonu. Tora's own seat was contested by Labour, whose candidate beat him. Outmanoeuvred, Tora refused to attend any of the People's Coalition rallies. Towards the end of the campaign, he became a vocal critic of the Labour Party, chiding Labour president Jokapeci Koroi for not forgiving Rabuka for his past actions and accusing Chaudhry of treachery (*Fiji Times* 7 May 1999). Tora refused to give preferences to his coalition partner, the Fijian Association Party, which had fielded candidates against his own. But by then, he mattered little. For once, the Machiavellian politician had been marginalised.

Veitokani Ni Lewenivanua Vakaristo/Christian Democratic Alliance (VLV/CDA)

This party was launched on 27 March 1999, on the eve of the election, by Fijians variously opposed to Sitiveni Rabuka and his government. Its support came from three sources. First, there were those who opposed the 1997 Constitution. Rabuka and his party had 'failed the Fijian people miserably',[11] the VLV charged. Rabuka had given away too much; he had 'exploited the indigenous Fijian institutions for his own glorification, even to the extent of selling out on the rights and interests of Fijians'. Unless the 'core interests' of the Fijians were addressed, there would be no political stability in the country.

We remind the PM of the VLV's primary platform that unless there is stability in the indigenous Fijian community, there will be no stability in this country in the future. It will all be fruitless and a waste of effort for all who have been trying to build and make Fiji a better place for all to live in.

In essence, they wanted to restore those provisions of the 1990 Constitution which would have kept power in Fijian hands and given substance to the notion of Fijian paramountcy.

Other members and supporters came from sections of the Methodist Church which wanted to turn Fiji into a Christian state (see *Daily Post* 31 March 1999). The very public blessing given to the party by the affable but malleable president of the Methodist Church, Reverend Tomasi Kanailagi, and the presence within it of such fire-breathing figures as former president Manasa Lasaro and Taniela Tabu, was powerfully symbolic. These people wanted the Sunday Ban re-introduced, which reversed the stance the church had taken when Dr Ilaitia Tuwere was president in the mid 1990s. Tuwere had argued that turning Fiji into a Christian state could not 'make it a better place for everyone to live in. It will neither further the cause of Christianity nor adequately meet the present wish to safeguard Fijian interests and identity'. And attention to 'man's careless disregard of the environment was more urgent than Sunday observance' (*Daily Post* 31 March 1999). Much depends on the character and vision of the person at the helm of the church. Nonetheless, religion is close to the heart of many Fijians, and most would not oppose the Christian state proposal. But others wanted to manipulate this deep religious attachment for their own ends.

The VLV claimed the support of 'members of the chiefly establishment'. To prove it, they made traditional approaches to Ratu Mara (Tui Nayau) and Adi Lady Lala Mara (Tui Dreketi), as well as Tui Vuda Ratu Josefa Iloilo. Most people believed that the president silently supported the party.[12] Close members of his own family were contesting the election on the VLV ticket, including his daughter and son-in-law, and Poseci Bune who was expected to 'strengthen and consolidate the Mara/Ganilau dynasty' (*Daily Post* 29 March 1999). Fairly or unfairly, the president was accused of harbouring dynastic ambitions. Many Fijians remarked on Mara's cool relations with Rabuka, and his desire to see the prime minister defeated. Many founding members of the Fijian Association were known to the president as members of the Diners Club formed in the early 1990s, with whom he shared his experiences and reflections on politics. Rabuka had defeated Lady Lala for the presidency of the SVT, which was not forgotten or forgiven. And Rabuka's claim, during the election and before, that he had been used to stage the coup, raised questions about who else was involved, including members of the chiefly establishment which now supported the VLV. Rabuka said that he was the fall guy who refused to fall. His comment, in Lau of all places, that a commoner candidate could be more accessible than a chiefly one, raised further questions about his loyalty to chiefs (*Daily Post* 7 May 1999). Mara's relations with Rabuka, never warm, had become decidedly chilly.

As the campaign proceeded, the VLV attempted to distance itself from extreme platforms, and proclaimed its commitment to socially progressive policies. These included reorganising and restructuring regional development, improving 'economic, social and human conditions in the rural areas,' and assisting the provinces to implement 'infrastructure plans and projects, industrial, business and commercial plans and projects, agriculture, forestry and fisheries plans and projects, and social/human development plans and projects', whatever these phrases, allegedly written in New York by an expatriate former Fiji public servant (Peter Halder) might mean, facilitating Fijian ownership of business, industry and commerce in each province and assisting Fijian landowners to 'utilise their lands for their own economic development and upliftment' (*The Review* April 1999). Bune, an experienced civil servant and former representative at the United Nations, got himself elected as party leader over Ratu Epeli Ganilau, the army commander who had resigned to contest the Lau open seat; but his elevation was contested by powerful party insiders who questioned his background and personal and moral credentials.[13] Nonetheless, the VLV fielded some well known and experienced candidates, including Ganilau and Adi Koila Mara Nailatikau, Fijian academic Asesela Ravuvu, trade unionist Salote Qalo, and lawyers Kitione Vuataki and Naipote Vere.

Among the smaller Fijian parties, the Fijian Nationalist Vanua Tako Lavo Party was the most prominent. Led by longtime Fijian nationalist Sakiasi Butadroka, it was the latest reincarnation of the original Fijian Nationalist Party founded in 1975 to keep 'Fiji for the Fijians.' Twenty years later, it had changed little, except in name. The party rejected the 1997 Constitution as a sell-out of Fijian interests, and wanted Rabuka punished for betraying the aims of the coup which, they said, was to entrench Fijian political control. Its manifesto proclaimed that 'in addition to the normal guarantees for 75 per cent support from the Great Council of Chiefs for amendments concerning the Fijian people, we will ensure that 100 per cent support will be needed from all 14 Provincial Councils before any changes can be made to the iron clad guarantees affecting the Fijian people'. The name of the country would be changed from the Fiji Islands to Fiji because 'we want to be identified overseas as Fijians not Fiji Islanders' (*Daily Post* 16 April 1999). The Fijian language would be taught in all schools, Crown land returned to the indigenous people, and special bodies would be set up to exploit natural resources in the interest of the Fijian people. Fine words, but the party was now a caricature of its former self, not a force of consequence. Some leading members (including Isireli Vuibau) had joined other parties, while ex-Taukei Movement member Iliesa Duvuloco was embroiled in financial difficulties. After the elections, Butadroka changed his trademark blood-red bow tie signifying violence if Indians ever challenged Fijian right to rule, to a black bow tie, mourning the political loss 'of the Fijian race'.

Issues

For the SVT/NFP/UGP coalition, the main question was which party or coalition was best placed to provide political stability. Reddy spoke for the coalition

> Experience around the world shows that political stability is a precondition for economic and social progress. Without political stability we will not be able to achieve anything. Political stability will lead to enlightened and progressive policies which, in turn, will generate business confidence, investment, economic growth and, above all, jobs for our unemployed.[14]

The NFP had always been the majority party of the Indian community, while the SVT 'is without doubt the majority Fijian party representing the widest cross-section of the Fijian community', and the UGP was the largest party of the General Electors. This coalition, he said, broadly based, representative, and with a record of working together was 'best placed to provide that political stability which will form the foundation for progress on economic and social issues'.

The SVT paraded its achievements, reminding Fijians of its pro-Fijian activities: more scholarships for Fijians, financial assistance, the promise to revert crown land to Fijian landowners. It reminded them of the new hospitals and health centres in Kadavu, Lami, Nabouwalu, Rabi and Rakiraki, improvements in infrastructure, including better shipping services to the islands under the Shipping Franchising Scheme; completion of major bridges; rural electrification; improved water supply in rural areas; the poverty alleviation scheme (F$4.4 million per year), and better housing for low income earners. But these achievements did not impress the voters, who remembered the scandals which had brought the country into disrepute and close to bankruptcy. There was widespread suspicion that a chosen few and those well connected had done well, but not the bulk of the citizens. In western Viti Levu, opposition parties said publicly that their region had been neglected, as in the past, and that the bulk of the development projects had gone elsewhere.

The SVT claimed credit for 'wide consultation in the comprehensive review and promulgation of the new Constitution, which laid the foundation for a united, free and democratic multi-racial Fiji'. It claimed credit for Fiji's readmission to the Commonwealth, and for restoring Fiji's link with the British monarchy. The Fijian electorate was unmoved. Many thought that the revised Constitution had somehow whittled down the Fijian position and deprived them of rights. The government claimed credit for establishing the 'framework for a multiparty government', when most Fijians wanted a Fijian government with some participation from the other communities, not equal partnership. The opposition Fijian parties, with diverse agendas and ideologies, united to condemn the SVT for compromising Fijian interests.

Rabuka's firm and decisive leadership had indeed been instrumental in negotiating the Constitution, without which the outcome could well have been different. Even his closest colleagues in cabinet had opposed the report of the Constitution Review Commission, and had tried to have the Constitution amended at the last minute. Eight of the 14 Fijian provinces had rejected the report; for their elected leaders now to claim credit was difficult. The hero of 1987 had become the villain of 1999, deserted by close supporters and friends and high chiefs with agendas of their own. They all wanted him defeated.

The NFP praised Rabuka to skeptical Indian audiences as the leader best suited to take Fiji into the next millennium.[15] Rabuka responded by apologising for the pain the coup had caused the Indo-Fijian community, and espoused an inclusive vision.

> I believe we cannot build a nation by tearing people down. No matter how they arrived in Fiji, they are a part of Fiji society. This is their land to till and make productive. We owe it to the indentured labourers, to cotton planters for what we have now. Let us leave our differences aside, have common interests in our hearts to build a beautiful Fiji (speech in Labasa, 10 April 1999).

Rabuka appeared genuine in his contrition, but it came late, and in the heat of an election campaign sounded expedient. As one observer put it, 'commitment to multiracialism and forgiveness for sins past' sounded all too vague. 'It is feel-good politics that blisters under the blowtorch of the Fijian Association Party–Labour call for new direction' (*Fiji Times* editorial 3 May 1999).

For the NFP, the successful constitutional review and the promulgation of the new Constitution was the main platform in the campaign. Much had been achieved through dialogue and discussion with a mainstream Fijian party, and it promised to continue that approach. If the Indian people wanted to resolve the land lease issue, they could only do so with the support of the main party of the Fijian people. It urged voters to take a longer-term view. Much had been accomplished, but much remained to be done. The NFP praised Rabuka as the man who had risked his political capital among his own people. They acknowledged his past misdeeds, but as Reddy said, 'this is the same person who has shown, by leading the revision of the Constitution, that he believes in genuine multiracialism, not just in parliament but more importantly in Government'.[16] He continued

> We are not in a partnership with token Fijians and General Voters, as in 1987, after which the coups took place. These parties will have the full force of their racial groups behind them. This Coalition will have real political authority and social backing to tackle the problems of our country, for example crime and ALTA (Reddy Final Campaign Speech 3 May 1999).

NFP wanted to eschew confrontational politics which 'only result in misery for people'. Instead, 'this is a time for moderation, reconciliation, and tolerance of all races, regions and cultures that grace this beautiful country of ours'. Reddy reminded voters of his party's record in opposition: 'The country knows that we have been in the forefront of bringing these issues (corruption, mismanagement of the economy, and inefficiencies) to the attention of the public, whenever the need has arisen'. Nonetheless, as Stewart Firth from the *Fiji Times* remarked, 'No answer could explain to an average Indian the reason why NFP leader Jai Ram Reddy formed a coalition with Sitiveni Rabuka's party' (*Fiji Times* 18 May 1999).

The NFP also made much of Labour's allocation of preferences. In 22 seats, Labour gave its first or second preferences to the VLV, a party whose policies were 'abhorrent, contrary to the spirit of our Constitution and against the interests of the Indian community'.[17] The VLV would reintroduce the Sunday Ban, make Fiji a Christian state and change the Constitution. The NFP placed the VLV last, and despite its competition with Labour it placed that party above the VLV 'as a matter of principle and morality'. For Labour, however, the election was not about principle and morality: it was about winning. To that end, it put those parties last which posed the greatest threat. Among these parties was the NFP, its main rival in the Indian communal seats. Labour's unorthodox tactic breached the spirit and intention of the preferential system of voting, where like-minded parties trade preferences among themselves and put those they most disagree with last. Political expediency and cold-blooded ruthlessness triumphed. Reddy was right about Labour's motives when he said that Labour wanted 'to get rid of Rabuka and the SVT [and Reddy and the NFP as well] at all cost'.

The Constitution, on which the NFP had placed such store, was for Labour an accomplished fact and a non-issue. It made no mention of it in the manifesto. When reminded, Labour belittled Rabuka's and Reddy's roles, saying that the Constitution was the work of the Constitution Review Commission and the Joint Parliamentary Select Committee. In any case, why should Rabuka be praised for rectifying a grievous mistake he had made in the first place. As Sir Vijay Singh put, 'in restoring the democratic Constitution', Rabuka 'did the Indians no favour'. He 'restored what he had stolen in the first place. He is deserving of some mitigation. If you were a criminal in court and you did some right thing, the court will deal with you lightly but it won't reward you' (*fijilive* 19 May 1999). It was a harsh, unforgiving judgement on Rabuka and what he had accomplished in the most difficult of circumstances and against powerful opposition from within his own party. Moreover, Rabuka was not alone in carrying out the coups. Some of Sir Vijay's own former colleagues in the Alliance Party (and now Rabuka's bitter opponents) had joined the colonel in 1987 to overthrow the 1970 Constitution. But these subtle points did not register.

Labour reminded the electorate of SVT's sorry record in government, and implicated the NFP in the mess, calling it the Rabuka-Reddy record:[18] mismanagement of public office; corruption at the top echelons of government; alarming crime rates; high unemployment; enforced redundancies in public enterprises brought about by privatisation and corporatisation; a high cost of living in an economy deep in recession with two consecutive years of negative growth; and the dreadful infrastructure with clogged up river systems prone to flooding, rundown roads and disrupted water supplies. This, Labour said, was the true record of the SVT government. The electorate understood. The sight of redundant workers at Nadi airport while the election was in progress reinforced the image of the government as uncaring and arrogant. The NFP said little; for Labour the pictures of the redundant workers were a godsend. 'The NFP', Labour president Koroi remarked, 'has been an ineffective opposition, frequently actively supporting the repressive measures of a government whose sole aim is to remain in power permanently' (*Daily Post* 2 April 1999). The electorate believed her.

Labour also promised policies and initiatives of its own. It would remove the 10 per cent value-added tax and customs duty from basic food and educational items, review taxation on savings and raise allowances for dependents, provide social security for the aged and destitute, and lower interest rates on housing loans. If elected, Labour promised to repeal legislation requiring farmers to pay back the F$27 million cash grant and crop rehabilitation loan made to drought-stricken farmers in 1998; establish a Land Use Commission, in consultation with landowners and tenants, to identify and access vacant lands; and oppose privatisation of strategic utilities such as water, electricity, telecommunications and civil aviation. 'We also believe that the overall control of the exploitation of natural resources such as forestry and fisheries must remain in State hands to maintain their sustainability. We will, therefore, reverse all moves to restructure and privatise them.'

Labour's partners broadly shared its policy platform, but their main target was Rabuka, for who he was and for the record of his government. The Fijian establishment, in whose name he had carried out the coup, jettisoned him as an ambitious commoner unfit to govern, a man who had overreached his authority and station. He had to be defeated almost at any cost. For Chaudhry, removing Reddy and his party was a major item.

Results

Voting in Fiji was compulsory for the 428,000 registered voters, but only 393,673 voted. Of the votes cast, 8 per cent were invalid. There were roughly equal numbers of invalid votes among Fijians (8.7 per cent) and Indo-Fijians (8.5 per cent). The percentage of Fijians not voting was slightly higher (10.9 per cent) than among Indo-Fijians (7.5 per cent). The Labour Party won 37 of the 71 seats in the House of Representatives, and thus was entitled to form a government in its own right. Its coalition partner, the Fijian Association Party, won 11, PANU 4 and the Christian Democrats 3. The UGP won 2 seats, the SVT 8 and, the biggest surprise, the NFP failed to win a seat. Fijian Nationalists won 2 seats and Independents 4 seats.

The Indian communal seats saw a two-way contest between Labour and the NFP. Labour won 108,743 of the 165,886 Indian communal votes cast (65.6 per cent of first preference votes) and the NFP 53,071 (32 per cent). Independents and other parties got 4,030 (2.4 per cent). Labour fared well in rural and urban constituencies, its electoral dominance evenly spread. Among the Fijian parties contesting the communal seats, the SVT won 68,114 or 38 per cent of (first preference) Fijian votes, VLV 34,758 (19.4 per cent), Fijian Association Party 32,394 (18 per cent), PANU 17,149 (9.6 per cent), Independents 7,335 (4.1 per cent), Nationalist Vanua Tako Lavo Party 16,353 (9.1 per cent) and Labour 3,590 (2.0 per cent). Labour's poor performance among Fijians should be seen in context. Although it fielded some Fijian candidates, Labour left Fijian constituencies largely to its Fijian partners. When the votes in the open seats are taken into account, there is evidence of large Fijian support for the party. There, of the 360,085 valid votes cast—428,146 were registered of whom 393,673 voted—Labour won 33.3 per cent of the votes, SVT 21 per cent, VLV 9.8 per cent, NFP 14.4 per cent, Nationalists 4.2 per cent, Fijian Association Party 10.8 per cent, Independents 2.1 per cent, United General Party 1.3 per cent and PANU 2.7 per cent.

Among General Voters, 11,981 voted from a total of 14,029. That is, 14.6 per cent did not vote and of those who did, 8.2 per cent were invalid. The United General Party won 5,388 votes (49 per cent), Fijian Association Party 1,052 (9.6 per cent), Independents 3,346 (30.4 per cent) and the Coalition of Independent Parties 1,156 (10 per cent). The strong support for Independents centered on personalities (Leo Smith and Bill Aull who were prominent sitting parliamentarians).

Why the massive swing to Labour? The NFP argued that Indian voters had taken revenge for the coups, that its pre-election coalition with Rabuka cost them the election. If NFP had not allied itself with the SVT and not revealed its hand, it would not have carried SVT's baggage. It would then have been able to mount an effective campaign in its traditional constituency and win enough seats to become a player in parliament. There is a grain of truth in this assertion. Certainly Labour advertised its campaign as a continuation of a brutally interrupted experiment of 1987, with Dr Timoci Bavadra's official portrait adorning many a campaign shed in western Viti Levu. Rabuka's public apologies unwittingly revived memories of disrupted careers, lost incomes and broken lives. The NFP's pre-election coalition may have cost it votes, but would an alternative strategy have made much difference?

The answer is not at all clear. In the public mind, Reddy was already hitched to Rabuka through the constitutional review, and any attempt by the two leaders to distance themselves from each other, after having worked so closely for so long, would have been hugely counterproductive for the politics of moderation and reconciliation they were preaching. Labour would not have left Reddy alone over Rabuka. They would have prodded and provoked and demanded to know why Reddy was not with the SVT leader. On the other side, the Fijian nationalists, unhappy with the new Constitution, would have accused Reddy of treachery, and of using Rabuka and the Great Council of Chiefs to amend the Constitution to suit the interests of his own community. The Fijian supporters of the SVT would have felt used and discarded.

Reddy argued that his party had taken the correct decision to ally with the SVT. The Coalition, he said

> was based on some very fundamental principles. And you don't abandon your coalition partners because they have done something wrong or they may be suddenly becoming unpopular. But I didn't see it that way. I saw the SVT as the mainstream Fijian party. They were founded by the chiefs. They seemed to have the support of the Fijian people. The important thing is that all these things we did with the utmost good faith. We did it because we believed in something. We believed that Indian and Fijian people and everybody else must be brought together in government (*The Review* June 1999).

He had been honest with the electorate. His coalition decision was not 'a grievous error of principle as well as strategy',[19] as some commentators noted, but a principled and courageous one.

The NFP's problem lay not so much in the message as in its failure to take it effectively to the voters. In hindsight, its focus on the Constitution, the great achievement that it was, to the virtual exclusion of any other issue was probably a mistake. Selling an untried Constitution, however good, to a skeptical, suffering electorate was not the same as criticising a demonstrably flawed one, as it had done successfully in 1992 and 1994. The fact that it could not use its solid performance as an opposition party, now that it was in partnership with the party in government, weakened its campaign. In short, the NFP was caught in a trap. A frontal attack on the SVT would have polarised the main communities, revived the hostilities and taken the country back to the tired politics of ethnic confrontation.

Labour's message was sharper and more effective, its criticism of government relentless. Its focus on bread and butter issues of employment, better health, social welfare and an accountable government, sat well with the electorate. Moreover, it had an extensive network to communicate that message. The Fiji Public Service Association, of which Mahendra Chaudhry was the head, covered the public sector unions. The National Farmers Union, of which Chaudhry again was the head, galvanised the farming community. And the Fiji Teachers Union, headed by Pratap Chand, a Labour candidate, reached out to primary and secondary teachers who play a pivotal social role in the community. They shape opinion and influence events. Farmers, workers and teachers were thus covered. The NFP's structure was less focused. Its once powerful working committees had become moribund, its decision-making and consultative function taken over by the Management Board. This change made the party more businesslike, but damaged its links to the grassroots.

Labour appealed to people who were desperate, and direct victims of government policies—400 redundant employees at the Civil Aviation Authority, 15,000 garment factory workers and their families, squatters and residents of low-cost Housing Authority flats, people threatened with job losses at the Fiji Electricity Authority, Telecom Fiji, the Fiji Sugar Corporation and in the public service, already reeling from the 20 per cent devaluation of the Fijian dollar. The NFP's appeal lacked focus. The Indo-Fijian community, whose interests it sought to protect, was increasingly divided in its interests and aspirations. The middle class, a constituency traditionally receptive to its message of gradual progressive change and with a keen eye on investment in a long term future, has been declining through migration. Over 70,000 have left since the coups while Labour's base of workers, farmers and teachers remained intact. For them, the immediate social and economic concerns were more important than saving for a rainy day. As one observer put it, the 'NFP achievements on the Constitution and talk of racial harmony were abstract issues while Labour promised tangible gains' (*The Review* June 1999), reducing prices, increasing exports, creating jobs. The NFP was perceived as a rich person's party, uncaring about the concerns of ordinary people.[20]

In the sugar belt, the heartland of the Indo-Fijian community, Labour outmanoeuvred the NFP. The National Farmers Union had displaced the NFP-backed Fiji Cane Growers Association as the most effective voice of the farmers. Ironically, it was the NFP which had paved the way for Chaudhry's entry into sugar politics after the coups, handing over to him a constituency that had long been the party's own but which Chaudhry would convert into his own solid base. To the drought-stricken farmers, Labour promised relief and concrete proposals: addressing the problem of milling inefficiencies, improving the transportation system, exploring diversification into agro-based industries, and writing off the F$27 million crop rehabilitation loan. Labour told the farmers that Reddy had opposed the cash grant, which patently misrepresented his position. The NFP cried foul, but the damage was done. The sugar belt turned to Labour as never before.

Rabuka's defeat was caused by several factors. His government's scandal-ridden performance was one. For many ordinary Fijians, life had not improved much since the coups. As Tamarisi Digitaki put it

> At the grassroots level, the standards of living have remained largely unchanged from ten years ago. While his [Rabuka's] government's performance on the national and international fronts has been commendable, it is in the rural areas that the goods have failed to be delivered. Poor roads, water supply, communication services, education facilities and shipping services to the islands only give rural people more reason to vote the government out of office (*The Review* February 1998).

Rabuka conceded that the complacency of his parliamentarians and a dormant party structure cost him votes, saying that 'while party leaders were busy resolving national issues, no one was really looking into bread and butter issues affecting its supporters.'[21] Labour and its partners capitalised on this rural disenchantment.

Rabuka's pursuit of moderate, conciliatory politics was always going to risk being outflanked by more extremist parties. Parties which court moderation in a multiethnic society tempt fate. Rabuka was accused of selling out Fijian interests, just as Reddy was accused of playing second fiddle to the Fijians. Further, Rabuka was not fully in command of his party. The 23 Fijian seats are contested on provincial lines, and candidates are selected in consultation with provincial councils. In some cases, candidates preferred by the party were overruled by the provincial councils, an example being the replacement of the highly regarded Education Minister Taufa Vakatale by Jone Kauvesi for the Lomaiviti Fijian seat. Provincial concerns and interests take priority over party. These problems of divided loyalties will plague Fijian politics as long as elections are fought from within provincial boundaries.

Rabuka also suffered from deserters from his camp. These included leaders of the Methodist Church, like Manasa Lasaro, Viliame Gonelevu and other earlier supporters. Now they had formed a party of their own, the VLV, which repudiated Rabuka's policies and accused him of being a traitor to his people. Joining them were opportunists like Poseci Bune and Asesela Ravuvu. Compounding Rabuka's trouble was the disdain of leading chiefs who were 'uncomfortable with a commoner being in power' and who believed that 'Fijian leadership should always remain with the chiefs' (*The Review* June 1999). Ratu Mara's disparaging assessment of Rabuka was no secret, fueled, it was said, by envy at Rabuka's success in getting the Constitution through parliament and his increasing national and international stature, as well as Ratu Mara's dynastic ambitions. Rabuka's anti-chiefly remarks, while appreciated by commoners, infuriated powerful chiefs, Ratu Mara among them.

The political fragmentation of Fijian society has distressed many Fijians, and Rabuka regarded this as a major causes of his defeat. 'Gone are the days when Fijians worked in accordance with what was required of them from their elders. Now when an order is given from an elder, they are asked to give the reason and if they are satisfied, then they can act' (*Daily Post* 27 March 1999). He was referring to the influence of urbanisation, multiracial education and the challenges and opportunities of a multiethnic society. The use of the provincial boundaries for electing members to parliament accentuated provincial rivalries and sentiments, to the detriment of a centralised party structure. The decline in the number of Indo-Fijians through emigration and a lower birthrate diluted the fear of Indian dominance, which fostered Fijian political unity. Finally, the absence from the national stage of strong and powerful chiefs—a Ratu Mara or Ratu Penaia or Ratu George and Ratu Edward Cakobau—opened up opportunities for others. It is unlikely that Fijian society will see the likes of these on the national stage in the near future.

The race to be prime minister

As the count proceeded and a change of government appeared likely, most people wondered what Rabuka's next move might be. The defeated SVT leader conceded defeat with exemplary grace and dignity. His words are worth recalling not only because of their symbolic importance but also as a measure of the man Rabuka had become. The people of Fiji had demonstrated to themselves and 'to the watching world that we have embraced democracy fully by the way the election was held and by the very nature of the result'. He congratulated the Labour Party, and told his supporters: 'Take heart that we have fought the good fight. We have given all that we could. Let us now, without rancour and bitterness or any sort of division, congratulate our fellow citizens who have won the day.' Rabuka lamented the apparent block voting by the Indo-Fijian community, but urged the new government to 'govern us all'. He would lend support when necessary, promising to be 'vigilant to ensure a just, accountable and honest government'. He urged the people 'to move to the centre ground, the middle ground', to 'genuinely come together to work for the common good of all our people'. It would be a terrible tragedy to 'dismantle the progress that we have made together'. Rabuka thanked Reddy for his support. Reddy knew the risks he was taking in coalescing with his party, but as a leader with 'deep conviction and strong principles, he courageously stuck to our agreement and it has cost him and his party dearly'. Not all was lost. 'I now give my assurances to him and his loyal supporters that their sacrifice and contribution in helping to lay the framework for lasting national unity, stability and progress in our country has not been in vain.'

To the Fijian people, he said

> We must find a way to come together to allow our collective voice to be heard. And to be a force in shaping the future of our country. We have allowed ourselves to splinter into different groups working against our common interest. We know the wise words that a house divided amongst themselves cannot stand. We have a lot of houses, our collective *yavu* and *vanua* have become divided. And the result is our voice in Government has been diminished (radio broadcast, typescript in my possession).

Rabuka promised to keep a watchful eye on the government, but before parliament met, he resigned his seat. In a stunning move, Rabuka then got elected chair of the Great Council of Chiefs by polling—the first time in history that chiefs had used secret ballot—32 votes to Tui Vuda Ratu Josefa Iloilo's 18. Rabuka described his victory as 'a sign of the chiefly support I have' (*Daily Post* 5 June 1999). His name was moved by Adi Litia Cakobau from the leading chiefly family of the Kubuna confederacy and seconded by Ratu Tevita Vakalalabure, the Vunivalu of Natewa.

Labour's victory put Chaudhry in the driver's seat. Within hours of the election results becoming known, Chaudhry convened his Labour parliamentary caucus which elected him as the party's nominee for prime minister. Soon afterwards, he was appointed prime minister by Ratu Mara. Chaudhry's other coalition partners were not consulted or informed, and they reacted angrily, claiming Chaudhry's appointment a breach of an implicit agreement to have an ethnic Fijian as prime minister. Adi Kuini Bavadra Speed, the Fijian Association leader, asked Mara, through Ratu Viliame Dreunimisimisi, to revoke his decision and appoint her as head of government because she was the leader of the largest 'Fijian' party in the winning coalition. Poseci Bune, the VLV leader, began canvassing the possibility of heading a broad coalition of Fijian parties in opposition. Tora threatened to pull out of the coalition altogether. The Fijian Nationalists proposed to march against the government.

Nothing happened. Chaudhry offered Speed the post of deputy prime minister which she accepted after Mara asked her to support Chaudhry, and after Labour threatened to invite the VLV into cabinet. Speed capitulated, quoting Mara's advice: 'It was basically appealing to us as leaders to consider the importance of cooperation rather [than] be at loggerheads with the new government' (*Fiji Village* 19 May 1999). Speed had been out manoeuvred. She could sit on the opposition benches with Rabuka, possibly as leader of the opposition, or become deputy prime minister. She chose the latter. Speed also opposed the VLV's inclusion in the cabinet, but was overridden. It was widely believed, but difficult to prove, that Mara wanted Bune and Adi Koila Nailatikau in the cabinet— and that might have been the reason for his surprisingly warm public support for Chaudhry. Be that as it may, both were offered and both accepted cabinet posts, as did members of PANU, despite Tora's objections. Later, Chaudhry praised Mara for his critical role in getting the Fijian dissidents to support his government. In truth, Mara did what the Constitution obliged him to do: to appoint as prime minister the member of the House of Representative who in his opinion commanded majority support. Chaudhry's numbers bolstered his position: he was unassailable; he could govern on his own. But a confluence of interests brought Mara and Chaudhry together. The eastern chiefly establishment had felt ignored by the Rabuka administration; it was now in a position to be represented in cabinet. Mara's waning influence was also reinvigorated. For Chaudhry, the president's daughter in cabinet, and Mara's public support for his government, shored up Labour's credibility among Fijians who might otherwise have distrusted an Indo-Fijian prime minister. Dislike of Rabuka brought the men together: my enemy's enemy is my friend.

In his first broadcast as prime minister, Chaudhry was at pains to emphasise his government's broad non-racial appeal. He stressed repeatedly that he was prime minister 'not for any[one] community' but 'for everybody'. He pledged his commitment 'to complying with the requirements of the Constitution for the equitable participation of all communities in government', promising to 'ensure that all communities fully benefit from the nation's economic development'. He would be 'guided by the wisdom and counsel [of the Great Council of Chiefs] on all matters affecting the interests and welfare of indigenous Fijians and Rotumans'. The business community too had nothing to fear. 'In working to uplift the conditions of life of the poor, the workers, and the less privileged in our society we are not being anti-business. We're just being pro-people.' His government believed in development with justice 'but we are equally committed to laying down economic policies that will encourage investors and business to grow' (Address to the nation 19 May 1999).

Chaudhry acted astutely in forming his cabinet. Eleven of the 17 ministers were ethnic Fijians, a gesture of reassurance to the Fijians that their interests were adequately protected. However, he himself controlled the key portfolios of Finance, Public Enterprises, Sugar Industry and Information. His Labour ministers controlled Foreign Affairs, Education, Labour and Industrial Relations, Commerce, Business Development and Investment, National Planning, Local Government, Housing and Environment, Justice, Regional Development and Multiethnic Affairs and Women, Culture and Social Welfare. Chaudhry knows that his success at the next election depends on his handling of the domestic social and economic agenda. People reacted cautiously and approvingly, though some Fijian nationalists as well as some defeated SVT parliamentarians wanted to oust Labour from power (*Daily Post* 28 May 1999). Rabuka was approached by people within his own party, including former senior ministers, to lead a 1987-style coup, but he rejected their overtures outright.[22] Things had changed: the majority of the Fijian people had rejected the SVT, and the overwhelming sentiment in the country was to give the new government a chance to prove its mettle.

Fijians would not be fooled again, a searching editorial in a Fijian newspaper wrote (*Volasiga* 31 May to 6 June 1999). It was typical of the reaction throughout the country.

> Sakiasi Butadroka and supporters of the Nationalist Vanua Tako Lavo Party are being mischievous and misleading in trying to scare the Fijians into believing the Indians have taken over Fiji...Buta is saying Ratu Mara and Mahendra Chaudhry are selling the rights of the indigenous Fijians. But we all know that no one on their own can sell the rights of the Fijians. No one who is not a Fijian, even if he or she is head of the Government, can remove the rights of Fijians to their land and resources. This will only happen if the Fijians themselves agree to it.

The editorial then drew attention to the problems facing the Fijian people which, it added, had little to do with other groups. 'When we look at our schools and their academic results, we see it is mainly the Fijians who are failing their exams. That's because there are weaknesses in our family life and within Fijian society.' The majority of those breaking the laws were Fijians. The biggest victims of sexually transmitted diseases were Fijians. Teenage pregnancies and single mothers were disproportionately Fijians. 'Who then is Butadroka fooling in Fiji? We are trying to catch up on the difficulties in life we are now facing and to reverse the general opinion that we are lagging behind.' To many Fijians, then, Chaudhry was not an adversary but an ally. It was their own leaders, drunk on power and dulled into complacency, who had deserted them.

Parliament opened on 15 June 1999. In his opening address, the president outlined the government's policies for its first term. The government's 'two crucial and central challenges' were to 'further strengthen the bonds of unity in our multiethnic and multicultural society' and to 'promote economic growth and social progress'. These challenges, said Mara

> are to be undertaken with a strong sense of social justice to ensure that development benefits all in our society, including the poor, the disadvantaged and all those who, through no fault of their own, need the helping hand of the State. Government will implement affirmative action and social justice programs to secure for all citizens and communities equal and equitable access to opportunities, amenities and services to better their lives.

How these appealing but uncosted promises were to be honoured would be watched carefully. The promises were impressive: removing value-added tax on basic food items, medical charges and supplies and essential educational items; establishing a minimum national wage scheme; providing social security for the elderly and removing the user-pay concept in health care; introducing a national health service; establishing a bank to service the farming community; reducing the cost of public utilities; establishing a land use commission to identify and access vacant land; upgrading equipment at the four sugar mills and building new ones in Sigatoka and Seaqaqa; revitalising and diversifying agriculture; and making investment capital and other inputs available to entrepreneurs at a reasonable cost. The Chaudhry administration delivered on some of its promises. The F$27 million loan repayment for crop rehabilitation was waived. The Rabuka government's privatisation of strategic public assets was halted. The prime minister insisted on more effective performance from his senior public servants. He has also ordered that all interest rates with banks and Housing Authority and Home Finance be decreased from 12 per cent to 6 per cent. But there was a long way to go.

Chaudhry made a concerted effort to assure the Fijian community that he would not undermine their interests. Soon after the election, he addressed the Bose Levu Vakaturaga; only the second Indo-Fijian (after Jai Ram Reddy) to do so, seeking their blessing and expressing his gratitude 'for their immense contribution in laying the foundation for freedom, democracy, unity and development in our country' (Ministry of Information Press Release 8 June 1999). His government agreed to honour a request by the BLV to transfer all state Schedule A and Schedule B land to the Native Land Trust Board. The decision was widely praised in the Fijian community. The government also pledged to continue the special annual education fund of F$4.5 million for Fijian education, and initiated programs to ensure that people on remote islands were 'not denied the benefits of development'.

It was not all plain sailing. There was hope of a long road ahead to translate a vision into reality. Fate willed otherwise.

Notes

I thank Donald Denoon, Stewart Firth, Padma Lal, Ron May, Robert Norton, Joeli Veiyataki and Christine Weir for their helpful comments which improved both the readability as well as the substance of this chapter. To Dilip Khatri, Davendra Nandan, Surend Prasad and Prem Singh of Nadi, Fiji, I owe many a conversation on the campaign trail which lightened the burden of research and forged friendships which will endure. None of them are responsible for my errors of judgment and facts.

1   For an overview of these periods, see Lal (1992, 1998).
2   See Fiji Constitution Review Commission (1996). A summary of the work of the Commission is provided in Lal (1997).
3   The words are from the *Pacific Report* 10 May 1999, but they are echoed in virtually every newspaper overseas and in Fiji. Fiji's most respected journal, *Islands Business*, even went on to predict the composition of the next Rabuka-led government.
4   The 52-seat house provided for by the Independence Constitution had 27 communal (racially-reserved seats, 12 each for Fijians and Indians and 3 for General Electors) and 25 cross-voting seats (10 each for Fijians and Indians and 5 for General Voters). The ethnicity of the candidate was specified, but all voters voted for them.
5   These were the Fiji Labour Party, National Democratic Party, National Federation Party, the Soqosoqo ni Vakavulewa ni Taukei, Fijian Association Party, General Voters Party, General Electors Party, Vanua Tako Lavo Party, Vitilevu Dynamic Multiracial Party, Party of National Unity, Veitokani ni Lewenivanua Vakaristo Party, United National Labour Party, Party of Truth, Natural Law Party, Coalition of Independent Nationals Party, Nationalist Vanua Tako Lavo Party, Farmers and General Workers Coalition Party, and Lio 'On Famor Rotuma Party.
6   ALTA was negotiated in the late 1960s under which tenants were given 30 year leases of native Fijian land. These leases have begun to expire. Landlords want their land back, placing the mostly Indo-Fijian tenants in a precarious position. Balancing the interests of tenants and landlords is perhaps the most thorny issue in Fiji at the moment.
7   For a study of the 1987 elections, see Lal (1988).
8   See *The Review*, March 1999: 'Divided they fall: selection of candidates split the General Electors'.
9   For more on this and the 1992 elections, see Lal (1993).
10   I owe this apt description to Robert Norton.
11   All the quotations in this section come from the party's campaign literature.
12   When he was confronted with this allegation, Ratu Mara reportedly replied that his 'conscience was clear'.
13   Among them, Colonel Inoke Luveni and Manasa Lasaro. They argued that Bune did not meet any of the criteria the party had laid down for leadership. These stipulated that the leader must come from a chiefly family and should be the offspring of a marriage; must not be divorced or separated from his wife and have a stable and happy family, and not have 'produced children' outside of marriage; be a Christian and a regular churchgoer, and must believe that Fiji should become a Christian state and that the Sunday Ban be reimposed. See *Daily Post*, 21 April 1999.

14 From Reddy's final campaign address, 3 May 1999.
15 As claimed by NFP's Dr Wadan Narsey (comments made in Labasa on 10 April 1999).
16 From Reddy's opening campaign speech. The quotations in the following two paragraphs also come from it.
17 From Reddy's closing campaign address, 3 May 1999.
18 This is based on the People's Coalition Manifesto.
19 Among them Sir Vijay Singh, former Alliance government minister and now a regular columnist for a local daily. See *Fiji Times*, 18 May 1999.
20 Reddy acknowledged this perception in his first post-coup press conference, but he saw this 'partly [as] the result of very successful propaganda', noting that in recent years, his party had extended its base to include as candidates trade unionists, teachers, and women.
21 Interview in *The Review*, June 1999; see also *Daily Post*, 21 May 1999.
22 Personal communication with Rabuka.

chapter four

Understanding the results of the 1999 Fiji elections

Robert Norton

The outcome of the most remarkable parliamentary elections in Fiji's history signalled the possibility of a new phase in political development: a government responding to popular interests that cut across the ethnic divide—the lost promise of the ill-fated Bavadra government of 1987.

While it would be mistaken to infer that the 1999 elections reflect a great weakening of racial or ethnic identities in national politics, it is clear that significant indigenous Fijian support for the still predominantly Indian Fiji Labour Party (FLP) was regained following the dissolution of their interest in it after the military coups 12 years ago. Labour received some of its Fijian support in direct votes, but most through the second and third preferences of its Fijian allies in both communal and open electorates: the Fijian Association Party (FAP), the Party of National Unity (PANU), and the Christian Democratic Party (VLV). Together, these three Fijian parties have followers throughout Fiji, though differing in their regions of greatest popularity.[1] They attracted 43 per cent of all first preference votes and 70 per cent of the seats in the Fijian communal contests, against the governing Soqosoqo ni Vakavulewa ni Taukei (SVT) Party's 34 per cent of the votes and 22 per cent of the seats in the communal electorates (Figure 4.1).

Leading government with stronger Fijian support than in 1987, the Labour Party had an opportunity to widen its popular base with programs aimed at improving the conditions of life of ordinary people. Its continued national leadership would depend on the success of this project in countering divisions of ethnic interests and agendas within the coalition. Labour's victory rested precariously on a conjunction of contradictory factors including quite disparate ethnic grievances (Indian and Fijian), growing 'class' discontent cutting across the ethnic divide, and the new system of preferential voting which especially favoured the party's strongest Fijian ally, the FAP.

Figure 4.1   Fijian communal contests: percentage of first preference votes and
              percentage of seats won

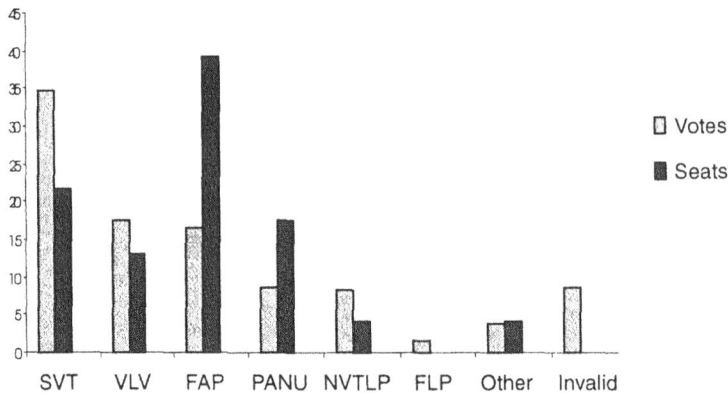

Key: SVT—Soqosoqo ni Vakavulewa ni Taukei; FAP—Fijian Association Party; VLV—Veitokani ni
Lewenivanua Vakaristo; PANU—Party of National Unity; NVTLP—Nationalist Vanua Tako/Lavo
Party; FLP—Fiji Labour Party.
Source: Fiji Election Office figures, May 1999.

Although interests and meanings of race (or ethnicity) have dominated
the shaping of national politics in Fiji, an important question for political
development has long been how realities of 'class' (such as economic
inequalities) that transcend ethnic difference might be given effective
expression in the democratic contest to control the state (Howard 1991;
Sutherland 1992). Shared interests as wage workers and consumers are
reflected in inter-ethnic cooperation in the powerful trade union movement
whose most influential leader, Mahendra Chaudhry, became prime minister.
At least 40 per cent of both Fijians and Indians now live and work, or are
unemployed, in urban centres, and increasing numbers of people in both
groups in the rural areas have interests in common as commercial farmers—
as reflected, for example, in the cooperation in elections to select farmers'
representatives to the Sugar Growers' Council.

However this inter-ethnic convergence in shared material interests has
ambiguous political implications. It brings the possibility of intensified
ethnic conflict no less than a prospect for unity. This was evidenced after
the victory of Bavadra's coalition in 1987 which seemed to promise the
political realisation of the class potential. Some of the strongest *Taukeist*
reaction against this coalition's win came from urban Fijians. The Labour
Party in that coalition had attracted about 9 per cent of votes in the Fijian
communal electorates. But after the coups Fijians began to split from the
party, due to the inevitable heightening of ethnic tensions. By the early
1990s most of Labour's leading Fijian stalwarts were rejecting the party for
having become an Indian concern.

So indeed it largely continued to be during the period of the first post-coup Constitution and the phase of constitutional reform from 1994 to 1997. In the first post-coup elections in 1992, Labour contested only four of the 37 Fijian seats, attracting from 3–9 per cent of the votes—a total of 2,654 votes, mostly in western Viti Levu. In the 1994 elections Fijian support dropped to a mere 555 in just two constituencies in western Viti Levu (Norton 1994). At the party's 1995 convention in Nadi, the heartland of western Viti Levu, there was a jarring contrast between its almost entirely Indian male audience and its ethnically and internationally variegated platform of speakers (including political figures from Australia and New Zealand). The event dramatised a tension between the post-coup pressures of ethnic politics, and the leaders' desire to preserve their original image in the hope that the political climate would change. The party continued to have a Fijian president, a former leader of the nurses' union, on whom the Indian principals relied to symbolise the interracial mission and to make aggressive declarations, such as urging Indians to 'agitate and demand' their rights *(Fiji Times* 3 June 1996:5).[2]

Yet it was in part a shared concern for the plight of the common people (farmers and urban workers) that had brought the Labour leader Mahendra Chaudhry and the coup-maker Sitiveni Rabuka together in 1992 for a short-lived alliance that enabled Rabuka to win office as prime minister against Fijian rivals. It was an astonishing irony, for Chaudhry had been the toughest fibre of the political force Rabuka had sought to demolish at gunpoint. Several months earlier, as his conflict with Prime Minister Ratu Sir Kamisese Mara intensified, the populist Rabuka had championed the cause of aggrieved mineworkers, sugar cane farmers, and nurses. He publicly drew an invidious contrast between Chaudhry and Mara. Chaudhry, Rabuka declared, was exemplary in his dedicated work for his people, the cane farmers, whereas Ratu Mara ignored the needs of the Fijians.

But Rabuka's flirtation with Chaudhry was encouraged more by fear of a political fragmentation among the Fijians which could undermine his power. This trend became clear in the 1992 and 1994 elections, particularly in the weakening of support for Rabuka's SVT Party in many areas of the main island Viti Levu, where the wage economy and urbanisation are most advanced and where everyday inter-ethnic relations are most common. Interestingly, however, support for the SVT on Viti Levu in 1994 was generally greater in the urban areas themselves (68 per cent on average) than in the rural areas (51 per cent) (Norton 1998). Even in 1999, when the Labour Party regained some urban Fijian support, the SVT's weakest areas were generally not the cities and towns. In fact the party attracted on average 35 per cent of urban Fijian votes, slightly greater than its overall support in the Fijian communal contests and far more than the urban support given to any other Fijian party (Table 4.1). The SVT remained the single most popular Fijian political party when first preference votes are considered (Figure 4.1).

The trend to Fijian political fragmentation had continued after the constitutional reform, encouraged by widespread Fijian dissatisfaction with Rabuka for having betrayed the political promise of the coups, as well as having failed to meet their expectations for improved living standards and opportunities. The trend finally overwhelmed his SVT Party in 1999. By contrast, division among Indian voters was far less than it had been since pre-coup elections. It was the unprecedented level of division among Fijians and a new trend to Indian unity behind the party that gave victory to Labour (Table 4.2 and Figure 4.2).

The electoral system

There were three innovations to the electoral system in the new Constitution: voting was made compulsory for citizens aged 21 years and over, 25 open electorates were superimposed on 45 communal electorates,

Table 4.1 **Support for parties in Fijian urban communal contests: first preference votes** (per cent)

	SVT	FAP	VLV	PANU	NVTLP	FLP	Other	Invalid
Tamavua/Laucala	40	27	26	-	-	-	-	7
Southwest Urban	39	21	18	-	6	8	1	7
Suva City	37	14	22	-	8	12	-	7
Nasinu	31	24	22	-	10	-	5	8
Northwest Urban	30	-	19	41	5	-	-	5
Northeast Urban	35	25	19	-	15	-	-	6

Note: SVT—Soqosoqo ni Vakavulewa ni Taukei; FAP—Fijian Association Party; VLV—Veitokani ni Lewenivanua Vakaristo; PANU—Party of National Unity; NVTLP—Nationalist Vanua Tako/Lavo Party; FLP—Fiji Labour Party.
Source: Fiji Election Office figures, May 1999.

Table 4.2 **Indian communal voting, 1992–99**

	1992		1994		1999	
	Seats	Votes (%)	Seats	Votes (%)	Seats	Votes (%)
FLP	13	47	8	42	19	60
NFP	14	50	19	54	-	29
Other	-	3	-	4	-	2
Invalid	..	..	..	..	-	9

Key: FLP—Fijian Labour Party; NFP—National Federation Party.
1992 and 1994 invalids not included.
Source: Fiji Election Office figures, May 1999.

and a preferential voting system (the 'Alternative Vote') replaced the old 'first-past-the-post' system. Voters' second and third preferences were distributed when no candidate gained more than 50 per cent of the first preference votes. The composition of the open electorates was multiethnic and their seats were not ethnically reserved. The ethnic composition of these electorates is shown in Figure 4.3.

From 1966 until 1987 there had been some 'cross-voting' electorates in addition to a majority of communal ones (Lal 1992; Lawson 1991; Norton 1990). They were introduced as a compromise with the longstanding call by most Indian leaders for fully common roll elections. Although they were multiethnic in composition, their seats were ethnically reserved. Most of these electorates each had an Indian and a Fijian seat, and every elector voted in both a communal and an encompassing cross-voting electorate. Like the communal contests, cross-voting contests could only be between candidates of the same ethnic group, so that elections could never alter the ethnic balance in parliament. Thus while it was true that Bavadra's government was elected very largely by Indian voters, there were no more

---

Figure 4.2   Indian communal voting: percentages of first preference support for the FLP and the NFP in the 19 electorates

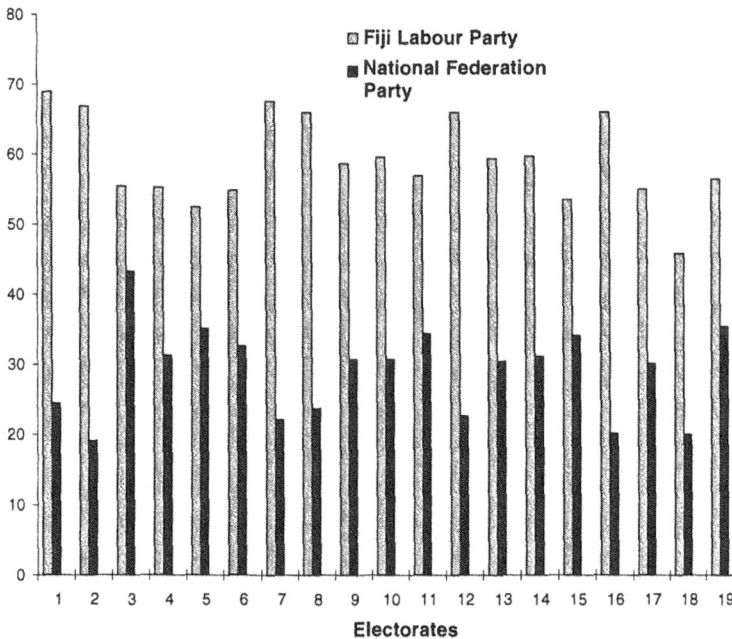

Key: 1. Nasinu, 2. Laucala, 3. Suva City, 4. Viti Levu South-Kadavu, 5. Tailevu-Rewa, 6. Viti Levu East-Maritime, 7. Tavua, 8. Ba East, 9. Ba West, 10. Lautoka Rural, 11. Lautoka City, 12. Vuda, 13. Nadi Rural, 14. Nadi Urban, 15. Nadroga, 16. Labasa, 17. Macuata East-Cakaudrove, 18. Labasa Rural, 19. Vanua Levu West.
Source: Fiji Election Office figures, May 1999.

Figure 4.3   Ethnic composition of the open electorates

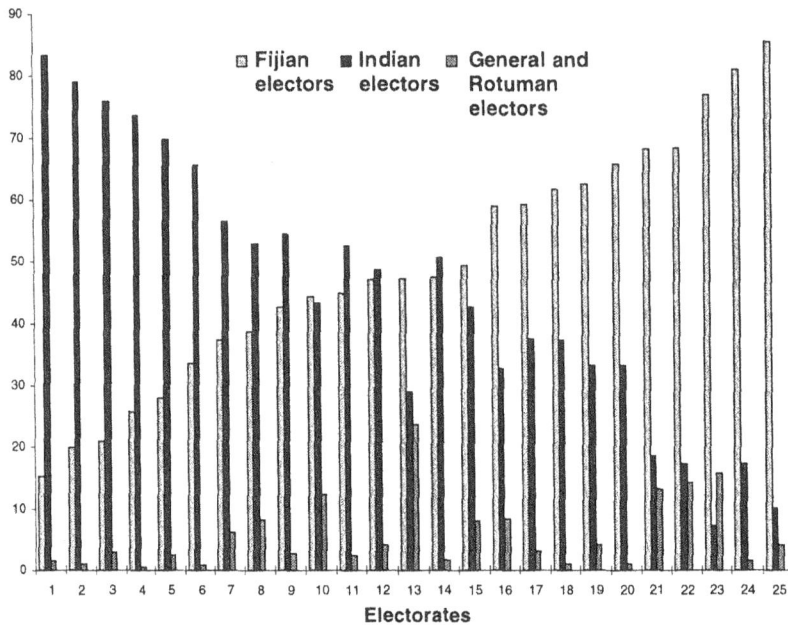

Key: 1. Ba, 2. Macuata East, 3. Labasa, 4. Magodro, 5. Vuda, 6. Yasawa-Nawaka, 7. Nadi, 8. Lautoka City, 9. Tavua, 10. Samabula-Tamavua, 11. Nasinu-Rewa, 12. Nausori-Naitasiri, 13. Suva City, 14. Nadroga, 15. Laucala, 16. Cunningham, 17. Bua-Macuata, 18. Ra, 19. Serua-Navosa, 20. Tailevu South-Lomaiviti, 21. Lami, 22. Cakaudrove West, 23. Lau-Taveuni-Rotuma, 24. Lomaivuna-Namosi-Kadavu, 25. Tailevu North-Ovalau.
Source: Fiji Election Office figures, May 1999.

Indians in the parliament than before. What had shifted, to some extent, were the party alignments of Fijian and Indian candidates, and of Fijian and Indian voters. Moreover, the cross-voting electorates did make it easier for a party such as Labour to appeal directly for Fijian votes.

The 1990 Constitution under which the 1992 and 1994 elections were conducted abolished cross-voting. There were only communal electorates, with 37 seats for Fijians, 27 seats for Indians, 5 for Generals, and one Rotuman. Rabuka's SVT Party, authorised by the Council of Chiefs, dominated the House of Representatives with a majority of the Fijian seats. The Council of Chiefs' nominees dominated the upper house (Senate). Indian leaders declined invitations to join the cabinet under this Constitution.

The Constitution Review Commission of 1995–6, headed by Sir Paul Reeves, recommended a new electoral system to comprise 45 open or 'common roll' electorates with no ethnic reservation of seats, and only 25 communal electorates each with an ethnically reserved seat. The objective was 'to encourage the emergence of a multiethnic political culture' (Reeves et al. 1996:309). However, the ratio was reversed by the Joint Parliamentary Select Committee which, under Rabuka's leadership, reviewed the Reeves report and decided the terms of the new Constitution. The two main Indian groups, the National Federation Party (NFP) and the Fiji Labour Party (FLP), were divided on this issue of the electoral system. The FLP urged accepting the Reeves Commission's proposal, while the NFP agreed with the Fijian and General leaders that communal representation should continue to predominate.

The communal seats included 23 Fijian, 19 Indian, and 3 General. There was also one Rotuman electorate and seat. Most of the Fijian electorate boundaries corresponded with those of the old provinces, but the three most populous provinces (Ba, Cakaudrove and Tailevu) were each split into two electorates. The 23 Fijian electorates averaged around 9,000 electors, but ranged very widely in size from Namosi 2,856 to Nadroga/Navosa 16,047, each with just one seat. The 19 Indian electorates averaged about 10,000, ranging from 7,760 in Viti Levu East/Maritime to 14,454 in Laucala (in Suva). The 3 General electorates ranged from Suva City 3,772 to Western/ Central 5,701. The 25 open electorates ranged in size from Suva City 15,566 to Nadi 21,020. They varied widely in their ethnic composition, but with an overall balance of some predominantly Fijian and some predominantly Indian electorates and a range of ethnic proportions between these extremes (Figure 4.3). As in the pre-coup system, voters were entitled to two votes: one in their communal electorate, and one in the open electorate of which their communal electorate, or a section of it, was part.

The introduction of open electorates, for the first time outside of town government, enabled direct contests between candidates of different ethnicity for the same seats, and hence allowed the election process to determine the ethnic proportions in the House of Representatives. More importantly, the change favoured the development of multiethnic political parties, though this potential has yet to be strongly realised.

An upper house, the Senate, was preserved, though altered in composition. It had 32 members appointed by Fiji's president, who was selected by the Council of Chiefs. Fourteen were nominated by the Council of Chiefs, 9 chosen by the Prime Minister, 8 by the Leader of the Opposition, and 1 by the Council of Rotuma. The chiefs were more strongly represented than they were under the pre-coup Constitution, but well below their strength under the 1990 Constitution.

The 1999 elections

The constitutional reform reconstructed, perhaps more surely than ever before, an institutional and ideological framework for containing Fijian ethno-nationalism and encouraging inter-ethnic political cooperation, both in election campaigning and in the formation and conduct of government.

Table 4.3   Fiji's population and registered voters by ethnicity

Population	No.	%	Registered electors	No.	%
Indigenous Fijians	393,575	50.8	Fijians	210,209	50.6
Indians	338,818	43.7	Indian	187,154	45.1
Part-Europeans	11,685	1.5	General	12,679	3.1
Rotumans	9,727	1.3	Rotuman	4,896	1.2
Other Pacific Islanders	10,463	1.4	Total	414,938	
Chinese	4,969	0.6			
European	3,103	0.4			
Others	2,767	0.4			
Total	775,077				

Note: General electors include mainly Part-Europeans, Pacific Islanders other than Fijians and Rotumans, Chinese, and Europeans. Tiny Rotuma is Fiji's Polynesian dependency, but a majority of the Rotumans reside on Fiji's main island, Viti Levu.
Source: Fiji Election Office figures.

The Constitution required that the prime minister must invite into his cabinet in proportion to their strength all parties whose membership in the House of Representatives comprised at least 10 per cent of the total membership of the House—in practice, 8 of the 71 seats.

In their joint campaigning, Rabuka and Reddy as leaders of the SVT and the NFP respectively, promised to strengthen 'multiracialism', political stability, and economic prosperity on the basis of their crucial collaborative roles in the achievement of the constitutional reform. NFP rhetoric sometimes warned of the danger of ethnic violence, pointing to recent tragedies in other parts of the world. The persistence of ethnically divisive issues concerning land and political power gave relevance to this platform. However, the new Constitution had opened the way for a new direction in political leadership on 'bread and butter' concerns of everyday popular life that transcended the ethnic differences.

The strategic alliance which devastated the SVT-NFP-UGP coalition was led by the FLP which, with its uncompromising universalist ideology, had been marginalised during the process of constitutional reform as Reddy, the NFP leader, dealt more effectively with Rabuka and the SVT (Lal 1998; Norton 2000). Ironically, however, Labour owed its victory not just to the new popularity of its ideology (mainly with Indian voters), but much more to the unprecedented political fragmentation of Fijians that had been provoked partly by resentment against Rabuka's compromising with Indian demands.

Some Fijian leaders denounced Rabuka for betraying the promise of his coups by agreeing to a change that would jeopardise indigenous power. They pointed out that a majority of the Fijian provincial councils had originally opposed the Reeves Commission's proposals for reform. While this issue was helping several Fijian parties to erode the SVT's popular base, Reddy's NFP was losing every seat to Labour. The catastrophic NFP defeat was due partly to the unpopularity of the party's alliance with the coup-maker and to anxieties about the future of farm leases. On the latter issue, the NFP often seemed more deferential to the Fijian owners than concerned to defend the Indian tenants, as many leases began to run out and, in some localities, landowner harrassment intensified.

Both the SVT and the NFP were weakened also by discontents over unemployment and poverty, and allegations of government neglect, mismanagement and corruption. Labour and its main Fijian allies (FAP and PANU) appealed to these concerns under the banner of 'The Peoples' Coalition'. Rabuka's strongest Fijian rivals had joined forces with the Labour Party in varying degrees and from differing motives, and Labour itself campaigned with a renewed Fijian participation, both in its leadership and among its candidates.

The splitting of the Fijians among several Fijian parties and the FLP (Labour), decimated the governing SVT Party both in the Fijian communal electorates and in the open electorates. In the communal contests, the SVT was reduced from the 65 per cent of votes won in 1994, to just 34 per cent. It was an unprecedented fall in popularity for a dominant Fijian political party (Figure 4.4). The party won only 8 seats (5 communal and 3 open)—11 per cent of the parliament. Labour won 37 seats (19 Indian communal and 18 open)—52 per cent of parliament (Figure 4.5). With its Fijian allies and the support of the sole Rotuman member, Labour held 56 seats (nearly 80 per cent). By ethnicity they were 30 Indians, 25 Fijians, and one Rotuman (Table 4.4).

Labour defeated the NFP in all communal Indian and in all open contests (Figure 4.2 and Table 4.2). Labour did not contest any of the three General seats, two of which went to independent candidates and one to the UGP in coalition with the SVT and NFP.

The effect of preferential voting

Preferences were distributed where no candidate achieved over 50 per cent of the votes on the first count. This was so in 18 of the 25 open contests, 16 of the 23 Fijian communal contests, 2 of the 3 General communal contests, but in none of the 19 Indian communal contests. The need to distribute second and third preferences was of course linked to the number of candidates competing for a seat—an average of 5.3 for the open seats, 4.3 for the Fijian communal, 4 for the General communal, but only 2.6 for the Indian communal seats.

In some cases 'dummy' candidates had been fielded to maximise the impact of preferences. For example, in several open electorates the SVT encouraged Fijians to vote for the NFP but also fielded its own candidate to help split the voting and to direct the preferences of supporters who would not tick the NFP. In several other contests the NFP used the same strategy when it favoured the SVT candidate (Table 4.5).

It is interesting to compare the election outcome with what would have been the result if the contests were all decided, as previously, by the largest first preference vote; that is, 'first past the post' (Table 4.6). Labour would still be the strongest group in parliament, with 33 of the 71 seats, though only 4 of its members would be Fijians, instead of 7. Only 4 of Labour's 18 open seats depended on preferences, and not one of its 19 communal Indian

---

Figure 4.4   Support for major Fijian political parties, 1966–99 (per cent)

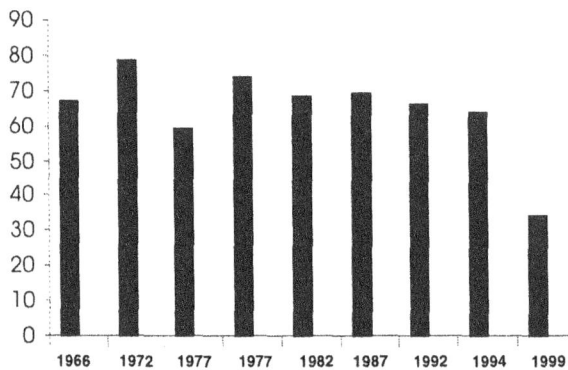

Key: 1966–87 Fijian Association (main body in the Alliance Party); 1992–99 Soqosoqo ni Vakavulewa ni Taukei (SVT).
Source: Norton, R., 1990. *Race and Politics in Fiji*, University of Queensland Press, St. Lucia (rev. ed); Norton, R., 1998. 'Politics in Fiji', in R. Chandra (ed.), *Atlas of Fiji*, School of Social and Economic Development, University of the South Pacific, Suva.

Figure 4.5   Support for parties in the open contests—first preference votes and seats won

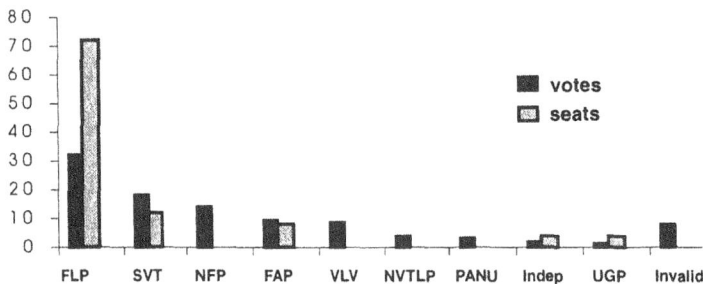

Source: Fiji Election Office figures, May 1999.

seats did—the party won every Indian seat by voters' first choice, which averaged twice the vote for the NFP (Figure 4.2).

But the fortunes of the SVT and its main Fijian rival (the FAP) would have been dramatically reversed. The SVT would have 18 seats instead of a mere 8 (11 communal and 7 open), and the FAP, Labour's major ally, would have only 6 seats instead of 11 (4 communal, 2 open). While Labour's other main Fijian ally, PANU, would still have its 4 seats, the VLV, informally a Labour ally, would have secured just 2 seats not 3. The SVT partner, the UGP, would have 4 seats rather than 2. Figure 4.6 shows the size of discrepancies between first preference and final votes for winning candidates in the open and the Fijian communal contests.

Clearly it was in the Fijian communal contests where the preferential voting system had the greatest effect. The SVT was isolated by the combined hostility of its Fijian rivals. Most directed preferences well away from the SVT leaving it at or near the bottom of their lists, and in the open electorates they shared preferences with Labour which often also ranked even the most conservative Fijian groups ahead of the SVT. The parties encouraged voters to endorse the parties' preferences by ticking the party box above the line on the ballot paper, rather than making their own rankings in a list below the line. Confusion over the new system often resulted in invalid votes (in some electorates as high as 14 per cent), and many Fijian voters later complained that they had not understood that endorsing their party's preferences could help the predominantly Indian Labour Party to victory.

But far more important for the Labour victory than the allocation of preferences was simply the political fragmentation of the Fijians. While in the Fijian communal electorates Labour gained indirectly from the victories of its allies who took 16 of these 23 seats, in the open electorates it owed 7 of its own 18 wins to the Fijian splitting (Laucala, Lami, Cunningham,

Table 4.4	Ethnic composition of House of Representatives, after 1999 elections				
Party	Fijian	Indian	General	Rotuman	Total
FLP	7	30	-	-	37
SVT	8	-	-	-	8
FAP	12	-	-	-	12
PANU	4	-	-	-	4
VLV	3	-	-	-	3
UGP	-	-	2	-	2
Other	1	1	2	1	5
Total	35	31	4	1	71

Note: FLP—Fiji Labour Party; SVT—Soqosoqo ni Vakavulewa ni Taukei; FAP—Fijian Association Party; PANU—Party of National Unity; VLV—Veitokani ni Lewenivanua Vakaristo; UGP—United General Party.
Source: Fiji Election Office, election results.

Table 4.5   'Dummy' candidates fielded by the NFP and SVT in 20 open electorates

Electorate	NFP	SVT
Nadroga	35*	6,377
Tailevu South Lomaiviti	22*	6,161
Bua Macuata	18*	5,897
Suva City	89*	1,040
Magodro	3,927	1,169
Cunningham	41*	4,833
Lami	-	-
Ra	-	3,495
Tavua	1,476	2,603
Macuata East	4,038	-
Ba	5,285	46*
Vuda	4,096	2,410
Laucala	68*	4,125
Nadi	5,653	156*
Labasa	4,246	-
Yasawa Nawaka	4,651	24*
Nasini Rewa	3,920	131*
Nausori Naitasiri	4,044	169*
Lautoka City	5,255	192*
Samabula Tamavua	4,726	565*

Note: *Number of votes received for 'Dummy' candidates.
Source: Fiji Election Office figures, May 1999.

Table 4.6   Effects of preferential voting: actual results compared with hypothetical 'first-past-the-post' outcome

	Actual number of seats won		Hypothetical seats won by voters' first choice	
	Communal	Open	Communal	Open
FLP	19	18	19	14
SVT	5	3	11	7
FAP	9	2	4	2
VLV	3	-	2	-
PANU	4	-	4	-
NVTLP	1	-	1	-
UGP	1	1	3	1
Other	4	1	2	1

Notes: FLP—Fiji Labour Party; SVT—Soqosoqo ni Vakavulewa ni Taukei; FAP—Fijian Association Party; VLV—Veitokani ni Lewenivanua Vakaristo; PANU—Party of National Unity; NVTLP—Nationalist Vanua Tako/Lavo Party; UGP—United General Party.
Source: Fiji Election Office figures, May 1999.

Figure 4.6(a) Effects of preferential voting—percentages of first preference vote and final vote for winning candidates: open electorates

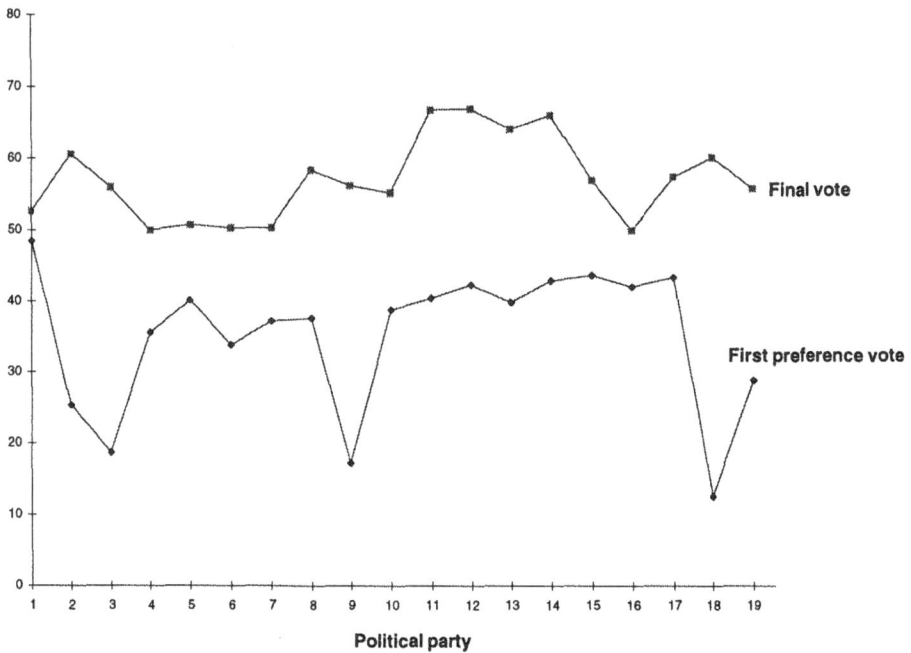

Key: FLP = 1–14; FAP = 15, 16; SVT = 17; Independent = 18; UGP = 19.
Source: Fiji Election Office figures, May 1999.

Figure 4.6(b) Effects of preferential voting—percentages of first preference vote and final vote for winning candidates: Fijian communal electorates

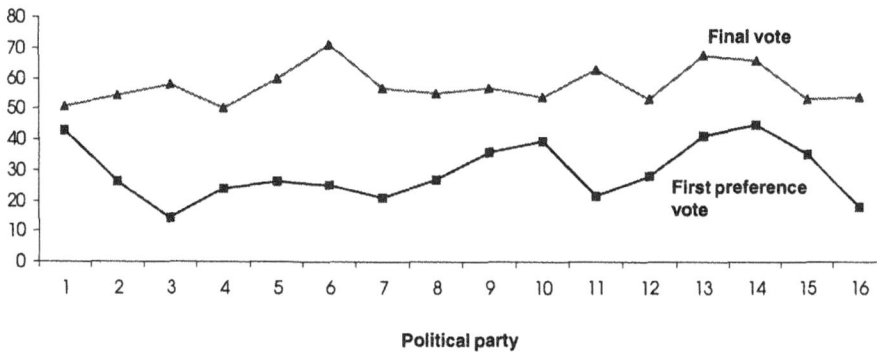

Key: FAP = 1, 3–9; Independent = 2; VLV = 10; NVTLP = 11; PANU = 12–14; SVT = 15–16.
Source: Fiji Election Office figures, May 1999.

Nadroga, Tailevu South/Lomaiviti, Bua/Macuata, Nadi). Fijian rivalries allowed the Labour candidates to emerge as the strongest contenders for these seats even on the first count.

The Fijian political fragmentation was encouraged partly by division among leaders of high chiefly rank. In its campaign rhetoric the SVT continued to emphasise that it had been formed under the authority of the Great Council of Chiefs. But several prominent chiefs, including the retired army commander and a daughter of Fiji's President, were now aligned with rival parties. One of the foremost chiefs, Adi Lala Mara, wife of Fiji's President, publicly repudiated the SVT claim to still have Council of Chiefs endorsement. An objective of the VLV, her daughter's party, was to restore a central role for the chiefs in national leadership which, it alleged, had been degraded by the Rabuka government.[3] PANU and the FAP, the other main challengers to the SVT, also enjoyed the leadership or support of important chiefs.

Labour's paradoxical gain from Fijian ethnic conservatism

The starkest irony of the elections was the massive popular rejection of the leaders who, over four years, had played the major roles in the dialogue and negotiation that enabled the reform of the racially-biased post-coup Constitution. They confidently relied on their momentous achievement to no avail in their election campaigning.

For both the SVT and the NFP, the constitutional reform was a double-edged sword. Its success had produced their coalition. But Indian voters at the very least either were not identifying the reform with the coalition, or they saw no continuing relevance of the coalition for their interests. Certainly their opposition to Reddy's electoral alliance with the coup-maker seemed to outweigh their perception of any likely benefits from the partnership—for all Reddy's reminders of tragic ethnic conflicts in other parts of the world and his urgings about the wisdom of working with the 'mainstream' Fijian political party to ensure harmony and achieve further reforms, particularly in respect to land leases. One of Labour's principal Fijian candidates, Tupeni Baba, before his Indian audiences, derided Reddy for trying to lead them to Rabuka's SVT just as Fijians were deserting it in droves! (Suva Civic Centre 5 May 1999). Rabuka's belated 'apology' for the hurt of his coups was occasioned, toward the end of the campaigning, by mounting criticism of the NFP for betraying the Indian people in uniting with the ruling party. The dramatic highpoint of Labour's last mass rally in Suva, was an indignant Mahendra Chaudhry playing a tape recording of Reddy's declaration during the 1994 elections that he would 'never endorse Rabuka for prime minister because of the suffering caused by his coups'. But Indians rejected the NFP also for joining with the party seen to be responsible in government for economic recession and corruption, after years of opposing it for these failings.

Many Fijians viewed the constitutional reform as a betrayal of the promise of the coups because its emphasis was on inter-ethnic power sharing. Certainly, for most Fijians, the constitutional reform was not a reason to vote for the SVT, and many were attracted by the promises of other Fijian parties to strengthen Fijian control over their lands at a time when Indian tenant farmers were becoming anxious about the future of their farms. A common question Fijians put to SVT candidates in villages and towns mirrored that being put by Indians to NFP campaigners: 'Why has the SVT joined with an Indian party?' Some candidates replied by stressing the importance of the new Constitution, the need 'to come together', and the correctness of this according to Christian values.

All the SVT's rivals, to varying degrees and in different places, encouraged Fijian discontent with Rabuka's compromising on the Constitution, as well as with his government's alleged economic mismanagement and corruption. This was especially true of the VLV and the Nationalist Vanua Tako Lavo Party (NVTLP). But each of Labour's Fijian party allies was characterised by a spectrum of outlooks and agendas, from ethno-nationalist to liberal. The VLV fanned ethnic sentiments with rhetoric about making Fiji a Christian state and bringing back the Sunday Observance Decree—though this call was eventually moderated for the sake of an informal alliance with Labour.

Ironically, the ethnocentrism encouraged by Fijian anti-SVT forces helped the ideologically universalist Labour Party by strengthening the popularity of its Fijian allies, and simply by splitting Fijian votes in the open contests. The party most strongly identified ideologically with constitutional reform, but which had been sidelined in the reform process, finally gained from Fijian opposition to reform.

Voting across the ethnic divide

Labour's pragmatic alliances in contravention of its ideological commitments do not account for its small but significant direct Fijian support, encouraged by some of the same discontents that compelled much of the party's Indian following. For urban audiences particularly, there was a striking contrast between the immediate relevance of the Labour Party's detailed criticisms and promises, and the SVT/NFP Coalition's platitudinous rhetoric about 'multiracialism', political stability, and economic growth. It was not that such goals were seen as unimportant, but simply that their proclamation could have little appeal against the powerful resonance of Labour's sharply focussed analysis of Fiji's problems, with widespread popular anxieties and frustrations: 'If the SVT/NFP Coalition wins government', Chaudhry warned his last Suva rally, 'they will inflict more pain and suffering on you!' (Suva Civic Centre 5 May 1999).

The SVT/NFP Coalition's faith in the power of their constitutional reform to carry the day for them seemed strangely out of touch with social realities. The period of the reform, from 1994 to 1997, had been a phase of redemption, of reconciliation and political reconstruction, after the trauma of the coups and an ethnically hegemonic Constitution (Lal 1998; Norton 2000). The tensions and uncertainties of this phase had kept ethnic concerns to the forefront and strengthened the identities of Reddy and Rabuka as national leaders. But the very success of the reform helped to free the political arena for new issues. There had been an accumulation of many sources of popular discontent, and it seemed that the achievement of a new Constitution opened the gate for an outpouring of the pent-up grievances.

Labour and PANU were the only parties with an ideological commitment to being multiethnic. But PANU, a Fijian group based in Western Viti Levu, fielded only one Indian communal candidate who attracted a mere 153 votes, and two Indian candidates for open seats (3,827 votes). The FAP supported three Indian and two General candidates for communal contests (the Indians winning 955 votes, the Generals 1,052). Even the VLV had an Indian candidate for an open contest in western Viti Levu (490 votes). But such inter-ethnic collaboration was intended mainly to assist in the splitting of votes.

The FLP (Labour) was clearly the only party that was substantially multiethnic in its leadership and popular following. A final rally packing the Suva Civic Centre auditorium three days before polling began included many enthusiastic Fijians. It was common to hear Fijians talking favourably about the party, and in some parts of Suva they held fund collecting drives (*soli*) for it. Labour contested four of the 23 Fijian communal seats, two of them in urban areas including Suva City, gaining from 7–12 per cent of the votes (3,352)—though only 1.7 per cent of all Fijian communal votes (Figure 4.1). The party left several other Fijian contests to its allies, the FAP and PANU. All seven of Labour's Fijian candidates for open seats were elected, five of them in electorates where Fijian voters equalled or outnumbered Indian voters (Tailevu South/Lomaiviti, Cunningham, Samabula/ Tamavua, Nadroga, Bua/Macuata West). In many other contests, both for communal and open seats, Labour encouraged support for its Fijian allies.

The communal figures do not reveal the magnitude of the direct indigenous Fijian support for Labour because the mere 1.7 per cent reflects the party's decision to leave most Fijian contests to its Coalition partners. However, the open results might reflect a considerably stronger Fijian interest in Labour. The FLP attracted 108,743 votes in the Indian communal contests, but 119,571 in the open contests. This increase of 10 per cent may comprise many Fijian and General votes.

A clearer indication of the possible scale of Fijian support for Labour might be found by comparing the ethnic composition of open electorates with the actual voting pattern, to gain a rough measure of the extent to which support for parties exceeded what might be expected if people voted simply on ethnic lines (Table 4.7 and Figure 4.7). Figure 4.7 makes two comparisons: (a) the total first preference votes received for the FLP, the NFP, and other Indian candidates in each of the 25 open constituencies, is compared with a hypothetical quantity of votes projected from the number of registered Indian electors in each constituency—the hypothetical vote is the portion of all actual valid votes in the electorate which we might expect to have been cast by the Indian electors; and (b) the total number of first preferences for Fijian candidates (other than FLP candidates) in the 25 constituencies, is compared with hypothetical quantities of Fijian votes calculated on the basis of the numbers of registered Fijian electors. The horizontal line represents equivalence of the figures in each comparison. The columns above and below this line show the extent to which actual voting exceeds or falls short of that hypothetical equivalence—that is, they represent the likely degrees of cross-ethnic voting.[4]

This is not an entirely reliable way of assessing the extent of cross-ethnic voting because we do not know the ethnic proportions of the actual voters, nor the ethnic makeup of invalid votes. I have assumed that these proportions are comparable to the ethnic composition of the registered electors. Average invalid voting in the communal electorates was about 9 per cent for Fijians and 10 per cent for Indians, suggesting that there may have been little ethnic difference in the invalid voting in the open electorates. Although the overall ethnic difference in the proportions of registered electors who voted was slight (92 per cent for Indians and 89 per cent for Fijians), the differences for particular open electorates are not known. My calculations also do not take account of the General electors and Rotuman electors whose combined strength among registered voters varied from 0.3–14.2 per cent, and averaged 4.6 per cent in the open electorates (Table 4.7). However, I do not think this would greatly modify the patterns in the figures.

If people had voted overwhelmingly on communal lines, we would expect to see a close correspondence between the ethnic composition of the registered electors in a particular constituency, and the division of votes between the predominantly ethnic parties. The number of votes for the FLP plus NFP (plus the few other Indian candidates) would be comparable to a figure projected on the basis of the number of registered Indian voters in the electorate, and the votes for Fijian parties and Fijian independents would resemble figures projected from the number of registered Fijian voters.

In fact, the pattern of correspondence and discrepancy between actual and projected figures indicates substantial degrees of voting across the ethnic divide, especially non-Indian support for the parties that have been identified as Indian or primarily Indian, the NFP and the FLP (the light-shaded columns above the line on the right side of the figure), and non-Fijian support for Fijian parties (dark-shaded columns above the line on the figure's left). There are several open constituencies, mainly urban, where the support gained by the 'Indian' parties must have included a substantial number of Fijian voters (Nos 16–25). Similarly, there are several open constituencies where the support for Fijian parties must have included a substantial number of Indian votes (Nos 1–9, especially 1, 2, 3, and 8).

Figure 4.7 presents the open electorates in order of the extent to which the totals of votes for FLP, NFP, and other Indian candidates fell below or exceeded the hypothetical projected votes by registered Indian electors. Toward the right of the figure, the volume of votes in excess of the projected votes corresponds with shortfalls of votes for Fijian parties and Fijian

Figure 4.7   Cross-ethnic first preference voting in open electorates

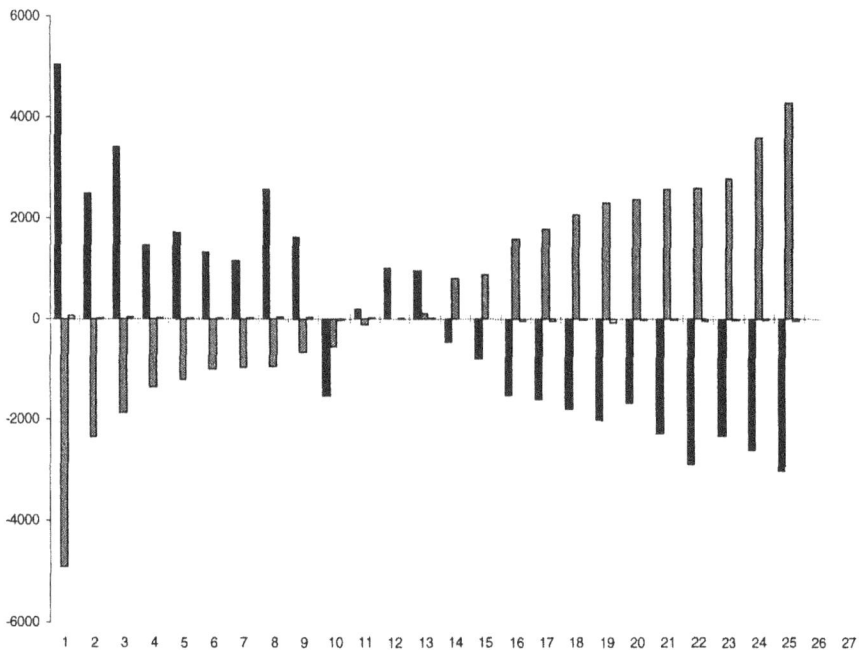

Key: Black: Difference between actual and projected votes for Fijian political parties and other Fijian candidates (other than those for FLP)
Grey: Differences between actual and projected votes for FLP, NFP, and other Indian candidates (calculations include 4,317 votes given to Indian candidates sponsored by the Fijian parties PANU and VLV).
Note: see Table 4.7 for constituency names.
Source: Fiji Election Office figures, May 1999.

independents (in relation to registered Fijian voters) in Nadi, Labasa, Yasawa/Nawaka, Nasinu/Rewa, Nausori/Naitasiri, Lautoka City, and most of all in Samabula/Tamavua where Labour fielded one of the most able of its Fijian leaders, Tupeni Baba; in five of these contests the Labour winners were Indians. All seven electorates are in urban or mainly urban areas throughout Fiji. In Samabula/Tamavua and Nausori/Naitasiri, Fijians and Indians made up almost equal proportions of the registered electors, and Generals and Rotumans were 9.6 per cent and 3.2 per cent respectively (Table 4.7).

Table 4.7   Cross-ethnic first preference voting in open electorates

		1	2	3	4	5	6
1.	Serua-Navosa	5047	-4906	62.6	33.3	2.5	0.4
2.	Lomaivuna-Namosi-Kadavu	2501	-2335	81.1	17.3	0.7	0.01
3.	Cakaudrove West	3404	-1853	68.4	17.3	11.5	0.3
4.	Tailevu South-Lomaiviti	1456	-1362	65.8	33.2	0.6	0.1
5.	Tailevu North Ovalau	1709	-1214	85.6	10.2	3.3	0.3
6.	Bua-Macuata West	1307	-999	59.3	37.6	2.0	0.1
7.	Nadroga	1143	-971	47.5	50.8	0.9	0.2
8.	Lau-Taveuni-Rotuma	2566	-942	76.9	7.2	3.6	8.4
9.	Laucala	1624	-668	49.3	42.7	3.6	3.3
10.	Suva City	-1542	-547	47.4	28.9	10.3	4.2
11.	Magodro	196	-121	25.7	73.7	0.4	0.1
12.	Cunningham	991	-21	58.8	32.7	5.3	1.7
13.	Lami	954	88	68.2	18.6	11.4	1.5
14.	Tavua	-476	788	42.7	54.5	1.1	1.2
15.	Ra	-798	870	61.7	37.3	0.4	0.1
16.	Macuata East	-1517	1577	19.9	79.1	0.3	0.01
17.	Ba	-1611	1781	15.2	83.3	0.9	0.1
18.	Vuda	-1795	2060	27.9	69.7	1.3	0.5
19.	Labasa	-2015	2288	20.9	76.0	2.0	0.1
20.	Nadi	-1657	2362	37.3	56.5	3.0	0.9
21.	Nasinu Rewa	-2279	2552	44.9	52.6	1.3	0.6
22.	Yasawa-Nawaka	-2888	2577	33.6	65.6	0.3	0.03
23.	Nausori-Naitasiri	-2328	2773	47.2	48.6	1.9	1.3
24.	Lautoka City	-2613	3591	38.7	53.0	4.6	2.0
25.	Samabula-Tamavua	-3010	4285	44.4	43.3	6.8	2.8

Notes:
1. Differences between actual and projected votes for Fijian political parties and other Fijian candidates (other than Fijian candidates of the FLP).
2. Differences between actual and projected votes for FLP, NFP, and other Indian candidates (calculations include 4,317 votes given to Indian candidates sponsored by the Fijian parties PANU and VLV).
3. Percentage of registered Fijian electors.
4. Percentage of registered Indian electors.
5. Percentage of registered General electors.
6. Percentage of registered Rotuman electors.
Source: Fiji Election Office figures, May 1999.

My observations in Suva at the time of the elections encourage me to believe that many of these votes were for Labour. However, it is not possible to determine how much of the Fijian support for 'Indian' parties was for the FLP rather than for the NFP. The chart partly reflects the success of the SVT/NFP/UGP Coalition's efforts to encourage 'cross' ethnic voting for shared candidates in many of the open contests. In some electorates the Coalition favoured an NFP candidate, and in others an SVT candidate, while also having the other party field a 'dummy'. The extent to which voters accepted the NFP/SVT coalition's true candidate regardless of party or ethnicity seems to be indicated by huge differences in the votes received by that contender and the 'dummy' (Table 4.5). These differences occurred in most of the electorates included in Figure 4.7.[5] The pattern on the left side of the chart shows the extent to which actual votes for the FLP, NFP, and other Indian candidates fell short of the hypothetical support projected on the basis of the number of registered Indian electors in each constituency, and the corresponding support for Fijian parties in excess of what might be expected from the numbers of registered Fijian voters.

The apparently substantial cross-ethnic voting for the NFP and the SVT is more likely to reflect the success of the coalition strategic sharing of contests rather than voters' identification with an ideology and program transcending the ethnic divide. Although the degree of Labour's success in directly attracting the popular Fijian vote remains unclear, the party has certainly made the most successful attempt to build a direct multiethnic following on the basis of ideology and policy. But alliances of primarily ethnic organisations continue to be the dominant form of political cooperation in Fiji, and these coalitions are likely to continue to be intermittently strained by their internal contradictions.

The election outcome

With 30 Indian and 7 Fijian members of parliament, Labour was the strongest group in the victorious Peoples' Coalition. Although at Labour's initiative, its leader, Mahendra Chaudhry, became the first Indian Prime Minister of Fiji, he selected a majority of Fijian ministers for his cabinet—11 of the 17 portfolios, including four from Labour, three from the FAP, and two each from PANU and the VLV. Several were of chiefly rank.

Fiji's president, Ratu Sir Kamisese Mara, refused a request by the FAP, Labour's principal partner in the Peoples' Coalition, that its high-ranking leader Adi Kuini Bavadra Speed, widow of Dr Bavadra, be appointed prime minister. Having faced the threat of losing his Fijian party allies a day before his swearing in, Chaudhry warmly acknowledged the importance of Mara's influence in persuading the FAP to accept Labour's leadership. Rabuka himself, while reproving Indians for a 'racial bloc' alignment with Labour and warning against actions that might threaten Fijian interests, nonetheless urged Fijians to support the new government—not least from his concern to demonstrate in Fiji and abroad his continued commitment to the Constitution he had played a crucial role in achieving.

Many people contacted the SVT headquarters to ask when 'the protest meetings would be held', only to be told they must accept the election result and perhaps had only themselves to blame for it. A protest march in central Suva organised by the NVTLP attracted little support. It is true that some people may have been deterred by the threat of the Police Commissioner, an ex-army Fijian, to make 'mass arrests' (*Fiji Times* 26 May 1999). However, the NVTLP had proved a generally weak contender in the elections, and the VLV, whose platform had also relied on ethnic appeals, had now been drawn into the new cabinet after sharing its vote preferences with Labour.

Within weeks of his victory, Chaudhry sought to dispel Fijian anxieties 'about my intentions and those of my government' in a speech to a specially convened meeting of the Council of Chiefs. He viewed the occasion as crucial for enhancing the legitimacy of his leadership of the nation, and his address echoed that of the first Indian to speak before the chiefs, Jai Ram Reddy, which had facilitated the constitutional reform (Lal 1998; Norton 1999). Chaudhry respectfully reaffirmed Reddy's 'assurances…that all communities…look to this great venerable institution for leadership and guidance in the good governance and well-being of our nation' (*Fiji Times* 14 June 1999:22–3). He promised especially to protect and advance indigenous interests and to consult with the chiefs.

Though many Fijians remained troubled by the appointment of an Indian prime minister, commonly exclaiming that 'this is our land, and a Fijian should lead!', the predominant reaction was acceptance in anticipation of action on Labour's ambitious electoral promises such as a minimum wage, tax reforms, and more jobs and job security. Some SVT leaders privately feared that Chaudhry, whose work and rhetoric had long focused on the plight of ordinary people, might now have the means to achieve an increasing popularity with indigenous Fijians.[6]

To some extent the FLP's success undoubtedly did reflect the widening of a popular base of shared inter-ethnic interests at a time of growing anxiety about employment and living conditions. Nonetheless, the party depended more on its ability to continue to lead an unstable alliance of groups with contradictory interests and agendas. Chaudhry had to contend with the ever-present potential for ethnic conflict within his coalition on such highly sensitive matters as land reform where he planned to improve the security of the tenants (mostly Indians), and over rivalries for cabinet and other government posts. Compounding his problems were imperatives of the international economy that were likely to impose obstacles to his attempts to tackle unemployment and poverty.

Rabuka regained his parliamentary seat, but quickly relinquished it to become full-time chairman of the Council of Chiefs where, still a potent icon of ethnic power, he had an enhanced capacity to encourage Fijians to either oppose or cooperate with Chaudhry's government. He could at times act as focal point of ethnic resistance, at other times as a mediator bridging the ethnic divide and promoting accommodation. In this respect his position might have been very like that which leading chiefs have long taken in the national political arena (Norton 2000; 1999). The crisis of expiring Indian farm leases, aggravated by Fijian resentment over the election outcome and posing a threat to national economic growth, might have proven to be Rabuka's first challenge in this role. During the months following the elections some traditional chiefs (including SVT members of parliament) reacted against the Labour victory by declaring that the leases in their districts would not be renewed: 'Fijians have given up the political control of their native land. They are not prepared to give up anything else. They will now be reluctant to share with others' (Tui Wailevu *The Daily Post* 23 June 1999).[7]

Postscript

Chaudhry's national leadership inevitably faced trouble over land, the issue of greatest sensitivity to Fijians. The Labour Party constituency included many Indian farmers anxious for the future of their expiring leases on Fijian clan lands. By demanding the retention of ALTA, the longstanding law that regulates the leasing and tends to advantage the tenants, he antagonised the Council of Chiefs and the Native Land Trust Board which wanted the legislation abolished and more control returned to the owners.

Several of Chaudhry's Fijian political opponents encouraged popular alarm on this and other issues, such as the proposal to establish a land use commission, and to extend to needy Indians a 'special loans' scheme originally introduced for Fijians. Aided by sections of the media, these politicians endeavoured to denigrate the new government's actions and policies as threatening indigenous interests. Chaudhry played into their hands when he ignored suggestions that he placate Fijian fears by consulting more with their authorities. For all his good intentions for the welfare of the ordinary people, he soon seemed to many Fijians to embody their long imagined threatening Indian leader. The antagonism toward him extended even to some of his own backbenchers. The orchestrated build-up of hostility created a supportive atmosphere for the violent seizure of his government by a 'rebel' group who masked their agenda for power and economic opportunity in the old familiar rhetoric of indigenous rights under threat from an Indian grab for political power.

The crisis has posed again Fiji's central dilemma: how can the indigenous demand for political pre-eminence accommodate the non-indigenous citizens who form nearly half the population and contribute so crucially to Fiji's wellbeing? The problem is compounded by rising Fijian expectations of political power. The principle of indigenous paramountcy has in the past been valued as a reassuring counterweight to non-Fijian economic and demographic strength. Ironically, while this constitutional privilege brought little material gains to most Fijians, it favoured continued Indian access to cheap leases and business opportunities.

At least since 1987, however, Fijians have seen control of the state not simply as a reassurance of security, but as a way to economic benefits (jobs, commercial opportunities, finance). The coups of 1987 and 2000 were influenced by these raised economic stakes of political power. The proposed strengthening of the Fijians' position in the state will not lessen the force of this factor, and the violent usurpations by Rabuka and Speight might well be repeated in future Fijian power struggles. As in 1987, the recent coup sparked Fijian rivalries along traditional and provincial divisions. A renewed exodus of Indians with their capital and professional skills can only aggravate such conflicts by contributing to economic recession.

Notes

Discussions with Brij Lal, Jone Dakuvula, Dale Keeling and Jonathan Fraenkel have helped me in preparing this chapter. However, any errors in negotiating the slippery psephological terrain are either mine, or those of the Fiji Electoral Office.

1   There were significant regional differences in the popularity of the Fijian parties, although some of this difference reflected an agreement between PANU and FAP not to contest in each other's main areas. The SVT was weakest in Ra in northwestern Viti Levu (13 per cent of communal votes), parts of southeast Viti Levu and in the Lomaiviti islands (18 per cent), and in Bua in Vanua Levu (19 per cent), and strongest in Kadavu (77 per cent), Cakaudrove (72 per cent), Lau (44 per cent), Macuata (43 per cent), and in the Suva city electorate of Tamavua/Laucala (40 per cent). PANU averaged 32 per cent of communal votes in the west Viti Levu Fijian communal contests, but had no candidates any where else. The FAP averaged 26 per cent in southeast Viti Levu, 9 per cent in the west, and 6 per cent in the eastern islands. The VLV averaged 30 per cent in the eastern islands, 14 per cent in southeastern Viti Levu, and 10 per cent in western Viti Levu. The most ethnocentric group, the Nationalist Vanua Tako Lavo Party (NVTLP), averaged 12 per cent in southeastern Viti Levu, 7 per cent in the west, and 4 per cent in the east. The Labour Party polled only 1.7 per cent of all Fijian communal votes, but from 8 per cent to 12 per cent in the four electorates where it fielded candidates, who helped split Fijian votes to the benefit of its allies. The Labour Party's Fijian allies each represented a wide spectrum of interests, from subsistence villagers and commercial farmers to urban wage and salary workers, and business people.

2   For the origins of the Labour Party see Howard 1991; Lawson 1991; Lal 1992 and
    Sutherland 1992.

3   Of the 12 winning candidates of designated chiefly rank only 3 were SVT, 6 were
    FAP, 2 FLP, and 1 VLV. Many more chiefly candidates lost their contests.

4   The vote totals do not include invalid votes. In five of the open contests there were
    no FLP, NFP, or other Indian candidates, and it is clear that here the support for
    Fijian parties included many Indian votes. These five electorates are very largely
    Fijian in composition: numbers 1, 2, 3, 5, and 8 in Figure 4.7 (Serua-Navosa,
    Lomaivuna-Namosi-Kadavu, Cakaudrove West, Tailevu North-Ovalau, and Lau-
    Taveuni-Rotuma).

5   The SVT's success in persuading its followers to support NFP candidates in several
    open contests is indicated also by the fact that in the seven contests where the SVT
    fielded 'dummy' candidates the average ratio of votes for the NFP against the FLP
    was 73 per cent, contrasting with an average NFP/FLP ratio of 46 per cent where
    the SVT supported its own candidates, and 50 per cent in the Indian communal
    contests (holding also for the urban Indian communals alone).

6   Many Indians were ambivalent at the prospect of an Indian prime minister, fearing
    a repetition of the 1987 coups. A Suva businessman remarked to me: 'The Fijians,
    they are good people…but they are immature politically. They are not ready to
    accept an Indian as prime minister and might react violently'. He feared that if such
    a reaction further damaged the economy, this would not much concern Fijians as
    they could simply return to their old subsistence way of life.

7   Immediately after Chaudhry's appointment as prime minister a PANU leader
    warned of a possible Fijian backlash against their Indian tenants. He claimed that
    there had been an understanding in the Peoples' Coalition that a Fijian would be
    nominated for prime minister (Apisai Tora quoted in *Fiji Times* 20 May 1999:3).

chapter five

Elections and the dilemma of indigenous Fijian political unity

Alumita Durutalo

The notion of indigenous Fijian political unity was a social construction which emerged after the establishment of the colonial state in 1874. Within Fijian society itself, the idea of political unity was adopted from indigenous forms of knowledge in which the philosophy of unity was embodied in customary leadership practices within the context of sociopolitical constructs such as the *I tokatoka, mataqali, yavusa, vanua* and *matanitu*.[1] The colonial administration under Sir Arthur Gordon reinterpreted and adopted these indigenous forms as a basis for national unity under the colonial state. Underlying the new approach was 'the colonial myth of homogeneity' (Routledge 1975:220) which proposed that there was a single form of cultural reality with uniform chiefly rule amongst indigenous Fijians in the different *vanua* throughout Fiji. British restructuring of Fijian social structures was facilitated by the system of 'indirect rule' involving the blending of the old and new systems of leadership under the authority of chiefs. The colonial government ruled Fijians through their chiefs (Durutalo 1997:66–7).

The introduction of indirect rule and the creation of various institutions to support it, resulted in the evolution of communal politics of which political unity has been the most essential aspect. The Fijian version of communal politics involves the process of politicking and competition for power which remains exclusive within a community which utilises traditional loyalties, ceremonies and values to solicit political support. Within indigenous Fijian communities, traditional loyalties to chiefs and the *vanua* became the foundation for political support to the chiefs and hence to the colonial state. The result was the emergence of patron–client politics.[2]

The colonial state and the politics of clientelism

Clientelism emerged through the system of indirect rule. Sir Arthur Gordon's Native (Fijian) Administration did more than preserve the Fijian 'race and culture';[3] it radically restructured relations in Fijian society. The major power brokers within the native administration were members of the Native Council (subsequently the Great Council of Chiefs) which sat at the apex of the institution. Members of the Council were mostly eastern Fijian chiefs and other commoners who were co-opted as officials in the Native administration. The native administration also included other structures such as the provincial governments, the Native Lands Commission (NLC) and (much later) the Native Land Trust Board (NLTB). All these structures had within them persons or 'lesser brokers' who were also answerable to the colonial state through the various layers of ranks which were above them. Within each *yasana* or province, for example, were a hierarchy of posts which began with the *Roko Tui*[4] at the provincial level to the *Turaga ni Koro*[5] (village headman) at the village level.

Fijian unity under the colonial state was imagined to have a neat hierarchy, at the apex of which was a chief who dictated to the assumed 'lesser' chiefs and commoners. The colonial state's restructuring of the chiefly system arrested a once dynamic institution where leaders had to earn the role and respect they were accorded. What emerged out of the system of indirect rule through the native administration was a very hierarchical institution which progressively became more powerful and authoritarian for the majority of the ruled. The system also gave rise to the 'new type of chief'[6] whose political supremacy was based on his loyalty to the colonial state which reciprocally supported him. That is,

> The colonial state, through the entrenchment of Indirect rule, created and maintained a patron–client relationship as a means of reaching grassroot[s] people…the creation of the Fijian administration in colonial Fiji served other important purposes than 'protecting' the Fijians; they were a direct link, through clientelism to the grassroot people. Those who controlled the colonial state needed political support…and confidence from indigenous Fijians (Durutalo 1997:50).

At Fiji's independence in 1970, the various administrative structures which had supported indirect rule were entrenched in the 1970 Constitution, including a communal or ethnically based electoral system. Both the former Alliance Party[7] (from 1970 to 1987), and the Council of Chiefs-backed Soqosoqo ni Vakavulewa ni Taukei (SVT) Party[8] (from 1991 onwards), utilised the massive network of patron–client politics through the Fijian Administration.

The Alliance Party and indigenous Fijian political unity

Amongst indigenous Fijians, the strength of the eastern Fijian-dominated Alliance Party lay in the system of Fijian administration. The party depended on the Fijian administration network for its survival. Communal patronage within the system had enabled the survival of the Alliance Party from independence in 1970 to the coups in 1987. For the Fijians, the party attempted to maintain the allegiance of all the groups in both the traditional and modern sectors, under the Council of Chiefs. On the multiethnic front, the party attracted mainly prominent Indo-Fijian business class and the European and the Chinese business community. At one end of the political spectrum then, was the effort to maintain indigenous Fijian allegiance through patron–client politics, and on the other, the maintenance of the multiethnic allegiance within the free market system.

Indigenous Fijian political unity under the Alliance reinforced obedience from those below to those at the top echelons of power and assumed the protection of indigenous rights and values through structures such as the Great Council of Chiefs, the NLC and the NLTB. However, the onslaught of modernity and the consequent demand for democracy at all levels contributed to the deconstruction of indigenous Fijian political unity. During its 17 years, the Alliance Party camouflaged class interests with ethnicity. Grassroots Fijians within the party supported an élite multiethnic group who were more accessible to the free market and its benefits than to them. This evolving class structure was supported by the unity of the 'have nots' (in modern economic terms), who had contributed significantly to the emergence of contradictions within the Alliance Party. The composition of the party was 'politically volatile' because ethnic Fijian grassroot unity was used to support class interests. The defeat of the Alliance Party and its re-appearance as the SVT exposed and led to other forms of contradictions within Fijian society.

At the intra-societal level, contradictions also emerged from the continued trend of traditional political rivalry between eastern and western Fiji. This rivalry can be defined in terms of 'internal colonialism' (Durutalo 1995) where the colonial state, since its inception, had favoured the eastern chiefly establishment for its role in stabilising the rule of the state through patron–client politics. This contributed to the dominance of eastern chiefs in the governance of the indigenous Fijians through employment in the native administration and the civil service. Chiefs in the more egalitarian *vanua* in western Viti Levu, have always regarded themselves as independent from eastern Fijian hegemony since they were never conquered by them prior to colonisation. Fiji's political history, therefore, reveals that western Fijian chiefs and their people have always shown an independent attitude towards the eastern Fijian oligarchy and their dominance in the new patron–client politics. Political dissent such as that shown by Apolosi Nawai and alternative Fijian political parties have always emerged in western Viti Levu. In the post-1987 era, the formation of alternative Fijian political parties has exposed the dilemma of Fijian political unity.

The deconstruction of an orthodoxy

The deconstruction of indigenous Fijian political unity continued in the postcolonial era. In the late 1970s, the Western United Front (WUF) was formed by western Fijian landowners after a conflict with the Alliance government over the payment of forest royalty, western Fijian chiefs claiming that their resources were being used without equitable compensation in monetary terms or otherwise. Within the realm of Fijian politics, the formation of the WUF was seen as a reaction against the eastern establishment. The western Fijian chiefs and their people saw their politico-economic marginalisation from the colonial to the postcolonial era, as similar to those of the descendants of the indentured labourers (*girmityas*). In this context, both were ruled by a government dominated by eastern Fijian élites and Fiji's ruling class. This was the beginning of a political consciousness which transcended the ethnic divide.

Challenge to Alliance rule and the orthodoxy of unity did not emerge only in western Viti Levu. Earlier in 1974, the ultra-right wing Fijian Nationalist Party (FNP) was formed by Sakeasi Butadroka of the province of Rewa. While indigenous Fijians in the WUF based their politico-economic marginalisation on traditional rivalry and the dominance of eastern Fijian chiefs within the colonial and postcolonial state, Butadroka argued that the Alliance Government was conceding too much to other ethnic groups while doing little for indigenous Fijians. The Fijian nationalists assumed that the presence of other ethnic groups was the cause of their economic marginalisation.

In the April 1977 general elections, Butadroka was able to sway about 25 per cent of Fijian communal votes away from the Alliance Party, causing its defeat. However, the Alliance was appointed to a minority government by the Governor General Ratu Sir George Cakobau when the National Federation Party (NFP), which had narrowly won the election, was unable to form government. In the second (September) elections of 1977, the Alliance was returned to power with a big majority. Two factors contributed to its victory. These were the split of the NFP into two factions, and the fear of Indian domination which was fanned by the nationalists and which contributed to the Alliance's victory. The 'fear of the unknown' was employed to rekindle Fijian political unity.

The most formidable threat to Alliance rule came with the formation of the Fiji Labour Party (FLP) in 1985. Its formation marked a new era in Fiji's history when an element of class consciousness was used by trade union leaders as a basis for forming a political party. Trade union leaders and workers who were members of the party, became conscious of economic exploitation across the ethnic divide and the use of ethnic politics to conceal class exploitation. The formation of the party posed a long-term challenge to ethnic politics in Fiji, especially in an era of increasing globalisation. The specific impetus behind the formation of the party lay in the IMF-required austerity measures in 1984–85 which recommended deregulation of the labour market, reduction in the size of government, a freeze on the expansion of the civil service posts, a wage freeze, privatisation of parastatals, and removal of price controls and subsidies (Durutalo 1996:134–5).

The multiethnic base of the party threatened a variety of interests. First and foremost, it threatened the Alliance Party and its dominant ruling class, including the Indo-Fijian business class, Chinese, Europeans and the indigenous Fijian chiefly and commoner élite. At another level, the FLP was a threat to the indigenous Fijian chiefly élite (mostly from eastern Fiji) who, since cession, had claimed custodianship of indigenous values and interests. The leadership of the FLP by a western Fijian (Dr Timoci Bavadra) was not only a threat to eastern Fijian political dominance but also to the facade of indigenous Fijian political unity maintained under the Alliance Party. The formation of the FLP, at a critical period of the Cold War, also threatened Fiji's allies (internal and external), who subscribed to the free market paradigm. The *Weekend Australian* (28–9 March 1987) described the Alliance Party as

> basically a conservative government…closely allied to the United States and Australia, in particular, and…solidly pro-Western and anti-communist. It welcomes American warships without asking questions, and has close defence links with Australia. It is seen as a pillar of Western interests in the South Pacific, and a powerful impediment against Soviet encroachments (in Lawson 1991:248).

Sitiveni Rabuka saw the formation of the FLP as 'foreign to the Fijian political scene and indicative of a trend towards socialism; they were, to him, warnings of an alarming change of direction in Fiji's national and international politics' (Dean and Ritova 1988:46).

This supports the *Weekend Australian's* thesis and reflects the real interests behind the existence of the Alliance Party. It also exposed a number of things: the intricate links between a Third World postcolonial political party and western free market interests; and how grassroots indigenous Fijian voters in the Alliance Party were used to support a government with class interests that linked the internal (local) to the external (international).

The 1987 military coups and indigenous Fijian political unity

The coup-maker, Lt Colonel Sitiveni Rabuka, explained that the military coups of 1987 were aimed at reinforcing chiefly leadership and protecting indigenous Fijian interests. He argued that

> the election of the Bavadra Government…had involved a leakage of Fijian votes to the coalition parties. This was…a reflection of a

changing society…[and] a breaking down of Fijian society and values.
Young Fijians were ignoring or defying the old values, their chiefs
and their elders (Dean and Ritova 1988:33).

The first major flaw in this argument was the claim that only young
Fijians had deserted the Alliance Party. In fact, as already seen, many high
chiefs had also over time defied the party. A high chief of Ba province whom
I interviewed in 1996 argued that the 'Fiji Labour Party election victory in
1987 was not bad at all. A number of chiefs from various *vanua* also
supported the party' (Durutalo 1997:169). The second major weakness was
the failure to define 'values' for all Fijians. It was evident that Rabuka
assumed that all Fijians in different sociopolitical and economic groupings
had the same values. The question that one should pose is 'what are Fijian
values and is voting for another party a reflection of a breakdown in values
or changing values?' Furthermore, when we talk about Fijian values, are
we referring to pre-European values, missionary values or colonially created
values?

This line of argument has been undermined with the SVT's defeat in
the 1999 general elections, and with the emergence of many Fijian parties
which challenged and undercut its power base. Perhaps indigenous Fijians
are looking for the type of political leadership which offers them more
than the empty rhetoric of protecting values. The coups brought to the fore
many contradictions within Fijian society itself. The first may have been
the exposure of the 'myth of homogeneity'. Political leadership was
originally the domain of a few and was maintained through the monopoly
of power in patron–client politics. The reaction against it led to other
reactions such as the invocation of independent *vanua* feelings. This, in
turn, has rekindled the pre-colonial political independence of Fijians in the
context of their *vanua* and leadership of their chiefs. The problem which
arises, then, is one of 'competing legitimacy'[9] and is part of the general
problem of trying to maintain unity in many Third World postcolonial states
where previously unity under the colonial state was maintained through
the 'invention of tradition' and the adoption of the 'myth of homogeneity'.

The coups themselves have been a catalyst for rapid social change
amongst indigenous Fijians, unleashing many forms of intra-societal rivalry.
Since the early 1990s western Viti Levu chiefs have met to discuss the
formation of *yasayasa Vaka-Ra* or western confederacy. This in itself implied
a number of things. First and foremost the chiefs wanted to reaffirm the
pre-colonial independence of the western Fijians, who were never
conquered by the eastern chiefs who now dominate them. Even eastern
Fiji did not have an overall hierarchical structure which everyone accepted
or understood. The colonial state introduced this through the Fijian
administration and its patron–client political system.

Amongst Fijians themselves, there are different levels of rivalry. Within each province there are subtle forms of competition based on pre-colonial *vanua* independence. In each province, for example, there are certain *vanua* which receive more from government than others. In the province of Nadroga and Navosa, the coastal Nadroga people have always been favoured over the inland Navosa people in terms of state resources for any development in the province. This has been a trend from the early days of colonisation when the Navosa people used to defy both missionary and colonial leadership. This has currently led to the move by the Navosa people to form their own province.[10]

At another level of rivalry, the various *vanua* on Viti Levu have increasingly regarded the arrival of people from the maritime provinces as a threat to their resources in what may be a milder form of the tension between the Guadalcanal and Malaitans in Solomon Islands. This was increasingly felt after the coups when the Viti Levu people realised that leadership after the coups only served to strengthen the political power of Fijians from Vanua Levu, Lau (the Tovata Confederacy), and other smaller islands, which contributed to the overwhelming support given to the Fijian Association Party (FAP) and other rival parties to the SVT on the big island of Viti Levu (see Tables 5.2 and 5.3).

In Tailevu, rivalry between the SVT and the FAP reached into chiefly households. With the change in constituency boundaries, Tailevu has been demarcated into two communal constituencies, namely Tailevu North and Tailevu South, and two open constituencies, Tailevu North/Ovalau and the Tailevu South/Lomaiviti. A number of prominent chiefs from the province competed against each other for the four seats. On the chiefly island of Bau itself, Adi Litia Cakobau (of the Mataiwelagi household), was the SVT candidate for the Tailevu North/Ovalau open seat and her cousin Ratu Tu'uakitau Cokanauto (of the Naisogolaca household), stood for the FAP,[11] and won the seat. In the Tailevu South communal seat and Tailevu South/Lomaiviti open seat, both SVT candidates lost to FAP and the FLP candidates respectively. One of the SVT candidates who lost was Ratu Apenisa Cakobau of the chiefly Mataiwelagi family. This trend of chiefly rivalry in party politics is recent. Perhaps, rivalry amongst chiefly households has always existed but was dormant until the increasing participation of indigenous Fijians in party politics.

At another level, the aftermath of the coups and the rise in the level of corruption and nepotism in government was not only blatant to Indo-Fijians and other ethnic groups but to indigenous Fijians as well, especially to those who did not support the coups. Perhaps the collapse of the National Bank of Fiji due to bad debts (by those close to people in power) epitomised the gravity of the problem.[12] A chief from the province of Tailevu who was interviewed in 1996 on his views on Fijian political unity argued that

Politicians use the notion of political unity as a basis of building their own wealth. If you look at the names of the bad debtors from the National Bank of Fiji, some of those involved hold a dual role of being a government minister as well as being a traditional chief. These people use both their modern and traditional roles as a means of earning money for themselves (Durutalo 1997:165).

Such practices unfolded the class nature of the coups and reaffirmed the truth that there was more to the coups than the ethnic explanations suggested. If some people benefited from the coups, the most crucial question to ask is which group of indigenous Fijians and people of other ethnic origins benefited?

The 1990 Constitution, and the SVT

The SVT was established in 1991 with the blessing of the Bose Levu Vakaturaga (Great Council of Chiefs).[13] The formation of the SVT was a deliberate and urgent attempt by the Fijian ruling élite to defend their status as the only defenders and promoters of ethnic Fijian values and interests. This move was seen by its supporters as crucial in a climate of increasing Fijian political dissent. The SVT, like its predecessor, the Alliance Party, was to utilise patron–client politics through the Fijian administration, which implied theoretically, that all indigenous Fijians registered in the Native Lands Commission's[14] Vula ni Kawa Bula (VKB)[15] were already members of the new party. Furthermore, the move was aimed at blocking the formation of any other indigenous Fijian political party.

The involvement of the Great Council of Chiefs and the Fijian administration in the formation of the SVT was enough to give the party a 'legitimate' look for most Fijians who over the years have come to internalise the myth of cultural homogeneity. A Malolo chief in the province of Nadroga who was interviewed in January 1996, explained the basis of his support for the SVT Party along 'legitimacy' lines: 'I support the SVT because it is a chiefly party. Other political parties are not part of the Fijian leadership system' (Durutalo 1997:166). However, the new party was not supported by all Fijians. A number of *vanua* chiefs in western Viti Levu viewed the move as another attempt by the eastern Fijian chiefly élite to retain political dominance. A high chief in the *vanua* Vatulevu of Nadi, whom I interviewed in January 1996, echoed this sentiment

The formation of the SVT was done by those in the top echelons of power in eastern Fiji. The formation of the SVT Party followed by various meetings was always done in Suva and never once were meetings decentralised to western Fiji. This is in spite of the fact that all [the] major resources that the Fiji government depends on are to be found in western Fiji. It is most obvious that the survival of the Fiji government is not determined by some coconut plantations on the island of Lakeba [in the province of Lau]. However, when it comes to government leadership, eastern Fijians dominate (Durutalo 1997:158).

The use of the Fijian administration as a political power base for the SVT was a deliberate attempt to infiltrate those *vanua* which otherwise would not have subscribed to the party. By doing this, the founders of the party exploited an institution which was supposed to be for the overall development of indigenous Fijians regardless of party affiliation. Indigenous Fijians from the 14 provinces who did not affiliate with the SVT Party saw this move as a blatant case of authoritarianism and abuse of power. A Fijian from Tailevu who was interviewed in 1996 argued that

> The use of the provincial offices to promote SVT agenda is not right because it contradicts the purpose that the provinces were set up for…as an integrative force amongst indigenous Fijians…What will happen is provincial service to the people will be neglected at the expense of preaching political propaganda (Duratalo 1997:179).

Along the same lines, a highly educated Fijian from Cakaudrove, and who was a minister in the Chaudhry government, had the following to say about the future of the Great Council of Chiefs in party politics

> That there is a clear distinction between an involvement in traditional politics and an involvement in party politics. Chiefs involvement in party politics implies that they support a political party as against other political parties…Increasingly, chiefs will alienate themselves from Fijians who do not support the party…If SVT falls, chiefs will fall with it. Inevitably their forming SVT is short sighted. By forming a political party, they are undermining their own traditional positions as chiefs (Duratalo 1997:177).

The 1990 Constitution was an attempt to recreate the rules to enable election victory and political dominance of the traditional élite. Out of the 37 indigenous Fijian seats, 32 seats were derived from the 14 provinces as shown in Table 5.1.

Underlying the 'over-allocation' of Fijian seats to the provincial constituencies was the belief that Fijians in the informal or rural sector of the Fijian society were still politically naïve and easier to control than those in the formal or urban sector. This is part of a characteristic of patron–client politics where the patrons exploit the ignorance of the voters for political gain. The electoral arrangement under the 1990 Constitution with its wholly communal and first-past-the-post voting system had indeed enabled overwhelming victory for the SVT Party in the 1994 general elections. Table 5.2 shows the details of the votes polled in these elections for the Fijian provincial and Fijian urban constituencies.

Table 5.1   Number of members in provincial constituencies

Province	Number of seats
Ba	3
Bua	2
Cakaudrove	3
Kadavu	2
Lau	3
Lomaiviti	2
Macuata	2
Nadroga/Navosa	2
Naitasiri	2
Namosi	2
Ra	2
Rewa	2
Serua	2
Tailevu	3

Notes: There are 14 provinces in Fiji: 8 are on the island of Viti Levu (Ra, Ba, Nadroga, Serua, Namosi, Rewa, Naitasiri, and Tailevu); 3 are on the island of Vanua Levu and surrounding islands (Cakaudrove, Bua and Macuata); Lomaiviti is composed of the islands in the centre of Fiji; Lau is made up of the eastern-most islands; and the island of Kadavu is the southern-most province. The boundaries of some of these provinces have been redrawn over the years, especially during the colonial period.
Source: Durutalo, A.L. 1997. Provincialism and the crisis of indigenous Fijian political unity, unpublished MA thesis, Centre for Development Studies, School of Social and Economic Development, The University of the South Pacific, Suva:136.

Despite the landslide, the victory of the SVT Party created its own dynamics and led to demands for change. For Fijians in the formal sector, the 1990 electoral system represented a gross under-representation of the majority of the Fijian taxpayers, with only four seats. The move was self-defeating both for SVT and the Great Council of Chiefs because later, Fijians moved out and formed alternative political parties. This may have been a direct reaction to the unequal distribution of parliamentary seats in the Fijian constituencies.

The formation of the All National Congress (ANC) in the early 1990s was one way in which the internal contradictions about the 1987 coups manifested itself. Maverick veteran politician and strong Taukei Movement supporter from western Viti Levu, Apisai Tora, applied political shrewdness when he formed the ANC Party. He distanced himself from the SVT and formed the ANC as an alternative Fijian political party. However, the ANC managed to secure only one seat in the 1994 general elections. Also in the early 1990s a more formidable political force was created by the late Josevata Kamikamica. The Fijian Association Party (FAP) was formed by a breakaway faction of the SVT which did not support the 1994 Budget,

Table 5.2   Votes polled by political parties in the 1994 general elections

Fijian provincial constituencies	Valid votes	SVT %	FAP %	FNP %	ANC %	FLP %	STV %	NDP %	IND %
Ba	11,769	55.8	2.8	1.1	40.3	-	-	-	-
Bua	4,428	88.2	2.8	1.2	-	-	-	-	7.8
Cakaudrove	10,550	93.3	6.7	-	-	-	-	-	-
Kadavu	3,855	96.9	2.2	0.9	-	-	-	-	-
Lau	4,957	41.9	57.8	0.4	-	-	-	-	-
Lomaiviti	4,815	84.6	2.8	4.1	-	-	-	-	8.5
Macuata	5,283	91.2	6.2	2.5	-	-	-	-	-
Nadroga/Navosa	8,719	48.5	-	-	13.9	-	37.5	-	-
Naitasiri	6,866	40.0	52.8	7.2	-	-	-	-	-
Namosi	1,650	80.2	-	17.4	-	-	-	-	2.3
Ra	5,392	24.9	2.6	18.2	-	-	2.4	-	51.9
Rewa	3,616	52.6	6.6	32.6	0.7	-	-	-	8.2
Serua	2,250	58.3	-	25.7	10.7	-	-	0.97	4.3
Tailevu	9,879	48.1	29.1	18.9	0.8	-	-	-	3.1
Total	84,029	62.7	14.5	6.8	8.4	0.1	3.2	0.02	4.3
Fijian urban constituencies									
Suva City	8,085	7.20	21.6	3.9	2.4	-	-	-	-
Serua/Rewa West	3,441	68.0	23.9	4.0	2.6	-	-	-	1.4
Tailevu/Naitasiri	9,977	69.9	25.1	-	4.9	-	-	-	-
Western Urban	6,008	61.7	12.0	5.8	8.6	5.1	-	-	6.9
Total	27,511	68.5	21.1	2.9	4.7	1.1	-	-	1.7
Grand total	111,540	63.4	15.3	6.3	8.0	0.2	2.8	0.02	4.0

Note: SVT—Soqosoqo ni Vakavulewa ni Taukei; FAP—Fijian Association Party; FNP—Fijian Nationalist Party; ANC—All National Congress; FLP—Fiji Labour Party; SVT—Soqosoqo ni Taukei ni Vanua; NDP—National Democratic Party; IND—Independents.
Source: Electoral Commission Report for 1 January 1994–31 December 1996.

leading to its defeat. Kamikamica and other members of the FAP had been concerned with Rabuka's poor leadership style generally. Kamikamica argued that Rabuka

> took over a role that he has not had the experience for, particularly civilian leadership because he's been in the army most of his working life. The principles and style of leadership in a democratic environment is different from the military…It [leadership] shouldn't really be a problem if you have some idea of what you're doing (*The Review* February 1994:25).

Rabuka's economic leadership was also considered a total failure by his critics. This had been a major factor in the defeat of the 1994 Budget. Kamikamica explained

Take the budget. He [Rabuka] could have resolved that very
simply…I faced a similar situation when he handed [the government]
over after the coups. He didn't hand over because he respected the
chiefs. He handed over when the economy was completely down. He
couldn't establish our trading and diplomatic links with other
countries…from the way he was carrying on—it was like a political
time bomb (*The Review* February 1994:25).

One of the major concerns of the FAP was to restore economic growth,
resolve the Agricultural Landlord and Tenants Act (ALTA) issue, and review
the 1990 Constitution.

The 1995 Constitutional Review and its impact on Fijian political unity

In 1995, the government established a Constitution Review Commission
to review the 1990 Constitution. The Commission recommended major
changes to Fiji's electoral system, including compulsory registration of
voters, compulsory voting, the adoption of an Alternative Vote (AV) system
in place of the first-past-the-post system and the introduction of open (non-
racial) seats. The Commission identified the following as advantageous
features of the alternative voting system: encouragement of multiethnic
government; recognition of the role of political parties; incentives for
moderation and cooperation across ethnic lines; effective representation of
constituents; effective voter participation; effective representation of
minority and special interest groups; fairness between political parties;
effective government; effective opposition; proven workability; and
legitimacy (Rigamoto 1999:1–2).

   The new changes incorporated into the new Constitution posed a direct
challenge to Fijian political unity labouring under the myth of homogeneity.
The review of the 1990 Constitution alienated ardent Taukei supporters of
the coups who believed that the review itself had undermined the whole
purpose of the coups—which was supposed to be the entrenchment of
Fijian interests. A message that emanated from the coups and which some
politically naive Fijians fell for is that Fijians should be aided without work.
This was clear in the type of leadership that Rabuka had demonstrated to
Fijians and for which his supporters gave him their support. As
Kamikamica, in *The Review*, explained: 'He [Rabuka], cannot have
everything his own way. Since the coups, he's had the habit of taking
whatever he wants…He should work for what he takes and not simply
take it because he has the power' (*The Review* February 1994:24).

   Demands of the new economic system and the failure in the delivery of
goods to the clients contributed to the erosion of the SVT's power base
during the 1999 elections. The implementation of structural adjustment

policies, which included public sector reforms, the move towards privatisation, and the 'logical' use of money in an increasingly free market society, was perhaps beyond the comprehension of grass root Fijian supporters of the coups. What Fijians did not understand is that, if the coups were really for Fijians, then why were many Fijians the poorer in the end?

In a discussion with Fijian *Vatuwaqa* squatters in Suva before the 1999 general elections, a Fijian woman said that she and her family and some other fellow squatters supported the Fiji Labour Party in 1987 and are still supporting it now in the hope of improving their living conditions. The woman believed that the party could devise policies to cater for the poor (interview with author, March 1999 Suva). For these marginalised Fijians, who have become part of the modern urban community, the choice of a political party is pragmatic and need-driven. Political pragmatism was also evident in the voting pattern of the SVT supporters. In the Kadavu Fijian provincial communal constituency, Jim Ah Koy, a Fijian Chinese millionaire of the SVT party, was elected overwhelmingly because of his business acumen and his contribution to development in his mother's province. Ah Koy secured the largest percentage of Fijian votes (83.40 per cent) in all the 23 Fijian communal seats (*Fiji Times* 20 May 1999:25).

Table 5.3 shows votes polled by Fijian political parties in the 1999 General elections.

Analysis of the 1999 elections and the formation of alternative political parties as an expression of Fijian political dissent

Perhaps the most outstanding feature of postcolonial and post-1987 politics within Fijian society has been the continuous demonstration of political dissent towards the ruling élite's ideology of unity. Dissent by Fijians such as Apolosi R. Nawai in the early years of this century are linked to the current general dissent in Fijian thinking now expressed through the formation of alternative Fijian political parties. Earlier forms of dissent were suppressed by the colonial state because the social construction of unity was aimed at ensuring the survival of the modern state in a society which previously had independent chiefdoms. Attempts to suppress Fijian independent political thinking were continued in the postcolonial era by the Fijian ruling élite. Rabuka's military coups can be viewed in that light. The irony is that the coups, which were aimed at reinforcing the myth of homogeneity through political unity, only served to encourage the growth of independent political thinking.

In the 1999 general elections, there were at least eight Fijian political parties, apart from candidates who stood independently. These were the:

Table 5.3   Votes polled by political parties in the 1999 general elections

Fijian provincial constituencies	Valid votes	SVT %	FAP %	NVTLP %	VLV %	PANU %	FLP %	COIN %	IND %
Bua	5,330	20.09	-	4.38	54.37	-	-	20.77	-
Kadavu	4,987	83.40	9.81	-	6.80	-	-	-	-
Lau	5,927	47.51	-	-	50.82	-	-	-	-
Lomaiviti	6,361	22.0	-	-	-	-	23.4	-	54.6
Macuata	7,926	46.29	-	-	53.71	-	-	-	-
Nadroga/Navosa	13,071	41.05	50.65	-	-	-	-	-	-
Naitasiri	8,992	-	71.21	28.79	-	-	-	-	-
Namosi	2,315	43.41	56.54	-	-	-	-	-	-
Ra	7,811	-	-	47.02	-	52.98	-	-	-
Rewa	5,193	-	59.70	40.30	-	-	-	-	-
Serua	3,345	37.28	-	62.72	-	-	-	-	-
Ba East	8,398	34.9	-	5.66	6.88	52.55	-	-	-
Ba West	10,052	34.47	-	-	-	63.53	-	-	-
Tailevu North	7,449	53.63	46.36	-	-	-	-	-	-
Tailevu South	7,110	40.38	53.59	6.03	-	-	-	-	-
Cakaudrove East	6,582	78.01	-	-	16.70	-	-	-	-
Cakaudrove West	7,920	68.94	6.94	-	24.1	-	-	-	-
No. of seats won		4	5	1	3	3	-	-	1
Fijian urban constituencies									
North East	10,182	68.94	6.94	-	24.1	-	-	-	-
North West	12,342	32.77	-	-	-	67.23	-	-	-
South West	9,475	43.24	56.76	-	-	-	-	-	-
Suva City	9,191	42.22	57.78	-	-	-	-	-	-
Tamavua/Laucala	10,014	45.19	54.81	-	-	-	-	-	-
Nasinu	9,096	49.57	50.42	-	-	-	-	-	-
No. of seats won		1	4	-	-	1	-	-	-

Note: SVT—Soqosoqo ni Vakavulewa ni Taukei; FAP—Fijian Association Party;
NVTLP—Nationalist Vanua Tako/Lavo Party; VLV—Veitokani Ni Lewenivanua Vakaristo;
PANU—Party of National Unity; FLP—Fiji Labour Party; COIN—Coalition of Independent
Nationals; IND—Independents.
Source: *Fiji Times* 20 May 1999.

Soqosoqo ni Vakavulewa ni Taukei (SVT), Fijian Association Party (FAP),
Veitokani ni Lewenivanua Vakarisito (VLV), Nationalist Vanua Tako/Lavo
Party (NVTLP), Party of National Unity (PANU), Party of the Truth (POTT),
Viti Levu Dynamic Multiracial Democratic Party (DMDP), and the Fiji
Labour Party (FLP). The most immediate impact of the emergence of these
parties has been the defeat of the SVT.

The implications of SVT defeat

The results of the 1999 general elections have been devastating to the Great
Council of Chiefs-sponsored SVT Party. Of the 23 Fijian provincial and
urban communal constituencies, it won only five, whilst the Fijian

Association Party won nine, PANU four, VLV three and NVTLP and Independent one each. Communal Fijian seats are an indicator of political legitimacy amongst indigenous Fijians. In this respect, the future of the SVT as well as 'chiefs in politics' has been marginalised. What was interesting in the 1999 general elections as far as Fijian politics is concerned, was not the percentage of votes that the SVT still controled overall, but the number of Fijian political parties which emerged to counter the 'legitimacy claim' of the SVT.

A number of questions have emerged in light of the defeat of the SVT: What is the future of Fijian political unity under patron–client politics? Has the defeat of the SVT spelled the beginning of the end of patron–client politics? Or have alternative parties simply taken it over on a smaller scale? Will the marginalisation of the SVT have an impact on the political power of the chiefly council? Will this in turn affect chiefly leadership as a whole? What about the role of the power brokers whose interests are closely linked with the maintenance of the status quo? Will they experiment with other political strategies to enable their political survival? Perhaps the recent resignation of former Prime Minister Rabuka from his parliamentary seat to become the president of the Great Council of Chiefs partially answers this question. Will the Great Council of Chiefs now operate along the system which is adopted in modern party politics? Will the council accommodate dissenting political views? How will this affect its traditional leadership roles? Are Fijians seeing the beginning of the acceptance of liberal democracy as a permanent part of Fijian politics?

The impact of the re-allocation of Fijian provincial and urban seats

The re-drawing of Fiji's electoral boundaries under the new electoral system has resulted in the overall reduction of communal seats in favour of open seats. Fijian provincial communal seats have been reduced from 32 to 17 while Fijian urban seats have been increased from 3 to 6. These changes have been accompanied by the overall redrawing of some constituency boundaries in line with five separate electoral rolls: for Fijian voters, Indo-Fijians, Rotumans, general electors, and an open roll which allows for multiethnic voting. The redrawing of the boundaries has had an impact on the redistribution of power within Fijian society. At one level the reduction of provincial seats has implied tougher competition in terms of Fijian political representation in parliament. Representation has been rationalised in terms of province size and population distribution and not political favouritism, which in the past resulted in small provinces like Lau having three parliamentary seats whilst bigger population bases such as Nadroga/ Navosa had two seats. Within each province, therefore, the process of selecting candidates has become more competitive.

In the redrawing of provincial boundaries, the three large provinces of Cakaudrove, Ba and Tailevu have been divided into two separate constituencies each and this has had an impact on the distribution of power in general at the intra-provincial level. In Tailevu, for example, there is now a Tailevu North provincial constituency and a Tailevu South Fijian provincial constituency. The division has affected provincial politics in the following ways. The basis of patron–client politics which had influenced the dominance of one or two *vanua* in party politics, since political independence, has been challenged. Bauan dominance was challenged with the defeat of two chiefly candidates: Adi Litia Cakobau (for the Tailevu North/Ovalau Open Constituency), and Ratu Apenisa Cakobau (for the Tailevu South/Lomaiviti Open Constituency). There has been a 'battle of the chiefs' kind of scenario amongst different parties in the two Tailevu constituencies. For instance, in the Tailevu North/Ovalau Open Constituency, cousins Ratu Tu'uakitau Cokanauto represented the FAP, and Adi Litia Cakobau represented the SVT. Ratu Cokanauto won. In the Tailevu South/Lomaiviti Open seat, Ratu Isireli Vuibau of the Fiji Labour Party defeated Ratu Apenisa Cakobau of the SVT.

In some subtle ways, party politics has served to aggravate traditional chiefly rivalry either in terms of household conflicts or *vanua* conflicts, influencing the support that each group has for different political parties. In Tailevu before the 1999 general elections, a Fijian Association Party candidate reminded the villagers that the SVT Party had undermined the contribution and the traditional leadership of the Tailevu people during its reign. This campaign reinforced that general feeling, causing the defeat of three SVT candidates in the province, including two from the chiefly Cakobau family. This may also have been because

> the province [Tailevu] had not had much of a part in the various regimes since the May coup, which had been dominated by native Fijians from further north and east (Macuata, Cakaudrove, Lau) and soldiers from the province had been lukewarm in their support for Rabuka (Howard 1989:30).

Tailevu was not the only province which changed its party preference in the 1999 general elections. In Viti Levu as a whole, the SVT managed to win only 1 out of the 23 Fijian communal seats. The defeat could be explained in terms of the reaction of the Viti Levu people in general, against the socioeconomic and political performance of the SVT government since its second term in power in 1994. Apart from its economic performance, many *vanua* on Viti Levu felt that since the coups and the formation of the SVT Party, Fijian politics had been dominated by people from Vanua Levu and other islands. Only two provinces which supported the SVT overwhelmingly in the 1999 elections were Cakaudrove (Rabuka's province) and Kadavu (Ah Koy's). One was a coup-maker and the other a very rich business man.

The role of 'seasonal parties' and alternative parties in Fijian politics

In the 1999 elections, the SVT Party was challenged by the emergence of 'seasonal parties' and the re-strengthening of alternative Fijian political parties.

Seasonal parties can be understood in terms of responses to needs that arise at a particular point in time. They act as indicators of 'independent thinking' among Fijians and use the modern political system to express dissent from the dominant mainstream political ideology of unity. Since Independence in 1970 seasonal political parties, as alternatives to the eastern Viti Levu dominated Fijian political parties, have always emerged in western Viti Levu. In the 1960s, Apisai Tora formed the National Democratic Party. This was a conservative indigenous Fijian party based on a similar political ideology to that of Butadroka's Fijian Nationalist Party. This party later merged with the Indo-Fijian dominated Federation Party, giving it the name National Federation Party (NFP). Tora was a member of the NFP when the party won the 1977 general elections. Another western Viti Levu seasonal party which emerged in the late 1970s to challenge the power of the eastern Fijian oligarchy was Ratu Osea Gavidi's Western United Front (WUF). In the early 1990s the All National Congress (ANC) emerged in western Viti Levu and led by Tora, himself an 'all seasons' western Fijian politician. In 1998 Tora formed the Party of National Unity (PANU), sponsored by the Ba Provincial Council. While the party won 4 out of the 23 Fijian Communal seats in parliament, Tora himself again failed to secure a parliamentary seat. Nonetheless, the idea behind the formation of the PANU has once again challenged the political power base of the SVT in western Viti Levu. In the 1999 general elections, the SVT failed to secure any Fijian communal seats in western Viti Levu. Sakeasi Butadroka's FNP failed to attract many followers, while the FAP won 9 of the 23 Fijian provincial and urban constituencies (see Table 5.3).

Towards the end of 1998, the Veitokani ni Lewenivanua Vakarisito (VLV), or the Christian Democratic Party, was formed by another breakaway group of the SVT Party. Former Methodist Church President, Reverend Manasa Lasaro, and other church members from mostly Vanua Levu and Lau fell out with Sitiveni Rabuka and this led to the formation of the VLV. While the party's support appears to be concentrated in the province of Lau and on Vanua Levu, this nevertheless poses a direct challenge to the political power base of the SVT in eastern Fiji as a whole. The Methodist Church has facilitated the survival of the eastern Fijian chiefly hegemony since its arrival in Fiji in 1835. One of the foremost tasks of the church was to legitimate the role of chiefs in traditional Fijian society because it depended on the cooperation of the people through their chiefs for its survival. The formation of a political party through the church is a direct attack on one of the main tenets of Fijian unity which is supposed to be grounded in the trinity of *vanua, lotu,* and *matanitu*.[16] In the 1999 general elections the VLV won three Fijian communal seats.

Conclusion

The myth of homogeneity has been constantly challenged since the establishment of the colonial state in 1874. Since Independence in 1970, challenge to eastern Fijian hegemony has been aggravated by the involvement of Fijians in party politics. Fijians have challenged the basis of unity under the colonial and postcolonial state and its ensuing patron–client politics by establishing seasonal or alternative Fijian political parties. Political dissent was regarded as a threat by those whose interests the system safeguarded. Over the years, unequal relationships in the form of chiefs dominating commoners or the eastern region dominating the western region have been entrenched. The 1987 coups can be viewed as a desperate attempt to re-strengthen the old order with its modern class interests. The coups, however, only served to throw up contradictions in a society whose unity was enabled through the formation of the modern state. The 1999 elections saw the re-emergence of pre-colonial *vanua* under the guise of alternative Fijian parties, including the FAP, the VLV and PANU.

Elections have always exposed the fragility and dilemma of Fijian political unity. The formation of *vanua*-based parties post-1987 continues a long term trend in Fijian political development. With the constitutionalisation of a multiparty cabinet, each regional party may attempt to forge a coalition with other parties of similar sociopolitical and economic interests. Perhaps, the present coalition in government has already set the pace for this new political development within Fijian society. The trend on the whole has imposed a permanent challenge to the colonial myth of homogeneity and the interests it used to protect since the formation of the colonial state.

Notes

1   *Itokatoka* is an extended family unit which is traced patrilineally. In some parts of Fiji the same extended family unit was known as the *bito* or *batinilovo*. Customary land use and tenure was mostly based on this kinship unit in pre-colonial Fiji (see France 1969). *Mataqali* is a sub-clan which is composed of one or more *I tokatoka*. It was made the basic landowning unit by the colonial government (see France 1969). *Yavusa* is the largest kinship group within the Fijian social system. It is composed of one or more *mataqali*. The word *yavusa* is derived from *yavu* which implies 'house

foundation'. The members of a *yavusa* are believed to have originated from a common house foundation and hence a common ancestor. A number of *yavusa* make up a *vanua*. In modern day Fiji, a number of *yavusa* would be found in a number of villages within a *vanua*. A *vanua* is a political construct which has been unified through warfare. A *vanua* chief therefore rules in a specific geographical boundary. Matanitu refers to the confederacy or the highest political formation beyond the '*vanua*'. It was found in some parts of Fiji towards the end of the eighteeth century. Unlike the more stable Yavusa, formed out of kinship alliances, the matanitu were composed of fragile alliances. They were formed through political processes and were regarded as power constructs articulated through the use of force. Currently there are only three recognised Matanitu in Fiji which are Kubuna, Burebasaga and Tovata. There were many more in pre-colonial Fiji.

2   Clapham (1985:59) argued that patron–client politics is founded on a premise of inequality between patrons and clients. Clients only benefit if they have anything to offer and it can also serve to intensify ethnic conflicts. Through patron–client politics, the roads are built in the wrong place or the wrong person gets the job, etc.

3   Conservative Fijian historians tend to highlight Sir Arthur Gordon's creation of the Native (later Fijian) Administration purely as an attempt to preserve the Fijian race and its culture. However, what they have not discussed is why it was necessary to have done this in terms of the establishment of the colonial state and its ensuing colonial capitalism.

4   This was and is the highest post within the provincial administration. Since the creation of provinces, most *Roko Tui* have been traditional chiefs. Such posts within the Native Administration facilitated the emergence of the 'new type of chief'. Since the creation of provinces in 1874, there has never been a female *Roko Tui* in Fiji. The words *Roko Tui* are two related Fijian words which are associated with the chiefly institution. *Roko* is a title which is conferred on people (including males and females) of chiefly birth in some parts of Fiji such as the various *vanua* in the province of Lau. *Tui* simply means chief; for instance, *Tui Levuka* or chief of Levuka.

5   This is the provincial administrator at the village level. Many chiefs refused to accept this post at the village level because they viewed it as a 'servant type' of job.

6   The concept of the 'new type of chief' began with the employment of chiefs in the system of indirect rule. Such chiefs thus assumed a dual role of being a traditional chief and that of being a 'state chief'. The chief's new role reinforced his traditional basis or rule and strengthened his political power.

7   The Alliance Party was formed in 1966. The party had three major ethnic components, namely the Fijian Association, the Indian Alliance and the General Electors. It was a unique political arrangement in which the concept of 'multi-racialism' was maintained through ethnic politics. The Fijian Association arm of the Alliance party was held together by patron–client politics through the Fijian Administration.

8   The SVT (roughly translated into English as 'the Fijian law making' party), was formed in 1991 as a replacement for the Fijian Association arm of the Alliance Party. The Great Council of Chiefs backed the formation of this party. Its major aims were to preserve the eastern Fijian chiefly hegemony which had emerged since the establishment of the colonial state; to contain Fijian political unity under this hegemony; and to re-strengthen the Fijian administration and its patron–client politics.

9   The Political situation within Fijian society in the post-coup era is one of 'competing
     legitimacy'. New political parties, for instance, have emerged from different regions
     of the country and have been supported by the various *vanua* and chiefs within the
     party. Each party defends its own rights to be the 'legitimate' representative of
     indigenous Fijians. This has been the case with the formation of the Party of
     National Unity (PANU) in western Viti Levu and the formation of the Veitokani ni
     Lewenilotu Vakarisito (VLV or the Christian Democrats), by mostly Methodist
     Church members in Vanua Levu.

10   Since the Labour Coalition government assumed leadership after the 1999 general
     elections, the people of Navosa had officially requested the Deputy Prime Minister
     and Minister for Fijian Affairs, Adi Kuini Vuikaba (a high chief of Navosa), to make
     Navosa a province of its own. The colonial government had put Nadroga and
     Navosa together to form a province. In this union, Navosa had always been
     neglected in terms of development.

11   Mataiwelagi is the sacred house foundation (*Yavu Tabu*) of the chiefly Cakobau
     family, which seats at the apex of the Kubuna Confederacy. Amongst the eastern
     Fijian confederacies of Kubuna, Burebasaga and Tovata, Kubuna is highest in rank.
     Naisogolaca is another chiefly household foundation whose members are closely
     related to the Mataiwelagi household.

12   The failure of the Government-owned National Bank of Fiji was perhaps the biggest
     blunder of the Rabuka government. Various cronies of the coups benefited through
     loans from the bank which after the coup was managed by a 'Rabuka handpicked
     Rotuman General Manager'. Such corruption revealed the real purpose of the coups
     (see *The Review* July 1995).

13   The Bose Levu Vakaturaga (Great Council of Chiefs or GCC) was initially created as
     the Native Council by Sir Arthur Gordon. It sits at the apex of the Native (Fijian)
     Administration. The Council was originally known as the 'Native Council' in 1874,
     then over the years it became the 'Council of Chiefs' and much later it had another
     name change to the 'Great Council of Chiefs'.

14   The Native Lands Commission was established under the Native Lands Ordinance
     in 1880. The NLC was to register all lands belonging to Native Fijians through some
     social unit. Thirty years later after many claims, and heated debates, G.V. Maxwell
     was able to draw up a Fijian land tenure system through the *mataqali* as a social unit.
     The NLC still exists and has an extensive record of Fijian landholdings and the basis
     of claims which formed the land tenure system.

15   The NLC has records of VKB. Indigenous Fijian land claims are based on one's registry
     in the VKB or the Fijian genealogy. To qualify for entry, one must have had a Fijian
     father through marriage or otherwise and the father must have been a registered Fijian
     through the VKB. Children born out of wedlock of Fijian mothers also qualify,
     provided that their mother is registered in the VKB. These children are registered in
     their mothers' *mataqali* and become landowners too through their mothers.

16   Fijian Unity is based on *vanua*, *lotu* and *matanitu*. *Vanua* refers to customary chiefly
     rule within the context of Fijian culture; *lotu* refers to Christianity and its teachings
     and *matanitu* is the state. The formation of both the FAP and the VLV has been a
     threat to those whose interests have been protected by the *vanua*, *lotu* and *matanitu*
     thesis. The formation of the FAP implies the breaking up of the *vanua*; formation of
     the VLV means the breaking up of the *lotu*.

chapter six

Peripheral visions?
Rabi Island in Fiji's general election

Teresia K. Teaiwa

In a paper on Rabi and Kioa prepared for the Fiji Constitution Review Commission, I described both resettled groups as 'peripheral minority communities' in Fiji. Rabi Islanders, also known as Banabans, were resettled to Fiji in two major waves, the first in 1945 and the second in 1947. They were resettled because colonial and capitalist interests wanted to mine Banaba for phosphate without the encumbrances of a native population. Rabi Islanders became Fiji citizens at Fiji's Independence in 1970, and apart from a period in the mid-to-late 1970s when they featured in the media with their legal case against the British Phosphate Commissioners, they have maintained an enigmatically peripheral profile in the nation.

While focusing on the Rabi Island community's position in the 1999 general election, I am dealing with two major 'peripheralities': the way Rabi exists for the most part in the peripheral vision of the nation, and the way the nation occupies the periphery of Rabi Islanders' imagination. By choosing to describe something so central to the development of national consciousness as a general election from the marginal position of Rabi, I am seeking to bring both these peripheral visions to the centre.

This chapter is based partly on observations made over seven days (8–15 May) on the island of Rabi. During this time, the North Eastern General Communal Roll issued by the Elections Office was carefully studied, and interviews carried out using a four-page questionnaire, administered between 8–11 May. I did not administer any of my own questionnaires on the polling days, 12–13 May. The questionnaire could be described as investigating two broad areas: first, the level and sources of voter awareness on Rabi in relation to the new electoral system and national politics; and second, the range of cultural and political identifications held by Rabi Islanders.[1]

The average running time for an interview in English was thirty minutes, and between forty and fifty in Gilbertese. I had initially hoped to conduct about a hundred formal interviews while on the island, but due to the need for extensive translations from English into Gilbertese, and constraints of intra-island travel, only 33 formal interviews were carried out.[2] Twenty-five interviews were carried out in Gilbertese, and the rest in English. Of the 25 interviews in Gilbertese, 11 were conducted with the assistance of interpreters and the rest were conducted unassisted.

All four villages: Tabwewa (6 interviews), Uma (5), Tabiang (13), and Buakonikai (9) were represented in the 33 interviews. Twenty of the interviewees were women and 13 were men. The slight over-representation of interviewees from Tabiang and of women, resulted from my position as 'researcher'. Because my family comes from Tabiang village, and since I stayed in our family home while on the island, I had more access to Tabiang villagers and my extended family. As a woman researcher, I found it easier to approach and talk with women; eleven of my interviews were conducted in the Women's Interest Centre at Nuku.

Although a quantitative breakdown of the survey results is presented in the Appendix, this research was not intended to produce definitive indicators. Rather, it should be seen, and is offered in this chapter, as an impressionistic representation of political consciousness on Rabi.

Rabi Islanders as Banabans

Many Fiji Islanders are uncertain about whether Rabi island is part of Fiji or not, and whether Rabi Islanders are Fiji citizens. Many people have asked me whether Rabi is in Kiribati, and whether Rabi Islanders have dual citizenship. Rabi Islanders are Fiji citizens who are entitled to a 'permanent residency' status if they entered Kiribati on a Fiji passport, because Banaba falls within the national boundaries of Kiribati. It bears repeating, though, that Rabi Islanders are Fiji citizens.

An added dimension to the peripheral perspectives I mentioned earlier, is my personal history as a Banaban/Rabi Islander. Born and raised neither on Banaba nor Rabi, I am a native speaker of English. Gilbertese is my second language. In the Gilbertese translation of my questionnaire, I unthinkingly substituted *te tautaeka* (the government) for 'the government of Fiji' in some of the questions. This translation sometimes caused interviewees to ask me for clarification, *Te tautaeka n ra?* (Which government?) Of course, I was thinking and talking about the government of Fiji, but the need for clarification arose precisely because the government of Fiji is not the only government for Rabi Islanders.

Under the *Banaban Settlement Act of 1970*,[3] amended in 1996, Rabi Islanders are administered by the Rabi Island Council, which is an elected body of Banabans representing each village. The history of the Rabi Island

Council—beyond the scope of this chapter—has been filled with drama, intrigue, and pathos.[4] For the present, it is enough to say that the Council is responsible for making and amending regulations on health, housing and social relations, levying taxes if necessary, and deciding on issues of development for the island and people. Te Kauntira, or the Council, is thus *te tautaeka* for Rabi Islanders.

As a fiercely democratic people,[5] Banabans value consensus, especially if it has been reached through struggle and competition. For this reason, authority is always challenged and privilege rigorously contested in the community. Local politics thus loom very large in Rabi Islanders' consciousness.[6] In a way, an event like the general election becomes an extension of local politics on Rabi. Furthermore, in the 1999 election, the Rabi Island Council did not publicly endorse any candidate, and Banabans were free to enjoy competition.

Rabi Islanders as Fiji citizens

When I asked interviewees whether they thought their community had contributed anything to the national good of Fiji, 8 were unsure and 24 responded in the affirmative. One respondent said Banabans contributed to the development of Fiji 'by developing Fiji'. Another respondent said, 'Yes, we contribute to the development of Fiji, but we don't remember how.' Others were more clear: 'We pay taxes, we work for the country'; 'We buy things'; 'Through agriculture and coconuts'. One respondent had a broad view: 'By teaching, working in government...I heard they contribute some money for the Fijians—we take part in Fijian functions and Banabans are friendly with Fijians'. Referring to Fijian provincial and Methodist church obligations, one respondent said, 'By giving *soli* to the province'. Another interviewee amplified this, saying, 'We've always contributed to different meetings in Taveuni and Suva'. Some respondents referred to contributions through phosphate (mined from the Banaban homeland) and phosphate monies (which add to Fiji's foreign exchange). So there was a diverse range of views among Rabi Islanders on how they contributed to the national good of Fiji. Some were unsure of their contributions—and this affects a community's relationship or identification with the nation.

Like other electors in Fiji, Rabi Islanders are entitled to two votes in a general election: a communal vote and an open vote. The two constituencies that include Rabi Island are the North Eastern General and the Cakaudrove West Open. The North Eastern General is geographically the largest of the three General Communal constituencies in Fiji. It includes Tailevu, Kadavu, Lomaiviti, Vanua Levu, Rabi, Taveuni, Kioa, and Lau.[7] The Cakaudrove West Open includes Savusavu Bay, Natewa Bay, Buca Bay, and Rabi, but interestingly excludes the neighbouring island of Kioa which is, instead, part of the Lau/Taveuni/Rotuma Open Constituency.[8]

The North Eastern General Communal constituency should have had approximately 6,000 registered voters to share one third of the estimated 18,000 in the national total of the General Communal electorate. However, the supplementary roll of registered voters issued on 6 April 1999 showed that only 4,553 were registered as voters in the constituency, of whom an estimated 1,317 were Rabi Islanders, constituting 28.9 per cent or almost one third of the total constituency.[9]

The current total population of Rabi Island is about 4,000. The number of voting age persons of Banaban descent living on Rabi Island and in other parts of Fiji is slightly higher than the registered 1,317. This is because some 600 of the total number of Banabans resident in Fiji (an estimated 300 of whom are of voting age) have yet to be confirmed as Fiji citizens.[10] In fact, at polling stations during the elections, a significant number of people lined up to sign affidavits confirming their illegibility as voters to avoid the F$50 fine for not voting.

Rabi Islanders as 'others' and general electors

At the last Fiji Census (1996), indigenous Fijians comprised 51 per cent of the total population, Indo-Fijians accounted for a little over 44 per cent, Rotumans 1 per cent, and 'Others' as they are so casually described, 4 per cent. As an ethnic category, 'Others' encompasses all non-Fijians and non-Indo-Fijians, including people of Pacific Islander descent, Europeans, 'part-Europeans'[11] and Chinese. Fiji's Pacific Islander community includes a number of groups, including Tongans, Samoans, Tuvaluans, Gilbertese, Banabans, Solomon Islanders and New Hebrideans (as they were known during the colonial period).[12] Each community has its own history in Fiji; some settled here by choice, others did not. Indeed, as a group, 'Others' is a motley crew which has had widely differing fortunes in Fiji.

'Others' are also known as 'Generals' for electoral purposes. While the category of 'Generals' pre-existed 1987, the rise of political parties specifically for 'Generals' is a decidedly post-coup phenomenon. Before the 1992 general election, 'Others' and 'Generals'—indeed Fijians as well as Indo-Fijians—could (and did) join any political party they wished.[13] But with the replacement of the racialist 1970 Constitution by a racist Constitution in 1990,[14] the re-segregation of the nation's electorate produced explicitly race-based political parties which discouraged cross-ethnic political affiliation. While there seemed to be some political rationale for the emergence of two different Fijian parties, the SVT and the FAP,[15] and the survival of the two pre-coup 'Indo-Fijian' parties, the NFP and the FLP,[16] there were dubious grounds for uniting 'Generals' under party banners.

The General Voters Party and the General Electors Association had regional support as their main difference, with the GVP strongholds centred in the Central and Northern Divisions, and the General Electors Association drawing its support from the West.[17] In 1998, the two parties explored unification, leading to the emergence of the United Generals Party. However, UGP was threatened with a revival of the GVP in 1999 as individual members not endorsed for seats broke away.

Rabi Islanders are significantly impacted by these so-called communal politics. Between 1970 and 1987, they had voted on the Fijian communal electoral roll.[18] This was rationalised by the special circumstances of the islanders: having been resettled from their home island of Banaba to Fiji after the Second World War by the colonial government, purchasing the island on which they lived, and paying customary tribute to the paramount chief of their province, Cakaudrove. With the abrogation of the 1970 Constitution, and its replacement with the 1990 Constitution, Rabi Islanders (along with 'Melanesians') were shifted to the General Electoral Roll, thereby becoming a minority within a minority.

When asked how they felt about being on the General Electoral Roll, most of my respondents said they were satisfied with their position. Some of the responses were uncomplicated: 'Because that's what we are', and 'We're not Fijian'. Others elaborated: 'Because we're special, different,' 'Sometimes it's better not to be counted with Fijians,' 'We have no Fijian blood—we are Fijians by citizenship' and 'We're different from Fijians: they're native, we're not'. Most of the answers reflected Rabi Islanders' concern for indigenous Fijians. They were careful to acknowledge their difference from Fijians, thus rationalising their presence on the General Electors Roll. But none of them commented on what it meant to them to be grouped with part-Europeans, Europeans, Chinese and other islanders. This blind spot, I believe, indicates that many Rabi Islanders have not fully considered the complex cultural and political implications of their designation as General Electors. In being careful not to tread on Fijian toes, Rabi Islanders have not been able to strategise for skillful negotiating with other General Electors.

In the two post-coup elections before 1999, Rabi Island as part of one of the five General Communal constituencies, was represented in parliament by GVP candidate and shipping magnate, Leo Smith.[19] GVP, of course, was then the coalition partner of the SVT. For Rabi Islanders, GVP's and Leo Smith's coalition with the SVT was highly desirable. Several levels of identification cemented the logic of Rabi Islanders' electoral representation by Leo Smith/GVP and SVT. Leo Smith comes from a Savusavu copra estate family he owns Consort Shipping Company whose vessel, the 'Spirit of Free Enterprise' (affectionately known by patrons as the SOFE), provides a direct service to Rabi Island at two crucial times of the year,[20] and claims descent from the *Tui Cakau*, the paramount chief of Cakaudrove, under whose traditional protection Rabi Island falls. Smith's effectiveness in representing his constituency, however, was severely undercut by his appointment to the SVT cabinet between 1992–99. Having their MP in Cabinet did not alter Banabans' peripheral status *vis-á-vis* the nation.

In any event, Rabi Islanders would have felt secure under a SVT government, a party created by the Bose Levu Vakaturaga, and led by Sitiveni Rabuka, a *kai*-Cakaudrove, and the erstwhile hero of the 1987 coups (the goals of which most Rabi Islanders implicitly supported).[21] Although Rabi Islanders, like most other Fiji citizens, had not previously had to cast a vote for or against Rabuka (because they were registered on non-Fijian rolls), the new electoral arrangements and Rabuka's decision to contest an open seat in the General Elections gave them this opportunity. For the first time, Rabi Islanders could elect a candidate who both could, and was likely to, become prime minister. Given this, in a sense then, they were not so peripheral.

Rabi Islanders and voter awareness

Q: Do you feel prepared to vote in this election?
A: Yes.
Q: Have you received any training or information on the new voting system?
A: No.

Q: Do you feel prepared to vote in this election?
A: Yes.
Q: Have you received any training or information on the new voting system?
A: Yes.
Q: Where did this training or information come from?
A: From Leo Smith's party.
Q: Please explain the voting system as you understand it.
A: We need to vote for Leo Smith because he's helped us already.

Q: Do you feel prepared to vote in this election?
A: Yes.
Q: Have you received any training or information on the new voting system?
A: Yes.
Q: Where did this training or information come from?
A: UGP.
Q: Please explain the voting system as you understand it.
A: Two voting papers—one for Vincent, one for Rabuka. I haven't seen a sample, so I don't know.

These three exchanges typify the range of responses I received. What became clear from my study was that while Banabans display a keen enthusiasm for exercising their political rights, they had an alarming lack of political education and information available to them before the election. So much so that of the 33 people I interviewed, 31 declared that they felt ready to vote in the election, but about half had not received any training or information on the new voting system. Of those who had, the overwhelming majority had done so from party officials and their campaign literature. None of the people I spoke to gave any indication that they had received information on the new voting system from the Fiji Elections Office. The Elections Office's educational campaign covered television, radio and print media, and some community visits and workshops. Television access in Rabi is limited by the lack of electricity on the island; the clearest radio transmissions come from the Island Network's Fijian language station (and, ironically, Tonga and Kiribati national radio); and the national daily newspapers are not delivered to the island regularly.

Most interviewees obtained the bulk of their understanding about the elections from party officials, candidates in-person, and word-of-mouth. Given this situation—where the transmission of information and education still depends on interpersonal communication rather than technology— Rabi Islanders would have benefitted greatly from an impartial presentation by the Elections Office.[22] As it was, many who relied on political parties for information were not told about their voting options. Very few people I spoke to could describe accurately the new voting system, and a significant number expressed surprise upon hearing that there was a new voting system at all. When asked to explain the voting system as they understood it, these are some of the things the interviewees said.

'I accept the coalition system that's been given to us.'
'There are two voting papers. Two sides.'
'I will vote above the line after checking for my name at the polling station.'
'Give a big tick. Two votes.'

In many instances, I found myself having to explain the new system to my interviewees. Because of the newness of the information, most interviewees were unable to answer this question: 'In the new voting system, which alternative do you think is better?' Of the few who did feel confident answering the question, five thought voting below the line was a better option, while eight preferred the above the line option, and two described them as equally good options. Some of those who expressed a preference for voting below the line gave the following reasons.

'Because it's my choice.'
'You can see their (the candidates') names.'
'Because that's what the preferential system is all about.'

Those who thought that voting above the line made more sense, had explanations like this

> 'It's the easier method for everyone, including old people.'
> 'Above the line is okay, especially if you don't know the candidates.'
> 'I trust the party.'
> 'Because I'm not sure my choices below the line will be good.'

While there are some convincing arguments for above-the-line voting, (for example, it produces a government, not just a parliament), what above-the-line voting also does is encourage peripheral communities like Rabi to abdicate their right and shirk their responsibility to understand and actively engage in national politics. Rabi Islanders were seriously under-educated (though not necessarily unprepared) for the 1999 General Elections, and were probably not the only community in this situation.

If most Rabi Islanders got what little information they had from political parties, which parties were they? Although Rabuka had visited the island (in fact, he only went to the administrative center at Nuku, and not to the villages) on the eve of the elections, he was so confident of the Rabi vote that he did not return. SVT's campaign on Rabi rode for the most part on the backs of UGP and GVP campaigns. None of the predominantly Indo-Fijian political parties campaigned on the island, mainly because there were no Indo-Fijian candidates running for the Cakaudrove West Open seat. The NFP and Labour parties have practically non-existent profiles on Rabi. However, apart from FAP, there did not seem to be any overt campaigning on the island by other Fijian parties either.

The two parties campaigning most vigorously on Rabi were UGP and the GVP; FAP had a modest following and COIN had fleeting visibility. The candidate for UGP was Vincent Lobendahn, GVP had the incumbent Leo Smith, FAP's candidate was Edward Daniel Reece, and COIN had Tony Fong. All four men had campaigned on the island, but during polling week, only three of them were physically present on the island (Lobendahn, Smith and Reece).[23] Interestingly, while most campaign material was in English, Leo Smith's campaign poster was the only one which utilised the Gilbertese language (see appendix). The only contest of any significance was between Lobendahn and Smith. Although Smith had the advantage of incumbency with the Rabi constituency, his defection from the UGP several months before the election, and the UGP's coalition with the ruling SVT, legitimised Lobendahn's campaign to a great extent. This General conflict had specific implications for the Rabi Islander electorate.

When asked to describe the various aspects of candidates' campaigns which had made an impression on them, these were some of the responses from interviewees.

'We've been with this party (GVP) a long time with no progress.'
'(The UGP candidate explained that) they are already in parliament.
We select two people to stand for us: one from SVT, one from UGP.'
'(The UGP candidate said) we'll vote for the party, and we'll be
represented directly in government. If an independent candidate goes
in, he'll have to go beg the government for me.'
'(The 'GVP' candidate) took power to us; he try to frighten us to vote.'
'(They say they're) trying to help the people here.'
'(They say we need) a change in government; (they talk about)
corruption.'
'(The UGP candidate) said that the government put up this
Constitution to include us…(that) the Rabuka government is
experienced. (The candidate said) he's introducing self-help projects
like seaweed and specialised fisheries for buyers like Joe's
Farm…(and that he'd be) improving the hospital and wharf.'
'Leo didn't make any promises. They all criticised each other. So I just
pray that when I go into the polling booth I'll know who to vote for.'
'Leo talked about the things he'd done—(improving) water, the
hospital—(he also said) the launch would come to Uma. Reece talked
about change.'
'Leo and the Tui Tunuloa were scaring us by saying that they'd close
the reef if we don't vote the way they want us to.'
'It doesn't matter (what others say) because I'll stay on Leo's side.'
'(The COIN candidate) said that our children and grandchildren's
future would be well looked after by him…(but) his stay was very
short, and (he) didn't say much.'

These answers present a complex picture of some of the concerns Rabi
Islanders had while facing this election. Issues of significance to the
islanders included: direct representation in government and improvements
to the quality of life on the island. Such interests would seem to not differ
greatly from other communities in Fiji.

A Rabi Island forecast

On polling days on Rabi, the candidates and their parties set up their bases
around the polling station. I visited the polling station at Tabiang on
Wednesday 12 May and the Nuku polling station on Thursday 13 May. At
both places, Reece's support, though strong, was clearly not as great as the
support for his two major competitors. At Tabiang, Smith and Lobendahn
seemed to have about equal numbers of supporters in their 'sheds,' while
at Nuku, Lobendahn appeared to have the edge. Of course, the politics of
'sheds' as indicators of support is complicated. In spite of the cultural value

given to competition, island etiquette dictates fair-play: an empty shed would delegitimise the whole contest. And so, as I observed, in some cases families would agree to send some of their members to one candidate's shed, while others would go to another's. Given the (ideal) secrecy of the ballot, though, the sheds are ultimately unreliable indicators—not to mention the questionable propriety of the policy which allows them to be erected in the first place.

Of the people I interviewed, 13 thought that SVT and its coalition partners would win the election, 1 expressed faith in the FAP and its coalition partners, and 19 declined to answer the question. Seventeen respondents thought Rabuka would be returned as Prime Minister of Fiji, 3 predicted Adi Kuini for the post, 1 said she was not sure, and 12 offered no answer. If we read the silent majority as an affirmation of the status quo, then it would seem that Rabi Islanders were to a large extent expecting that SVT and its coalition partners to win the election, and Rabuka returned as prime minister. As it turned out, of course, neither was to be. The SVT captured only 8 seats, NFP none, and the UGP only two. The Labour/ FAP/PANU 'People's Coalition' won the majority of seats in parliament, and Mahendra Chaudhry became the first Indo-Fijian Prime Minister of Fiji.

Election results and results of results

In the Cakaudrove West Open Constituency, Sitiveni Rabuka won easily. Of a total of 14,066 votes cast, Rabuka polled 9,190, (2,618 more than the required majority of 6,572), and 69.92 per cent of vote. His nearest contender, Aisake Kubuabola of the VLV polled 1,936 votes or 14.73 per cent. In the Northeastern General Communal Constituency, Leo Smith won on the fourth preference. On first preferences, Smith had polled 1,305 votes. Vincent Lobendahn had been leading on first preferences with 1,636 votes. However, this was 152 votes short of the required majority (of fifty per cent plus one). All of Lobendahn's four rivals had given him and the UGP their fifth preference, while Leo Smith had received the fourth preferences of COIN, FAP, and Ian Simpson. Leo Smith ended up winning the seat with 1,879 votes, leaving Lobendahn behind with 1694 votes.[24] Significantly, the Northeastern General Constituency had 287 invalid ballot papers. We cannot know what percentage of those invalid votes were from Rabi. However, even if all the invalid votes came from Rabi, it would still indicate that the majority of the islanders were fairly well prepared for the new voting procedures.

What did the outcome of the election mean for Rabi? Having returned Rabuka to parliament, they lost him when unexpectedly, before the first sitting of the newly elected parliament of 1999, he resigned his seat to become the chair of the Bose Levu Vakaturaga. When the new parliament convened on June 15 1999, the open constituency of Cakaudrove West was not represented.[25] It was, however, represented by Leo Smith, the member for the Northeastern General Communal Constituency, who had campaigned as an independent under the unofficial banner of GVP, and in an unofficial coalition with SVT. Before parliament convened, though, Smith and his GVP colleague, Bill Aull, joined the government coalition. In this sense, the words of one of my interviewees takes on new meaning

'...If an independent candidate goes in, he'll have to go beg the government for me.'

Smith, the 'Independent' MP, made an unorthodox, but perhaps necessary move given the paradigm-shifting results of the 1999 General Election. Rabi is now represented by a government backbencher, though it is hardly the government they expected to get.

Peripheral visions?

My research and analysis of Rabi Islanders and the Fiji General Elections of 1999, pulls towards reassessing my initial description of the community as peripheral. Although I suspect that the welfare of our community is not high on the agenda of the present government, we can only hope that our representatives in parliament will indeed be advocates of our minority interests. But being a minority does not necessarily mean we have to be peripheral. European, part-European and Chinese interests are minority interests without being peripheral. Like other rural communities, Rabi Islanders will always be geographically peripheral in Fiji, but that does not necessarily translate into political or cultural peripherality. Whether Rabi Islanders are effectively represented or empowered in Fiji's national politics might be instructively illuminated by a different elections process.

On Saturday 28 August 1999, a young woman named Joanne Terubea[26] was crowned Miss Hibiscus, the premier beauty pageant title in Fiji, and, I contend, an important indicator of racial and cultural politics in Fiji. Hailed as the first Banaban Miss Hibiscus by the media (see *Fiji Times* and *Daily Post* 29 August 1999), it does indeed seem that Fiji is ready, at least at the level of popular culture, to embrace Rabi Islanders in the national imaginary. Indeed, in her press statements, Joanne has been careful to insist that she is a Fiji Islander first and foremost.

Notes

1   Although both sets of questions will be discussed in this chapter, this same survey is
     also being used as the primary source material for another paper, more explicitly
     dealing with the issue of minority rights.

2   This sample amounts to roughly 3 per cent of the total electorate on Rabi. Though this is, in objective terms, a small proportion of the community, it is fairly representative in its distribution.

3   From my survey, only 8 out of 33 respondents had actually ever read the Banaban Settlement Act. By comparison, only 6 out of the 33 said that they had read the Fiji Constitution.

4   See the Aidney Report (Aidney et al. 1994) for an inventory of financial mismanagement by successive Councils which culminated in a 'coup' of sorts when Rabi Islanders overthrew an elected council in 1991.

5   Grimble and Maude (see Maude 1989) have irresponsibly tried to inscribe a chiefly or hierarchical system on Banabans, but except for those few families who are privileged by Grimble and Maude's records, the majority of Banabans maintain that they did not and do not have a chiefly system. Rather, each family or clan has a role to play which integral to the whole of the society. This is similar to other island traditions in Kiribati, especially Tabiteuea, whose name announces its democratic belief system: *e tabu te uea*. This may be translated to mean that either a) no chiefs are allowed; or b) everyone is a chief.

6   In a forthcoming article to be published by the International Working Group for Indigenous Affairs, my sister, Katerina Teaiwa describes the way that Banabans refer to Rabi as *abara*—meaning not only our land, but our country.

7   The 1999 General Election candidates in this constituency included (in alphabetical order) Anthony Fong (COIN), Vincent Lobendahn (UGP), Edward Daniel Reece (FAP), Ian Mitchell Simpson (Independent), and Leo Smith (Independent/GVP). Other parties which listed preferences in this constituency were FLP, VLV and NVTLP.

8   The 1999 General Election candidates in this constituency included (in alphabetical order) Mosese Gere (*Na Vanua Tako Lavo* Party), Aisake Kubuabola (VLV), Epeli Ligamamada (FAP), and Sitiveni Rabuka (SVT). Other parties which listed preferences in this constituency were UGP, NFP, COIN, and FLP.

9   Banaban statistics are not normally disaggregated from 'Other' indicators and statistics in Fiji. This makes acquiring information about Banabans from nationally-collected data quite difficult to obtain. The total number of Rabi Islanders registered in the North Eastern General Communal constituency was arrived at by a careful survey of the Electoral Roll, identifying Banaban names (as opposed to Gilbertese or Kioan names), and place of residency. A certain margin of error must be allowed for this method which yielded these approximate figures: 1,171 Rabi Islanders on-island; 146 Rabi Islanders off-island (but still within the same constituency). The Elections office, however, expected a total of only 1033 ballot papers to be cast on Rabi.

10   My father's brother, who was born in Kiribati and came to Fiji as an infant, and has lived here all his life, was unable to register to vote because he was told he was not yet a Fiji citizen—even though he has lived in Fiji for 52 years. Several hundred Banabans are in similar situations. The Immigration Department is requiring these people to pay F$800 fees to become Fiji citizens, which seems unfair and unreasonable to many Banabans. The Rabi Island Council is seeking alternative avenues for confirming all Banabans as Fiji citizens.

11 Fiji is the only country I know of which uses the term 'part-European' to describe people of mixed European and Pacific Islander descent. Common in Native American usage is the term 'mixed-blood' or *metis*; in Latin America and the Caribbean the terms *criollo* and *mestizo* are used. In Hawaii, people of mixed descent are described as *hapa* or *hapa-haole*; in Samoa they are described as *afakasi*, in francophone Tahiti as *demi*. While the term 'half-caste' is sometimes used colloquially in Fiji, only 'part-European' appears on bureaucratic forms as a subsection of the category 'Others'.

12 The New Hebrides became the independent nation state of Vanuatu in 1980, and the people of Vanuatu are called ni-Vanuatu.

13 An Independent Candidate in the 1999 general elections, Arthur Jennings was a National Federation Party candidate in the late 70s or early 80s. However, most 'Generals' (like Charles Walker, the Stinsons, John Falvey, Ted Beddoes, Fred Caine, et al.) tended to make their home through the General Electors Association within the governing Alliance Party headed by Ratu Sir Kamisese Mara. (The Alliance comprised three groups: the General Electors Association, the Fijian Association, and the Indian Alliance.)

14 I make the distinction here between 'racialist' and 'racist' though some may argue that there is no difference or that any form of racialism is inherently racist. However, the 1970 Constitution of Fiji was not forged in quite the same overtly racist spirit in which the 1990 Constitution was. Although the 1970 Constitution of Fiji inscribed race-based electoral politics (12 communal seats each for Fijians and Indians, and 3 communal seats for Generals), it also provided for multicultural or inter-communal identifications (10 seats each for Indian and Fijian candidates on a national roll, and 5 'national' seats for Generals). The 1990 Constitution, however, did away with open seats altogether, and radically decreased the proportion of Indian seats in parliament (in a parliament of 70, Fijians held 37 seats while Indians had 27 and Generals held 5).

15 The SVT was set up in 1990 by the Great Council of Chiefs or Bose Levu Vakaturaga to contest the 1992 elections (its contenders then were the Fijian Nationalist Party headed by Sakeasi Butadroka, and the Western-based ANC headed by Apisai Tora); the Fijian Association Party emerged in 1993 as part of a dissident group of former SVT supporters led by the late Josefata Kamikamica (see the *Fiji Times* 7 August 1999 for an interesting letter to the editor which provides a genealogy of mainstream Fijian political parties).

16 While the NFP claims roots in the cane-belt, it has, over the years, become increasingly identified as the party of Indo-Fijian business and the professional class; the Labour Party, on the other hand, is solidly identified with both rural and urban Indo-Fijian working classes and has loyal support from a small multicultural urban working class and segments of the intelligentsia.

17 The GEA, which formed to contest the 1994 election, drew its membership from the ANC (led by the ubiquitous Apisai Tora) which had contested the 1992 election. The leadership of both of the 'Generals' parties has tended to come from Europeans and 'part-Europeans.' All elected 'Generals' in 1992 and 1994 were 'part-Europeans' (David Pickering, Bill Aull, Leo Smith, Harold Powell, Vincent Lobendahn). Attempts to increase support across their traditional borders have often taken the

form of unscrupulous bribing and herding of Melanesian and Micronesian voters to rallies and polling stations.

    In addition to regional differences, however, there do seem to be cross-cutting issues of class and culture determining the political factioning of 'Generals.' For instance, the symbolic (though not formal) resurrection of the General Voters Party in the 1999 Elections, under the leadership of the late Phillip King, Fred Caine, and Peter Howard in support of successful independent candidates Bill Aull (Central General Constituency) and Leo Smith (Northeastern General Constituency). In the Central General Constituency, Bill Aull's campaign was identified as solidly working class and subtly Polynesian or islander-oriented. His main rival, Robin Storck, of the United Generals Party, on the other hand, was identified with European and business interests. Leo Smith is the owner of Consort Shipping, and very rarely identified with working class interests, his alignment with the 'GVP' group thus was pragmatic.

18   A history of Rabi Islanders' electoral representation in Fiji between 1970 and 1987, would greatly illuminate the manner in which different communal interests were expressed and investments or disinvestments made in the Rabi Island community. This, however, is beyond the scope of this chapter. Forthcoming work by my sister, Katerina Teaiwa, will shed more light on this time period.

19   In 1992 Rabi Islander, Teiwaki Benaia (ANC) and Gus Billings (Independent) ran against Leo Smith. While Teiwaki's genealogy (being the grandson of the Reverend Tebuke Rotan, for many years the Chairman of the Rabi Island Council) might have carried a lot of weight with other Rabi Islanders, he was not able to pull in voters from other parts of the Northern General Constituency.

20   Otherwise, getting to Rabi from Suva involves an inter-island (40 minute) plane or (overnight) boat trip to Savusavu, a (2½ hour) car or (4 hour) bus ride to Karoko landing, and a (½ hour) punt ride to Rabi. The cost of a direct and one-way trip from Suva to Rabi on the SOFE is about F$50. By plane and taxi from Suva a one way trip costs F$210. By boat to Savusavu and bus to Karoko it costs F$80. A direct flight service to Rabi Island has been proposed by Air Fiji to be launched in 1999. The cost of a one way ticket has been set at F$120. The high cost of interisland travel contributes greatly to Rabi Islanders' isolation.

21   I recently heard about a fantastic rumour which had been spread among some Rabi Islanders after the coup that the Australian government was willing to evacuate Banabans to Australia!

22   In a presentation to the Citizens' Constitutional Forum Elections Audit 17/7/99, Elections Office Information Officer, Suzie Naisara-Grey admitted that her office had indeed neglected Rabi while offering workshops in other communities in the General electorate like the Suva-based Chinese Association. Naisara-Grey's statement is ironic when we remember that her father, the late Jone Naisara, was a representative of Cakaudrove (and Rabi Island) in pre-coup parliaments.

23   COIN's Tony Fong's absence during polling week was noticeable. He had declared in the COIN brochure that one of his main ambitions was to find a wife of either Rabian or Kioan descent, but apparently, when he had come to campaign he only spent an hour in total on the island!

Significantly, Lobendahn came to the island alone, and relied completely on a local Rabi Islander support-system. Leo Smith arrived on the island with an entourage of Gilbertese and some Rabi Islanders drawn from the Savusavu area. Daniel Reece came to the island accompanied by a Fijian woman who spoke fluent Gilbertese.

24 It would be interesting but impossible to find out where exactly within the constituency Smith picked up his slim majority of 185. Detailed information from the Elections Office regarding ballots from Rabi will not be available—ballots from individual polling stations are placed into a common bin so as to preserve their secrecy, and make it impossible to identify localised voting patterns within a constituency.

25 A by-election was to be held in September 1999 with a new VLV candidate standing: Ratu Epeli Ganilau. This, of course, raises a whole new set of cultural and political issues for the Cakaudrove West Open Constituency—which unfortunately, cannot be analysed here!

26 Being the daughter of Reverend Rongorongo Terubea, the Chairman of the Rabi Island Council who was deposed in a popular uprising on the island in 1991, complicates the local reception of Joanne's crowning as Miss Hibiscus.

Appendix—Breakdown of survey results

Village		Party affiliation		Male (13)
Tabwewa	(6)	UGP	(9)	Female (20)
Uma	(5)	GVP	(2)	
Tabiang	(13)	None	(22)	
Buakonikai	(9)			

Age		Religion		Education	
21–30	(3)	Catholic	(13)	Primary	(12)
31–40	(11)	Methodist	(13)	Secondary	(12)
41–50	(10)	Other	(7)	Tertiary	(2)
51–60	(8)	Unstated	(7)		
61–70					

1. Do you feel prepared to vote in this election?
   Yes: 31   No: 1   No response: 1

2. Have you received any training or information on the new voting system?
   Yes: 16   No: 15   No response: 1

2a. Where did this training or information come from?
   Political party: 15
   Elections office: 0
   Other: 0

2c. In the new voting system, which alternative do you think is better?
   Below the line: 5   Above the line: 8   Both: 2

3. Have you been visited by any candidates for this election?
   Yes: 17   No: 13
   One candidate or representative: 5   (UGP)
   Two candidates or representatives: 3   (UGP and "GVP")
   3–4 candidates or representatives: 6   (UGP, GVP, FAP, COIN)
   More candidates or representatives: 1

3c. Do you feel you have a good choice of candidates in your constituency?
   Yes: 27   No: 4

3d. What factors influence your opinion most? Please rank in order of priority
   experience #1   (18 + 3 #3 ranking)
   race   #5
   reputation   #8
   wealth   unranked
   personality   #7
   religion   #6
   speaking ability #4
   education   #2 (10 + 5 #1 ranking + 5 #3 ranking)
   work habits   #3 (7 + 1 #1 ranking + 5 #2 ranking)
   gender   #8

4. What is your main source of news on the election campaigns? Please rank in order of accessibility.
   a. radio   #3 (4 #1 + 2 #2)
   b. newspapers   #2 (7 #1 + 1 #2)
   c. party manifestos, brochures   # 1 (16 #1 + 3 #2 + 1 #3)
   d. Elections Office literature   #4 (1 #1 + 2 #2 + 1 #3)
   e. candidates in-person   #2 (3 #1 + 6 #2 + 2 #3)
   f. your own travels to town or
      city centres   unranked
   g. word-of-mouth   #3 (1 #1 + 4 #2 + 5 #3)

5. Are you happy with Banabans' inclusion on the General Electors roll?
   Yes: 25   No: 4

6. Have you ever read the Constitution of Fiji?
   Yes: 6   No: 27
   6.i. 1970
   6.ii. 1990

6a. Have you received any training or information about the 1997 Constitutional Amendment?
Yes: 1   No: 32
6b. Where did this training or information come from?
The Citizens' Constitutional Forum—'Your Constitution, Your Rights' handbook

7. Have you ever read the Banaban Settlement Act?
Yes: 8   No: 25
7.i. 1970
7.ii. 1996 Amendment
7a. How did you get access to the Act?
From the Rabi Council of Leaders
From the Rabi Community Library
A personal copy
7b. What caused you to read the Act?
Work related
Personal interest
Educational

8. In your opinion, do Banabans contribute to the national good of Fiji?
Yes: 24   No: 8   Unsure: 1

9. Is being a citizen of Fiji important to you?
Yes: 32   No: 1

9b. Can you sing the national anthem of Fiji?
Yes: 30   No: 3

9c. On what occasions do you commemorate or celebrate your citizenship in this country?
October 10th
December 15th

9d. Which of the languages spoken in Fiji are you fluent or conversant in?
English   #1 (30)
Fijian   #1 (30)
Hindustani   #2 (5)
Rotuman   #3 (1)
Tuvaluan   #2 (5)
Chinese   unranked

9e. Does being a citizen of Fiji make you feel you have a bond with all Fiji Islanders?
Yes: 10   No: 1   No response: 22

9e.i. Which ethnic group of Fiji Islanders do you feel closest to? Please rank:
Fijians   #1 (19 #1 + 8 #2 + 1 #3)
Indo-Fijians   #6
Rotumans   #5
Europeans   #5
Part-Europeans   #4
Chinese   unranked
Gilbertese   #2 (10 #1 + 14 #2 + 2 #3)
Kioans   #3 (2 #2 + 12 #3)

10a. Which parties do you predict will form the next government of Fiji?
SVT: 13   Other: 1   No response: 19

10a.i. Do you think the voting system will greatly affect who wins the election?
Yes: 5   No: 1   No response: 27

10a.ii. Do you prefer the new voting system or the old one?
New: 8   Old: 7   No response: 18

10c. Who do you predict will be the next Prime Minister of Fiji?
Rabuka: 17   Adi Kuini: 3   Undecided: 1   No response: 12

chapter seven

Land, Lomé and the Fiji sugar industry

Padma Lal

The Fiji Sugar industry faces an uncertain future. With the ongoing negotiation over the renewal of the preferential access under the Sugar Protocol of the Lomé Convention, the renewal of native land leases, declining productivity and high costs, the industry is facing major challenges. The viability of the industry will depend on the reforms the industry and government make in the short to medium term. These reforms would need to be underpinned by significant research on crucial aspects of the industry.

The Sugar Commission of Fiji (SCOF) has identified in its Sugar Industry Strategic Plan a number of reforms needed to increase efficiency in the transportation and milling subsectors. Reforms to the cane payment system to increase farmer incentives to produce sugar cane with high sugar content and the establishment of an independent Sugar Cane Research and Extension Centre are also planned. While these strategies will help increase crop and sugar yield, they are not likely to be sufficient to encourage improvements in farm efficiency.

This chapter discusses the types of policy issues the Sugar Commission of Fiji is likely to face in the light of expected changes in land tenure, the international sugar trade reforms, declining farm productivity and high production costs. It outlines gaps in the industry's proposed reforms. More specifically, the chapter outlines the reforms needed in the Sugar Cane Research Centre and its research portfolio to cope with medium term challenges.

The Fiji Sugar Corporation (FSC) must move beyond concentrating on just increasing yield through farm husbandary, breeding, crop agronomy and pest control. The proposed Sugar Cane Research Institute must adopt a systems approach to research and development to include in its portfolio economic and other social science research. Moreover, the Institute should also embrace a more participatory approach to research and involve all relevant stakeholders, including growers and policymakers, in the identification of research needs, prioritisation of research and design and implementation of research. Such an approach will help the Commission develop appropriate economic policies and farm level strategies aimed at increasing farm productivity and economic profitability and efficiency. It will encourage farmers to consider the technical and economic feasibility of sustainable farming systems, including crop diversification.

The Fiji sugar industry

The value of the sugar industry's production is about F$230 million, equivalent to about 43 per cent of the value of Fiji's agricultural production. Although its contribution to the nation's GDP has fallen slightly in recent years, sugar remains the single most significant source of primary production, contributing about 23 per cent of GDP. Other major contributors are the 'service' sectors, such as transport and communication (12.6 per cent), finance, insurance, real estate and business services (14.1 per cent), hotels and restaurants, wholesale and retail sectors (16.5 per cent), and community, social and personal services (17.5 per cent).

Sugar is Fiji's largest export earner, accounting for around 40 per cent of the country's total export earnings. Much of this depends on two sets of preferential arrangements that Fiji has enjoyed since 1975. Under the Sugar Protocol of the Lomé Convention and the Special Preferential Sugar (SPS) Agreement, exports to the European Union (EU) have accounted for some 59 per cent of Fiji's total sugar exports and Fiji has enjoyed prices well above free world sugar prices and a guaranteed quota of about 197,000 tonnes of sugar. In 1997 this was equivalent to 56 per cent of Fiji's total sugar production. Apart from relying on the EU markets, Fiji also has preferential arrangements for sugar exports to the United States, supplying an annual quota of about 18,900 tonnes in 1997, equivalent to a little less than 1 per cent of US total sugar imports. Fiji has in the past also supplied sugar to Malaysia, China, Korea, Canada, New Zealand and Japan. In 1997, only Malaysia and Japan took Fiji's sugar under bilateral agreements. Domestic consumption of sugar is about 1 per cent of total production.

In 1998, there were 22,130 sugar cane farmers with the average farm holding of about 4.6 hectares. Farm numbers have risen by about 30 per cent from a low of about 17,000 in 1975. The area under sugar cane has also increased since the implementation of the preferential access agreement in 1975, from about 45,000 ha to about 74,000 ha of sugar cane in 1997 (see Table 7.1). The average area harvested has increased from about 2.5 ha to 3.4 ha per grower. The status of farmers—whether they are full-time or part-time, relying on other sources of income—is unknown. Average sugar cane production is about 52 tonnes/ha, with farmers receiving on average about F$50/tonne.

Table 7.1   Sugar cane production and payments received by growers and millers, 1995–97

	1997	1996	1995
Number of growers	22,100	22,304	22,449
Area under sugar cane (ha)	73,378	73,981	73,977
Tonnage per grower	148	196	183
Yield per ha	44.7	59.2	55.6
Cane crushed ('000 t)	3,280	4,380	4,110
Sugar output ('000 t)	347	545	454
Price per tonne cane F($)	50	45	54
Income to growers (F$million)	164.2	196.3	221.0
Income to millers (F$million)	69.3	79.1	89
Employment direct (no.)	36,991	37,422	36,754
Cane cutters (no.)	14,891	15,118	14,305

Source: FSC Annual Report 1998 and Current Economic Statistics (Jan–Oct 1997).

Cane is transported by rail or truck to the four Fiji Sugar Corporation-operated mills at Lautoka, Rarawai and Penang in VitiLevu and Labasa on Vanua Levu. Altogether these mills employ about 4,500 workers. In addition, there are about 14,300–15,000 cane cutters and about 2,000 lorry operators whose livelihood depends on a viable sugar cane production sector. Thus the sugar sector is a major employer in the rural areas, employing about 25 per cent of the country's active workforce.

Challenges facing the industry and research needs

The sugar industry faces many challenges. The renewal of native land leases and the renewal of the Lomé Convention are two urgent problems that need immediate action. In the short to medium term, the industry will also need to address the problem of low and declining farm productivity and inefficient transport and milling sectors. These challenges will have to be met through reforms underpinned by rigorous research, and some hard decisions.

Agricultural land lease renewal

The most pressing challenge facing the industry is the renewal of expiring native leases. Seventy three per cent of farmers in Fiji are cultivating land under native leases from indigenous Fijian landowners. These leases were offered for a period of 30 years, under the 1969 Agricultural Landlord and Tenant Act (ALTA). Native leases began expiring in 1997 and over 70 per cent of leases will expire by 2001 (see Table 7.2).

Renewal of ALTA leases is currently being negotiated between the growers, landowners and the government. Before the May 1999 elections, of the 134 expiring leases, 90 per cent had been renewed. The challenge

Table 7.2   Expiry of agricultural farm and cane leases in Fiji, 1997–2005

Year	Agricultural leases	Sugar cane leases
1997	45	26
1998	189	129
1999	231	168
2000	1,828	1,215
2001	1,808	2,536
2002	479	325
2003	645	466
2004	332	231
2005	288	244
Total	5,845	5,340

Source: World Bank, 1995. *Fiji: restoring growth in a changing global environment*, The World Bank, Washington, DC.

facing the new government is to negotiate renewal at a time when many landowners, upset about the defeat of the SVT party in the election, are threatening to withhold renewals.

Because of the importance of security of land tenure to investment and to productivity, the outcome of the land negotiation will have a far reaching effect on the industry as well as on the efficiency and sustainability of sugar cane farming in Fiji. Moreover, depending on the outcome of the lease negotiations, the industry will need to develop different types of practical strategies.

At the industry level, if a large proportion of leases are not renewed, the total sugar production will doubtless decrease. Depending on the category of land for which the agricultural lease is not renewed, the impact could be greater than the proportion of land taken out of sugar cane. The impact on displaced rural households could also be significant. However, the extent of any impact is difficult to predict, particularly as the options being considered include separation of the agricultural lease from the area used for housing purposes. In some cases, farmers have other sources of income. Moreover the government has recently decided to offer F$28,000 as an incentive for farmers to leave the industry if they desire. While a few farmers have decided to take up this offer, a large proportion still await the outcome of the ongoing negotiations.

If land leases are not renewed and the indigenous landowners continue to grow sugar cane, cane production will very likely still decline. Currently, 25 per cent of farmers are indigenous Fijians. In the past indigenous Fijian farmers had generally lower sugar cane yields than their Indo-Fijian counterparts (Reddy 1998). According to Reddy, the cane yield from Fijian farms is about 46 tonnes/ha as compared with 64 tonne/ha for Indo-Fijian farmers. Fijian farmers are also believed to be economically less efficient, although in global terms both Fijian and Indo-Fijian farmers are highly inefficient. From a study of 397 farm households, Indo-Fijian farmers are estimated to achieve efficiency of about 50 per cent of their potential (at the production frontier) as compared with the 35 per cent of Fijian farmers. It appears that Fijian farmers make less use of inputs such as chemicals, fertiliser and labour, and more use of financial capital. Lack of farming experience and sociocultural differences could also explain the difference in productivity. Ethnic Fijian farmers have only recently become involved with sugar cane farming in large numbers, and the level of expertise is low compared to that of the Indo-Fijians who have been farming cane for over 100 years. However, this conclusion needs to be treated with caution because the analysis is based on only 0.2 per cent of the farm population.

The productivity of farms also depends on the timing of input applications which, to some extent, depends on experience as well as the sociocultural characteristics of a community and their value system. In Fiji, it is widely acknowledged that for indigenous Fijians, maximising income is not the only goal. Maintaining social harmony is equally important, and this has often meant the use of human resources in other competing social activities, at the expense of cane yield. This situation should be adequately considered when developing and designing government policies and industry strategies.

If the land leases are renewed but the tenure is short and insecure, the industry will suffer. It is generally accepted that secure land leases encourage long term investment in productivity-enhancing technology (Feder 1987), and promote socially optimal use of resources, including capital and labour. Long and secure leases also encourage soil conservation practices, and pesticide and fertiliser use aimed at minimising environmental costs by adopting strategies such as integrated pest management, as well as encouraging farmers to produce other more valuable, but perennial crops. Whatever the duration of tenure, detailed bioeconomic research will be required to develop appropriate government policies and farm-level management strategies. Such issues have either been totally ignored or have only been marginally addressed in the past. Given the expected volatility of world sugar prices, farmers would also need to adopt strategies that would help minimise risks. For this, sugar cane-based farmers could consider diversifying into crops other than sugar cane, particularly fresh fruits and other horticultural commodities, for which demand has been growing at a rapid pace. The European Union market alone for tropical fruits, such as papaya, pineapple and mango—crops for which Fiji has shown it has comparative advantage—has more than doubled since the early 1980s. As discussed below, diversification of agricultural activities on sugar cane land could be one of the important options available to farmers to cope with expected changes in the sugar markets resulting from obligations under the World Trade Organization (WTO).

The Sugar Cane Research and Extension Centre of FSC has in the past carried out many field trials to identify, for example, agronomically suitable other crop species and farm management practices for different categories of sugar cane land. On the basis of these experiments they then promoted, through extension services, adoption of particular crops and farm management practices. Such an approach reflects traditional scientists' general concerns with production yields only and ignores any associated demands on farm labour or input costs. Farmers, however, concerned with both costs and returns as important determinants of their farming practices, have thus often ignored extension advice. Future research must include considerations of crop diversification on sugar cane-based farm-level profitability.

Whatever the nature of the final outcome of the lease renewal negotiations, the impact on the industry will be significant. To improve production efficiency on sugar cane farms, the industry will need to adopt very different types of policy decisions and strategies to help Indo-Fijian farmers and Fijian farmers. To design appropriate farm-level strategies, it is important not only to consider the land classes involved but also the underlying causes of inefficiency in different categories of farms: small farms, large farms, Indo-Fijian-managed farms, Fijian-managed farms, freehold farms or leased land. Given the underlying institutional constraints, it will also be important to identify optimal resource reallocation options available to improve farm-level efficiency. Such issues cannot be addressed unless major reforms are undertaken in the Sugar Cane Research Centre.

The Lomé Convention and the WTO

Fiji is a small producer of sugar cane in global terms, contributing only about 0.5 per cent (350,000 tonnes) of annual world sugar production. It relies heavily on preferential access to European Union markets under two sugar arrangements: the Sugar Protocol of the Lomé Convention which was first signed in 1975 and the Special Preferential Sugar Agreement (SPS) signed in 1995, and to a lesser extent a United States import quota. The prices paid under these preferential access arrangements have been up to three times world free market prices.

As a result, Fiji has enjoyed a price subsidy from the EU equivalent to about 3.72 per cent of Fiji's GDP. In 1992 the subsidy was estimated to be worth US$41 million or about F$90 million (MacDonald 1994 cited in Prasad and Ackram-Lodhi 1997). Although the Sugar Protocol, as explicitly noted in Article 1, is of indefinite duration, and the Protocol sugar tonnage is contained in the EU schedule of Market Access Offers under the Uruguay Round, its status is unclear under the WTO.

Until recently, the Lomé Convention was recognised by WTO under a waiver arrangement. However, any renewal of the waiver to cover any successor agreement to the Lomé Convention runs the risk of failing if WTO Contracting Parties, not parties to the Lomé Convention, vote against such a renewal—as is likely judging from recent performance. However, it is unclear what the outcome of the next round of negotiations will be, and what changes may be required for these to be compatible with the WTO's requirements. Under the WTO, the European Union (and Fiji) is bound by three guiding principles: prohibition of import restrictions of all types other than tariffs which are subject to negotiation; encouragement of countries to adopt equal treatment or non-discriminatory strategies when importing products from all foreign sources and internally; and undistorted competition limiting use of domestic and export subsidies (Roberts 1997).

While these arrangements have been in place for some time, they have come under pressure since the GATT Uruguay Round negotiations and the establishment of the WTO. The industry is facing a potential threat of losing its preferential access to the EU market as a result of the European Commission's proposed review of the Sugar Protocol of the Lomé Convention in response to the criticism of the Common Agricultural Policy (CAP) from the WTO. The Fiji sugar industry, like those of the other African, Caribbean and Pacific (ACP) countries, is therefore facing serious threats to its guaranteed quotas from the EU and USA at preferential margins. If the preferences are lost, Fiji and other ACP countries will face the vagaries of free world sugar markets, which have been highly volatile. The world sugar price has fluctuated in the order of 41 per cent, whereas the EU price has changed by about 9 per cent (Hermann and Weiss 1995). Any loss in preferential access if Fiji were forced to sell its sugar at world prices would affect everyone directly or indirectly associated with the cane industry: growers, harvesters, those involved in transporting, and mill workers who have benefited from the welfare transfer. In the long term, Fiji may be forced to become more efficient and better utilise its limited resources. In the short term, however, the adjustment costs could be quite significant.

Currently, Fiji is negotiating the continuation of the Protocol and a longer transition period during which the Protocol will continue to operate as it does presently. The ACP countries want a 10-year transition period instead of the five years being offered by the EU (Dakar (Senegal) Meetings of the ACP Council of Ministers and the ACP-EU Ministerial Negotiations 6–10 February 1999). But this arrangement will only be an interim measure. Ultimately, the preferential arrangement will cease and the severity of the impacts will depend on how rapidly the preferential margin is reduced.

National level impacts

It is speculated that a fall in sugar prices of 15 per cent by the year 2000 could result in a F$7 million decline in household wages and salaries (Chand and Abello 1997). This could exacerbate rural poverty. Prasad and Akram-

Lodhi (1997), using secondary data, note that farmers who produce less than 200 tonnes of cane could be classed as living below the relative poverty line. They suggest that over 65 per cent of growers are likely to be seriously exposed to poverty. However, this study does not take into account other sources of income that cane farmers may have. Partly because of the insecurity over land tenure and the government's various economic policies, most of the Indo-Fijian families have encouraged at least one member to seek off-farm employment. Many households—the exact number is unknown—in semi-urban areas in western VitiLevu and Vanua Levu have non-farm sources of income; in many cases sugar cane farming has become a part-time activity. Such aggregate-level analyses are useful in raising overall awareness of the social impacts. However, they do not provide a detailed understanding of which category of farmers, where, or on what soil types, are likely to be most affected. This raises the question of appropriate responses to expected trade reforms.

The national impacts of alternative trade reform scenarios are difficult to estimate in the absence of robust base-line data as well as key analytical tools, including an operational economy-wide analytical computable general equilibrium (CGE) or macroeconometric model for Fiji. In Fiji, many economy-wide models have been constructed, usually by expatriate consultants with minimum involvement of Fiji nationals. Mark Sturton and Chris Murphy constructed macroeconometric models in the late 1980s and early 90s (Sturton 1989; Murphy 1992). However, their models have had minimal use in Fiji since their departure because of poor modelling skills within the key ministries. Although training was provided in the use of the models, sustainability of such models is always an issue when the limited core of trained staff have moved on. An adequate core of staff trained in model use and maintenance of their underlying database needs to be maintained to insure against the loss of users through the normal processes of job movement. These measures were not in place in Fiji to ensure the sustainability of the models constructed previously.

Many of these models, moreover, relied on the 1981 input–output database that was constructed using a 1979 survey of various sectors and industries in Fiji. Since then much has changed in Fiji not only because of the impact of the 1987 coups but also because the underlying economic structure has changed. Researchers in the past updated some of the parameters in the input-output table based on their assessment of the industry structure. However, this is less than satisfactory, particularly since the Bureau of Statistics no longer updates the input-output tables although they continue to collect industry specific data.

A new input–output table has recently been developed under an Australian Centre for International Agricultural Research (ACIAR)-funded project, in addition to a new CGE model. Such a model could be used to carry out simulations of policies that could help to minimise economy-wide impacts of changes in sugar export arrangements. Such analysis should also become part of the Sugar Commission of Fiji's (SCOF) research agenda, as should farm-level bioeconomic analysis to identify potential farm-level impacts.

Farm-level impact

Any changes in the prices paid for Fiji sugar will have significant impacts on the production sector as well. Reddy (1998) predicts the gross return per hectare could drop from about F$3,050/ha to about F$2,200/ha for small farms. For large farms, the gross returns could fall from F$2,800/ha to F$1,500/ha under world free prices. In terms of financial viability, there is not much difference between the two categories of farms, each having a net return of about F$500/ha. However, as noted above, these estimates are based on the assumption that farmers maintain their current farming practices and there are no shifts in the input mix. Moreover, the results are based on a very small sample size. Before firm conclusions are drawn and policies formulated to tackle the impacts, a more in-depth economic research using a larger and better stratified sample should be undertaken.

It is believed that long-term viability of farms is uncertain because of declining farm productivity. Average farm level productivity is said to have decreased by 0.6 per cent per annum over the last ten years (SCOF 1997a). However, it is not clear whether this decline in average productivity is due to declining yields or because of more cane being planted on marginal land. Since 1989, sugar cane area has increased by about 15 per cent, mainly in hilly areas. To assess the apparent cause in productivity decline, spatially disaggregated analysis of production by soil type would be relevant. Even in terms of total factor productivity measures, which is a ratio of an index of output to an index of all inputs, Fiji has experienced a slight decrease in total factor productivity over the last 25 years (Reddy 1998). This is despite the introduction of new fertilisers and varieties. Many farmers continue to plant the traditional crop varieties, the reasons for which need to be examined before continuing to breed new varieties and promoting the use of new fertilisers.

If Fiji is to compete on the world market, it must reduce its costs of production. Fiji's average farm level cost (including transportation costs) as a proportion of the total costs of sugar production is amongst the highest in the ACP region (Landell Mills Commodity (LMC) International 1998). About 70 per cent of the cost of producing sugar in Fiji is attributed to on-farm and transportation costs, as compared with 40 per cent in Barbados, 60 per cent in Swaziland, and 50 per cent in Guyana. At the same time the cane yield is amongst the lowest. There is a considerable scope for reducing costs at the farm level as well as in the transportation sector. Farmers rely on rail and trucks to transport cane to the mills. The rail system of sugar transportation in Fiji has, however, steadily and significantly deteriorated over the years because of under-investment in rail maintenance, inefficient harvesting and loading systems, poor labour practices and incentive systems, lost and inadequate skills, and the institutionalised disempowerment of management (Davies 1997). Other contributing factors to the declining efficiency are the age of locomotives, high repair bills and frequent breakdowns. It is also believed that there is unfair competition from road transport. The industry has already identified the need to increase the efficiency of its transportation sector and is seriously considering reforms, including the introduction of a user-pays system for the rail service. Currently, farmers using rail do not pay for transportation of their cane to the mills.

Industry leaders agree that farm-level costs have to fall by 15–20 per cent, at the same time as efficiencies in the transportation and milling sectors are achieved. However, farm costs cannot be reduced in isolation from the whole household production system and without taking biophysical and socioeconomic factors into account. Cost per unit of output is determined by economic, social and environmental factors as well as agronomic practices, crop management, pest and pathogens control. The Sugar Cane Research Centre's 1995 annual report shows that with good farm management practices present average yield of 55 tonnes/ha can be increased to 70 tonnes/ha. However, such an increase in yield cannot be achieved without a shift in input mix with increased costs.

The FSC has concentrated on providing advice to farmers to increase sugar cane/sugar yield. Currently, the Sugar Cane Research Centre's mission statement commits it to 'advancing industry by excellence in research to improve productivity' and 'to increase[ing] productivity, profitability and sustainability of the industry by producing high yielding disease resistant varieties and by facilitating an efficient extension services.' Consistent with this, research and extension activities carried out by the Fiji Sugar Cane Research Centre (FSRC) have largely been concerned with screening and testing new varieties, detecting pests and diseases and improving crop protection, and agronomic trials to determine optimal fertiliser and agrochemical applications. Fiji Sugar Commission annual reports (for example, 1995, 1996) summarise the results of various agronomic trials. In 1996, FSC conducted research on the effects of nutrition and chemical ripeners on cane yield and sugar content. This research, although limited, highlights the large gap between attainable yield and potential yield on farmers' fields—a phenomenon not restricted to Fiji. Past results suggest that with better farming practices farmers could increase their yields to between 80 and 120 tonnes/ha from an average yield of 55 tonnes (FSC Sugar Cane Research Centre Annual Reports 1996). In Australia too, such differences can be found between yields in farmers' fields and potential yields identified through experimental trials (Muchow et al. 1997). However, such increases are only possible if agronomically optimal levels of inputs such as fertilisers, herbicides and pesticides are applied at the appropriate times and if these recommended practices are economical. The recommended rates often do not reflect the cost of the inputs and the expected benefits in terms of increases in yields. The implicit assumption has been that productivity and profitability can be increased primarily by increasing cane output.

The opportunity costs of farm household labour are also important determinants of the input mix that farmers utilise. The challenge is therefore to look beyond the potential increases that can be achieved just through improvements in agronomic practices, disease controls and high yielding disease resistant varieties, as has been the practice so far. For Fiji to compete on the world market, the industry should also aim to encourage the use of input and output mix that reduces the variance of net revenue, in addition to providing appropriate incentives to produce sugar cane with higher sugar content.

Without such an approach, industry reforms and adjustments advocated in the strategic plan may not be able to increase industry-level efficiency, farm-level productivity and profitability to the point required to compete without preferences on world markets. Moreover, without such an approach, the sustainability of sugar cane-based farming systems and the environment cannot be addressed. To identify management strategies that reflect the simultaneous consideration of biophysical (natural resource), social and economic factors, integrated bioeconomic research is necessary. Such strategies would need to consider the suitability (in bioeconomic terms) of current sugar cane lands for sugar cane and farm-level resource reallocation options under alternative world market conditions. Much of the information needed for designing such strategies is currently not available.

Integrated biophysical and socioeconomic assessment can help identify appropriate (efficient and profitable) farm-level resource reallocation options under alternative world market conditions. To identify resource use options and design farmer strategies, nested analysis using crop-level biophysical models, farm bioeconomic and household bioeconomic models will be helpful. For this to be possible, the mandate of the Sugar Cane Research Centre needs to be changed to include economic and social science research, adopting a systems approach to its research.

Currently, extension services are aimed at promoting better farm management practices without explicitly taking into account financial costs and benefits. Extension programs encourage farmers to adopt cane varieties suitable for different soil types and environments, the correct timing of planting and improved planting methods, weed control, appropriate fertiliser use and trash management (FSC Sugar Cane Research Centre Annual Reports 1996). But extension services should also aim to improve farm profitability and resource use efficiency. The recommended strategies are not likely to be adopted without directly linking research and extension services to the needs of the users of the outputs.

The Industry Strategic Plan and proposed restructuring of research and extension

In 1997 SCOF, the peak industry level policymaking body, noted that the industry must embrace the concept of efficiency increases in all sectors and at all levels. SCOF, with representatives from key stakeholder groups (including the government, the FSC, the sole miller, and the Fiji Sugar Cane Growers Council), developed the Industry Strategic Plan (SCOF 1997a, 1997b). The Sugar Commission of Fiji notes that the purpose of the Plan is 'to underpin an industry reform process to improve efficiency in milling, and infrastructure development and sugar cane production' (SCOF 1997b). Its reform agenda primarily deals with increasing efficiency in the transport, infrastructure and milling sectors, as outlined in Table 7.3.

To achieve these targeted efficiency improvements, the Commission has begun industry restructuring. Under the Strategic Plan, a new committee structure comprising the Quality Cane Subcommittee, Industrial Relations

---

Table 7.3   Agenda of reform for the Fiji sugar industry

Phase	Focus	Main strategies
1997–2001	Investing in efficiency	Introduce productivity payments
		Reorganise industry institutions
		Revitalise rail transport
		Invest in mill efficiency
		Improve public/grower awareness
		Phase in mechanical loading
		Start Land Utilisation Board
		User-pay charges on rail
2002–06	Quality cane benefits	Introduce quality cane payments
		Set sector based targets
		Improve rail/farm interface
		Selective mechanical harvesting
		Optimal mill efficiency/capacity
2007–20	Best practice culture	Maximise sugar content/acre
		Expand in Vanua Levu
		Automated mills
		Increase mill capacity to 4.6 mt

Source: SCOF, 1997b. *Industry Strategic Plan—Action Plans*, 1997–2000, Lautoka.

Subcommittee, Railway Restructuring Committee, Harvest and Delivery Subcommittee, Industry Investment and Mill Efficiency Advisory Committee and the Sugar Cane Research Advisory Committee has been created. These committees do not make policy but are required to act as inter-organisational teams developing proposals for the Commission, facilitating the implementation of agreed programs, and acting as reference panels. I will discuss two of the subcommittees that have direct implications for sugar production.

Quality Cane Subcommittee

The sugar industry is considering changing the cane payment system to give farmers incentives to produce sugar cane with a higher sugar content. On average, the quality of cane in terms of sugar recovered has declined. In 1968, 7.5 tonnes of cane was required to produce one tonne of sugar (SCOF 1997a). The volume of cane required increased to 9.44 tonnes in 1997 (FSC Annual Report 1998).

The current cane payment system, which is based on the weight of cane delivered, does not encourage farmers to produce cane of high quality. The growers receive about 73 per cent of the total sugar proceeds, with the rest going to the FSC. A cane payment system based on quality rather than volume provides an incentive to farmers to grow those varieties of cane and adopt those farming practices that produce the highest sugar content, consistent with their objective of maximising net revenue.

Choice of the appropriate premium is difficult. Where there is competition in the milling sector, the choice of the premium is left to the market. A single mill competing without taxes or subsidies in the world market is under pressure to provide appropriate incentives. However, this is not likely to be the case in Fiji for some time. With a monopoly miller, the price paid to farmers is best decided administratively by the SCOF, in which all the stakeholders are represented.

Sugar Cane Research Advisory Committee and Sugar Cane Research Institute

The Sugar Cane Research Advisory Committee is one of the six committees established under the Commission. The Committee, chaired by the Deputy Executive Director of Fiji Sugar Marketing, is set up to facilitate the creation of independent research and extension services. However, the focus is still very much to provide 'advice on optimal mix of cane varieties for different soil types, improve farm viability and give a scientific basis to quality control' (SCOF 1997a:11–12).

The Advisory Committee has proposed the establishment of a Sugar Cane Research Institute to replace the existing Sugar Cane Research Centre.

The Centre, which replaced the original Agricultural Experimentation Station, was established to 'breed and release new varieties of cane'. Its focus has remained much the same (FSC Sugar Cane Research Centre Annual Report 1995), concentrating on: detecting and controlling pests and diseases in the cane field; screening new varieties for resistance to disease; determining the nutritional requirements of cane; and deciding on the use of herbicides, pesticides and other agricultural chemicals.

The proposed Sugar Cane Research Institute may have a similar focus. According to the draft Bill, the objective of the Sugar Cane Research Institute will be to enhance the productivity of the Fiji Sugar industry through research aimed at increasing quantity and improving the quality of sugar cane products, improving the method of producing sugar cane products and/or diversifying sugar cane products. The Bill also suggests that the Institute may undertake research required to minimise environmental damage, and maintain the quality of land to sustain sugar cane crops.

The proposed structure of the Institute, as outlined in the Industry Action Plan (SCOF 1997b), reflects a biophysical approach to research. There are to be three research programs: 'Agronomy', 'Breeding and variety' and 'Crop protection'. In addition the deputy director of extension will be responsible for activities such as 'technology transfer, training and library'. The industry, in its Industry Plan, has identified a number of strategies, including those to establish a Land Utilisation Board, to create a policy to penalise farmers who break minimum regulatory standards, to map productivity of all cane farm types, and to measure, and notify all cane farms how to maximise their income' (SCOF 1997a). Whilst such strategies do recognise the need to consider profitability as well as productivity of farms, these needs seem to have been approached in a piecemeal and somewhat *ad hoc* manner (the strategies are considered in the Industry Action Plan under the section heading 'Update the Method of Quality Control'). If the industry is to improve its competitiveness in the world sugar market, the Institute's mandate should adopt a more systems approach and systematically identify the needs of growers and policymakers aimed at increasing and sustaining farm productivity and profitability (efficiency) and environmental sustainability. This would require reorienting research away from increasing the quality and quantity of sugar products, and towards improving efficiency in resource use in a sugar cane-based farming system (including land, labour and capital) and environmental sustainability. The research should also reflect the whole farming system in the context both of international trade as well as in its social and institutional context. Herein lies another challenge—a methodological one—that of developing an integrated analytical framework.

Integrated analytical framework

Analytical frameworks integrating agricultural trade reform scenarios, regional farm level supply characteristics, and household welfare have only recently been attempted. Traditionally, agricultural research and development was dominated by a fragmented sectoral approach, which was suitable only for addressing simple agricultural issues. More recently, a farming systems approach has helped to encourage technology-focussed developments (Collinson 1987). Farming systems research (FSR) has adopted farming systems as the focus of analysis while recognising the socioeconomic constraints on production. However, in practice, the FSR framework has generally failed to accommodate socioeconomic and cultural contexts (Davidson 1987). Generally, there is an absence of integrated methodologies that take advantage of recent developments in individual disciplines and carefully analysed case studies. Many of these approaches are either at a conceptual stage (Grimble and Wellard 1997) or have been applied only in specific case studies.

More recently, integrated approaches such as the Integrated Catchment Management (ICM) approach have been recognised as a useful framework to encourage stakeholder involvement and for the sustainability of development, resource use and decision making (Lundqvist et al. 1985; Easter et al. 1986; Ewing et al. 1997). The ICM approach has been used in most states in Australia to encourage stakeholder inputs in the design of catchment-wide management strategies. This model too, has been criticised for not integrating resource management, socioeconomic development, and implementation strategies (Margerum 1996).

In the face of these shortcomings (RAC 1993; Wallace et al. 1996), a new approach based on the Integrated Resource Management (IRM) paradigm is emerging. This approach recognises the interdependencies of natural, political and social systems, and the inherent characteristics of natural resource use (Bellamy et al. 1996). It also recognises the relevance of insights from scientific domains other than agriculture including ecology, policy science, economics and social science. What is emerging is a new paradigm based on an adaptive approach to ecosystem management and collaborative decision-making (Holling 1995; Wallace et al. 1996).

A number of other integrated frameworks based on computer-based expert systems are currently being developed. For example, at the Centre for Resources and Environmental Studies, ANU, an Integrated Water Resources Assessment and Management (IWRAM) framework based on an unpublished discussion paper prepared by Padma Lal in 1990, is being developed and trialed in Thailand. This framework matches the hopes and plans of stakeholders with known natural and human resources in order to generate alternative development options. In its application, transdisciplinary methodologies are adopted (see Jakeman et al. 1997; Walker et al., forthcoming). The Cooperative Research Centre for Sustainable Sugar Production (CRC Sugar) is currently developing a Strategic Regional Resource Assessment (SRRA) framework which embodies resource assessment, systems modelling, and options analysis as part of its integrated planning (Mallawaarachchi, pers. comm. 1998). None of these models, however, includes international sugar trade considerations. MacAulay and Owen (1999) developed a comparative static spatial equilibrium economic model of the Australian dairy industry incorporating trade reform scenarios, and state-level supply and demand characteristics and policies to assess the effects of reform on milk producers in different states.

Research and extension link

The work of the Institute must be applied, adaptive, problem-solving, demand-driven and responsive to stakeholder needs. To improve the relevance of research, the Institute must move away from the classic paradigm of top-down, state or industry-sponsored research promoted through extension agents, or experts who identify and conduct the research, and provide technical solutions. Such expert-led and officially sponsored innovations, with a break in relationship between researchers and extension, has been found throughout the world to be highly ineffective in encouraging farmers to adopt new technologies or better farm management practices (Tabor and Faber 1998). Policymakers too have not had the benefit of much of the research carried out by scientists because of the gap between them. There has to be a direct link between stakeholder needs and the research process, and an institutional mechanism needs to be established that encourages greater collaboration and cooperation between researchers, extension staff, growers and policymakers.

The Research (and Extension) Institute must also be proactive by developing a strategic research plan. It must develop an approach that leads to the identification of relevant research priorities of farmers and policymakers. To this end, farmers and policymakers should have a direct say in the research agenda of the Institute. Currently, farmers do not have a voice in the activities of the Research Centre, although they contribute to its costs. The requirements of the policymakers, which may not be the same as the growers or the millers, must also be reflected in the research undertaken. Growers, policymakers and agricultural scientists often view problems in different ways. A grower, focusing on the immediate problem may think purely in terms of financial returns, while scientists, depending on their own disciplinary training, may view a natural resource problem in terms of biological, physical and chemical factors affecting the resource use. For their part, a policymaker may consider the problem in terms of likely economic and political consequences. All the different perspectives need to be considered when setting the research agenda for the Institute. The stakeholders could then collaboratively determine the nature, scope and combination of disciplines required to address the priority issues facing them, and the Institute's research would then be problem-oriented and its outcomes focused. The proposed structure of the Institute's Board, which includes representatives of various stakeholders (growers, millers and the government), would help in this regard.

However, this needs to be strengthened through the Commission establishing an institutional mechanism for research identification and prioritisation involving the Board and the researchers. To bring about change, the Institute must encompass strong components of information, communication and research-development integration; a mechanism for effective on-farm adaptive research, information and liaison, and farmer-extension and training. The Bill must also provide the means for the Institute to develop a three to five-year research strategic plan in order to encourage it to take a more proactive and forward-looking approach to research rather than just reacting to immediate problems.

To achieve this, a major shift in the research and extension philosophy is also required, focusing on outcome-oriented (action) research (King et al. 1994). Action research, as the name implies, has the dual aim of action and research simultaneously. The aim of the action is to bring about change in a community, amongst policymakers, or within a program through outcome-oriented research that involves farmers, policymakers and other stakeholders throughout the project cycle—from identification of the problem, and planning (analysing the problem and designing a project), to implementation and monitoring and evaluation. Once the Institute takes a proactive approach to research, it could also benefit by prioritising the research, allocating internal research funds and/or seeking external support.

Partnership and alliances with other research institutes

The draft Bill provides for the Research Advisory Committee to include an officer from the Ministry of Agriculture and a representative from the School of Pure and Applied Sciences of the University of the South Pacific. However, to take advantage of expertise available in Fiji and abroad, the Bill needs to provide for partnerships and alliances with other research agencies as well. Alliance and collaboration with the University of the South Pacific and other government agencies, particularly the Ministry of Agriculture, Forestry and Fisheries (MAFF) and Ministry of Planning and Information (MPI), must be fostered. This could help the Institute access research skills across a wide range of disciplines available within Fiji.

Given limited resources in Fiji, the new Institute may not have to repeat much of the traditional scientific research but instead could 'borrow' technologies and results of research undertaken elsewhere in the world. There is a wealth of information that is available from other ACP countries and others such as Australia, India and Thailand, that Fiji can access. The results of other work could be adapted for use in Fiji and the Institute could then focus on research that is unique to Fiji. Moreover, there are many International Agricultural Research Centres with interests in developing countries which have both expertise and results that the Institute could tap into. As noted by Eyzaguirre (1996), small countries such as Fiji must concentrate on intelligently using external knowledge and relating the results to local needs, networking with other research nodes and managing partnerships with external research bodies and donors.

Proposed institutional structure

To fully embrace the philosophy and strategies suggested above and focus on a more outcome-oriented research and development, a different institutional structure for the Sugar Cane Research Institute would be desirable. The industry has proposed a vertical division of programs into agronomy, breeding and variety, and crop protection, summarised in Figure 7.1. This structure emphasises science-driven research focusing on traditional divisions in research around activities and inputs rather than outcomes in terms of profitability/efficiency. If a purely biophysical approach to research is adopted and the resulting input combination is suggested, farmers are most likely to adopt this because 'benefits versus costs' is most likely to be the main criteria when choosing between farm management strategies.

It is recognised that research related to irrigation, pests and diseases, and intercropping are important, but given the proposed structure and research tradition, it is very likely that the Institute will mainly consider the biophysical aspects of these. Research into costs and benefits of these activities are likely to be ignored or treated as an after-thought under the proposed institutional structure. This is reflected in a proposed structure where the agricultural economist is expected to be responsible to the Head of Extension, as reflected in Figure 7.1.

An appropriate institutional structure is one of the most important preconditions for collaboration and cooperation (Eyzaguirre 1996), and integration of disciplines. For outcome-oriented research it is desirable to organise multidisciplinary teams of 'experts' around problems. This would encourage greater interaction between disciplines, with researchers producing outcomes based on innovative farm-level strategies that also reflect both biophysical and socioeconomic considerations. The Institute would also be able to more effectively utilise its limited expertise and resources in biophysics and economics and other social sciences. An appropriate institutional structure is highly desirable if a research institute

Figure 7.1   Input-based institutional structure proposed in the industry action plan

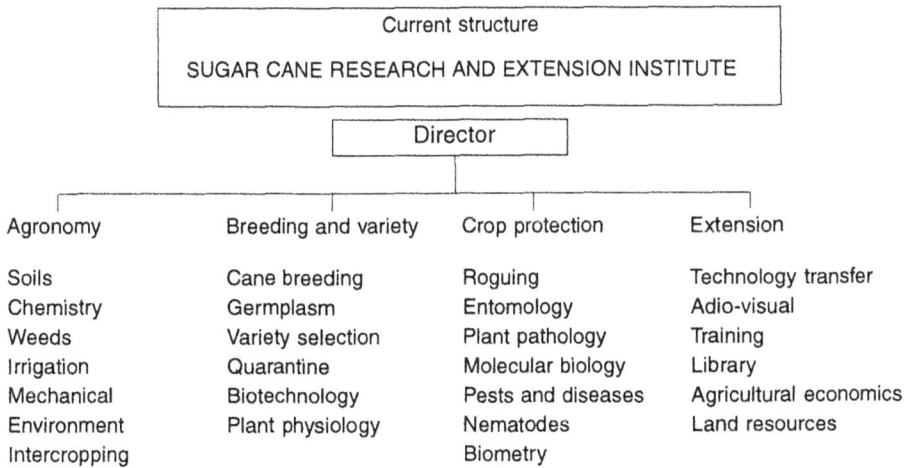

```
┌─────────────────────────────────────────────────────────────┐
│                      Current structure                        │
│                                                               │
│        SUGAR CANE RESEARCH AND EXTENSION INSTITUTE            │
└─────────────────────────────────────────────────────────────┘
                        ┌──────────────────┐
                        │     Director     │
                        └──────────────────┘
```

Agronomy	Breeding and variety	Crop protection	Extension
Soils	Cane breeding	Roguing	Technology transfer
Chemistry	Germplasm	Entomology	Adio-visual
Weeds	Variety selection	Plant pathology	Training
Irrigation	Quarantine	Molecular biology	Library
Mechanical	Biotechnology	Pests and diseases	Agricultural economics
Environment	Plant physiology	Nematodes	Land resources
Intercropping		Biometry	

Figure 7.2   Proposed Sugar Cane Research and Extension Institute structure

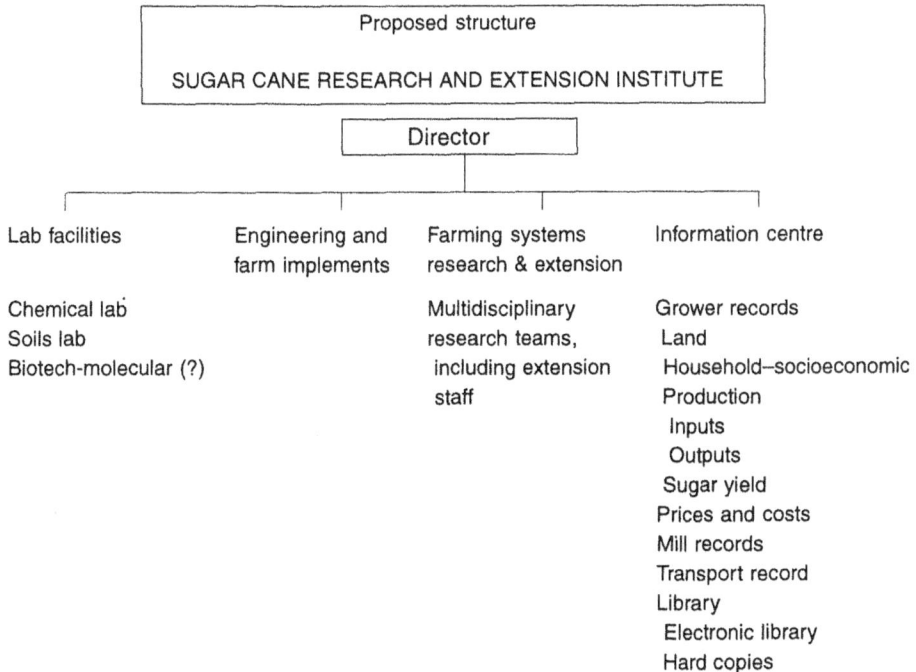

```
┌─────────────────────────────────────────────────────────────┐
│                     Proposed structure                        │
│                                                               │
│        SUGAR CANE RESEARCH AND EXTENSION INSTITUTE            │
└─────────────────────────────────────────────────────────────┘
                        ┌──────────────────┐
                        │     Director     │
                        └──────────────────┘
```

Lab facilities	Engineering and farm implements	Farming systems research & extension	Information centre
Chemical lab		Multidisciplinary	Grower records
Soils lab		research teams,	Land
Biotech-molecular (?)		including extension	Household–socioeconomic
		staff	Production
			Inputs
			Outputs
			Sugar yield
			Prices and costs
			Mill records
			Transport record
			Library
			Electronic library
			Hard copies

is to become more relevant to the needs of the growers and policymakers, and provide information and analyses that the stakeholders can adopt.

To improve the effectiveness of research and extension, an alternative institutional structure, as outlined in Figure 7.2, is proposed. It is suggested that the Institute have three divisions: Farming Systems Research and Extension (which will also include various laboratories and field experimental stations); Engineering and Farm Implements; and a Sectoral Data Centre (including a library). Under such a structure, the Division of Farming Systems Research and Extension will be the centre of all research (field-based trials as well as desk-based bioeconomic modelling and agricultural economics analyses). Bridging the disciplinary divide through the integration of disciplines is only possible if there is a regular dialogue between people trained in the respective disciplines. The Division of Engineering and Farm Implements and the Sectoral Data Centre will, in this alternative arrangement, play a service role. The Sectoral Data Centre could become the centre for all records, farm-level information on things such as input and outputs, prices, costs, plant varieties, diseases and pests, and Government Information Services (GIS). A library of electronic information and hard copies of papers, reports and publications about the sugar industry in Fiji and elsewhere, could also be maintained within this centre. Such an arrangement could help collate and consolidate all published and unpublished material relating to the sugar industry in one place overcoming the current difficulty in identifying information about the industry.

Research capacity

In recent times, the FSC Sugar Cane Research Centre has been denuded of trained and experienced research staff, even in the traditional fields of research undertaken at the Centre. For industry-level assessment and economic policy analysis, Fiji has tended to rely on external consultants, often from Australia and New Zealand. Although their studies have provided valuable analysis, and in some areas of expertise (such as international trade analysis) the industry may continue to rely on expertise drawn from elsewhere, such arrangements are not satisfactory in the medium to long term. The industry must develop in-house capacity to undertake farm-level bioeconomic and policy analyses to identify policies and farmer strategies needed to increase farm-level productivity, profitability and sustainability. While economy-wide impact assessments and broad government policy assessments are the responsibility of the government, the industry needs to build its own capacity in various disciplines if it is to meet the challenges that lie ahead.

In recent discussions between the Australian Centre for International Agricultural Research (ACIAR), FSC, MAFF and MPI, the urgent need to enhance capacity in the FSC Research Centre (and in Fiji more generally) in order to undertake such transdisciplinary biophysical–economic research was acknowledged. The FSC Research Centre's staff are primarily agronomists, breeders, chemists, and specialists in crop protection. The new Research Institute must also employ researchers with economic and social science research skills to encourage it to adopt a systems perspective and develop a multidisciplinary research program. The foundation for such a systems approach to research will be laid once the recently approved ACIAR project is implemented.

The ACIAR Project

The ACIAR is currently developing a four-year collaborative and interdisciplinary research project titled 'World trade liberalisation and the Lomé Convention: potential impacts and future options for Fiji's sugar industry'. The overall goal of the project is to assist the Fiji Government, the Fiji Sugar Industry and most importantly, the small-hold sugar cane farmers to adjust to the expected reduction and eventual loss in preferential access to the European and USA markets.

The specific objectives of the project are to: identify ongoing and expected international market reforms, including the potential loss of preferential access under the Lomé Convention and other agreements, and estimate their impact on the national economy; assess the bioeconomic viability of sugar cane-based farming systems under current and alternative market reform scenarios; and assess the relative merits of alternative options under the Alternative Trade Arrangements (ATA), for Fiji (ACP)-EU negotiations and identify key farm/household-level options to improve and stabilise household incomes.

To address these objectives, the integrated international trade, bioeconomic and institutional framework outlined in Figure 7.3 will be used. The project is organised into three subprojects, each with specific objectives and expected outputs. A number of analytical tools will be used, taking advantage of recent methodological developments in relevant disciplines. Generally, empirical analysis will be undertaken using nested scales of analysis, as outlined below, adapting appropriate, readily available models to suit the situation in Fiji (see Figure 7.4). The project will make use of an existing international trade model (SUGARBARE), a computable general equilibrium model for Fiji (developed under ACIAR funding), and existing GIS databases in Fiji.

The key challenge in this project will be to develop farm-level biophysical and bioeconomic models—a sugar cane crop model for Fiji and household-based bioeconomic models for different categories of sugar cane farming systems in Fiji. Another major challenge will be to obtain relevant data required for the modelling. Much of the data will need to be collated from

Figure 7.3   Integrated systems analytical framework

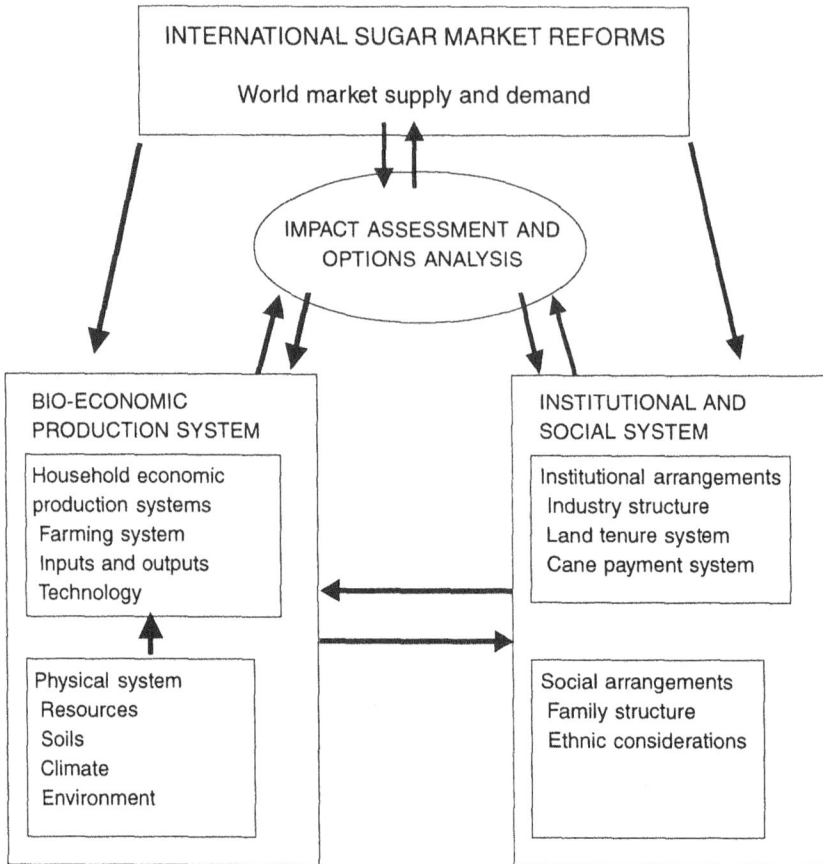

existing biophysical and production data available with the FSC and its
research stations. However, baseline household-level socioeconomic
information and production data will also need to be collected. Biophysical
and economic information will need to be integrated to assess and define
appropriate responses by Fiji to reforms in the international sugar markets.

This will draw on multidisciplinary research skills across a number of
leading research organisations to address these issues. The National Centre
for Development Studies, the Australian National University, and the Fiji
Ministry of Planning (with the Fiji project leader from Fiji Sugar Marketing
Ltd) will lead the project. Expertise in agricultural science, agricultural and
resource economics, and geographic information systems will be drawn
from the Australian National University and the CSIRO Division of Tropical
Agriculture in Australia. Fijian counterparts include the Land Use Division
and the Economics and Policy Section of the MAFF, the Centre for
Development Studies, The University of the South Pacific (USP) and the

Figure 7.4   Nested scales of analysis

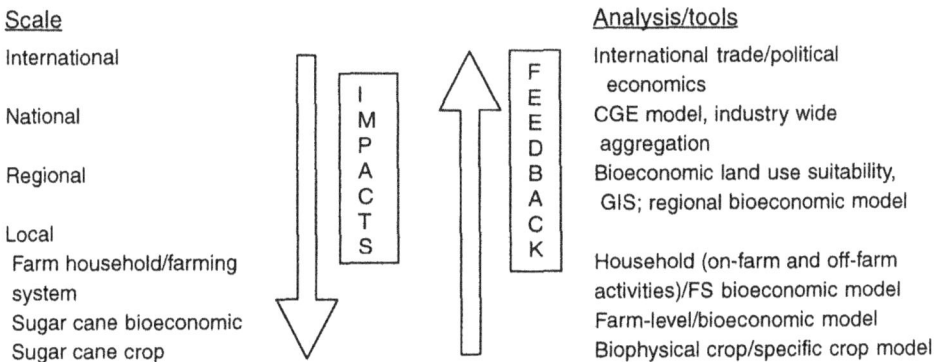

Scale		Analysis/tools
International		International trade/political economics
National		CGE model, industry wide aggregation
Regional		Bioeconomic land use suitability, GIS; regional bioeconomic model
Local		
Farm household/farming system		Household (on-farm and off-farm activities)/FS bioeconomic model
Sugar cane bioeconomic		Farm-level/bioeconomic model
Sugar cane crop		Biophysical crop/specific crop model

Ministry of Lands. Fiji Sugar Commission will also be a significant collaborator, particularly through active participation of the Fiji Sugar Marketing Ltd in the international subproject. Fiji Sugar Cane Growers Council and Fiji Sugar Corporation will provide data, advice and guidance.

Conclusion

With ongoing reforms in the international sugar trade the Fiji sugar industry is facing major challenges not only in the transport and milling sectors, but equally importantly in the production sector. The results of ongoing negotiations over the renewal of land leases will pose additional challenges, particularly if a large proportion of the leases are not renewed. The government will have to deal with the major downturn in the sugar-based national economy. The industry will need to pay greater attention to ways of increasing the production efficiencies of farms managed by indigenous Fijian farms, for whom profit maximisation may not be the only objective. The proposed Sugar Cane Research Institute will need to move away from its traditional research focusing on fertiliser and pesticide trials to focus on increasing profitability and production efficiencies of sugar cane-based farming systems. The production sector reforms will need to be underpinned by rigorous and integrated biophysical and socioeconomic research reflecting social, economic and environmental considerations. The government has a golden opportunity now to embrace the innovative and holistic approach to research as it lays the foundation for the new Sugar Cane Research Institute.

Note

Comments on an earlier draft received from Professor Ron Duncan and an independent reviewer are gratefully acknowledged.

chapter eight

Inshore fisheries development in Fiji

Joeli Veitayaki

Inshore fisheries, which includes the artisanal and subsistence sectors, is arguably one of the most important resource sectors in the Fiji economy, but it is undervalued and poorly understood. Its value and contribution is still based on estimates. However, the value of inshore fisheries is substantial for a variety of reasons, including its contribution to the protein requirements of the majority of the population, the savings to the economy through import substitution, the livelihood of the people who rely on it for income and employment, and the increasingly threatened nature of the resource due to changing environmental conditions (South Pacific Commission (SPC) 1994).

The recent survey of subsistence and artisanal fisheries in Fiji noted that on Viti Levu, half the households interviewed have at least one member who fishes. Two-thirds of them fish for subsistence and one-third are artisanal operators who supply their villages and the urban markets (Rawlinson et al. 1995). The survey estimated the total annual catch on Viti Levu at some 10,000 tonnes, with the subsistence catch accounting for 3,500 tonnes and artisanal 6,206 tonnes. At the weighted mean 1996 price of F$3.75 per kilogram, the total value of subsistence and artisanal fisheries on Viti Levu alone would be around F$37.5 million (Ministry of Agriculture, Fisheries and Forests 1996). The Fisheries Division estimated the inshore supply for the country in 1996 at around 23,000 tonnes which, with the weighted mean value of F$3.75 per kilogram, was worth F$86 million (Ministry of Agriculture, Fisheries and Forests 1996). During the same period, the artisanal sector contributed 4,580 tonnes of finfish worth F$17.18 million and 2,148 tonnes of non-finfish worth some F$8.06 million.

The total subsistence production for Fiji for 1999 is estimated to be around 17,800 tonnes. This is based on a figure of 14,000 tonnes for 1980 and a yearly increase of 200 tonnes. The retail price ranges between F$1 and F$10 per kilogram. At the weighted mean price of F$5.75 per kilogram, this fishery will be worth approximately F$102.4 million. The reliability of these estimations is difficult to judge, but the importance of the fisheries sector to the national economy is beyond doubt.

Since 1995, the Fisheries Division has been trying to undertake the second phase of the subsistence and artisanal fisheries survey, but it has been hampered by lack of funds. This remains a major concern, because it will be difficult to understand the contribution of inshore fisheries unless more information is made available on its contribution and status. All the current planning, policies and strategies are based on estimates from a survey in the late 1970s.

Over the last decade, the development and management of inshore fisheries has become an important priority because of its importance to the local economy and its vulnerability to over-exploitation. Local community groups dominate inshore fisheries, which are labour intensive and flexibly organised. As both the population and coastal development increase and technology improves the power of inshore fishers, it is crucial that the management of the reef and lagoon fisheries resources be improved. This is important because the national desire for self-sufficiency and maximum inshore fisheries production has to be balanced with the need for prudent management and the sustainable use of the resources (Kailola 1995; Pita 1996).

Fisheries development policy

Fisheries development objectives during the Development Plan 7 period (1976–80) were to: promote and consolidate the development of village and commercial fisheries in order to provide additional income especially in areas where fish resources were adequate but agricultural potential low; develop local capability to fish skipjack tuna through appropriate institutional arrangements; encourage the commercial development of fish, oysters and other marine species of animals and plants; avoid over-exploitation of fisheries resources; train fishers and bring extension workers to test, modify and develop appropriate technology to increase the efficiency of fisheries enterprises; encourage the processing of fish and other fishery products in Fiji; provide adequate and effective machinery for inspection, protection services, law enforcement and regulatory activities; and liaise closely with other fisheries agencies in the region (Fiji, Central Planning Office 1975).

During this period, the emphasis was on the development of small-scale artisanal fisheries through the introduction of motorised craft; improvements in fishing gear and methods; processing of export items; establishment of a marketing and transportation system, ice making, and storage plants; and the improvements of landing and berthing facilities at the main fishing centres. The National Marketing Authority (NMA), a statutory body, was created to purchase, distribute and market fish and fish products nationwide. At the same time, fish culture trials were conducted in Raviravi, Naduruloulou and other parts of the country.

Between 1981 and 1990, the period of Fiji's eighth and ninth development plans (DP8 and DP9), the major objectives of the fisheries sector were to generate further employment opportunities in the exploitation and processing of marine resources, increase production for local consumption, enhance the value added in fish production for exports, and to regulate and control the exploitation of fin and non-fin fishery products (Fiji, Central Planning Office 1985).

To pursue these objectives, the Fisheries Division promoted four major fisheries sector programs.

1 The Rural Fisheries Development Program, designed to
   - promote the development of the fisheries potential of remote regions of the country
   - provide basic protein requirement
   - create further opportunities for employment and income generation and integrate rural communities into the formal sector of the economy.

2 The Commercial Artisanal Fisheries Development Program, designed to
   - provide suitable fishing vessels to commercial fishers to enable them to fish around the reef in areas more distant from larger urban centres
   - ensure adequate ice supply, storage, improved markets, fishing gear and equipment provide technical assistance, training and facilitate credit
   - provide berthing and slipping facilities.

3 The Industrial Fisheries Development Program, designed to
   - expand the skipjack tuna industry
   - expand the utilisation of tuna-processing capacity and
   - encourage alternative fishing methods such as purse-seining and longlining or a combination of such methods where applicable.

4 The Rural Aquaculture Extension Program, designed to
   - provide an alternative protein source for the inland population, release grass carp into rivers and waterways throughout Fiji as a biological control measure for introduced water weeds
   - provide fish fry to fish farmers as part of government support
   - promote fish farming as a viable business and a source of employment in the rural sector
   - provide training to fish farmers.

Two of the above programs (1 and 2) concern the utilisation of inshore resources, which illustrates the importance of the sector. However, most of the failed fisheries projects referred to here were formulated during this period, when government policy favoured decentralisation through the deployment of infrastructure and extension staff to rural areas. Unfortunately, this strategy resulted in the over-exploitation of inshore fisheries and caused the collapse of the fisheries development activities.

Under the Rural Fisheries Development Program, several rural fisheries schemes and fisheries cooperatives were established in various parts of the country, and people were encouraged to take up artisanal fisheries. A number of schemes such as the 'West' Hurricane Oscar Fisheries Rehabilitation Program (Evening 1983) involved the collection of fisheries products by vessels or trucks from predetermined collection points for sale in the urban markets. The scheme was geared for chilled fresh fish rather than frozen fish. Hence, five one-tonne per day ice plants and 20 three-tonne iceboxes were provided for the scheme (Shepard and Clark 1984). All these projects were aimed at allowing people in distant rural areas access to the high prices in urban areas, enabling them to improve their living conditions.

Under the Commercial Artisanal Fisheries Development Program, people were encouraged to improve their fishing technology and gear through the Rural Fisheries Training Program (RFTP) and take follow-up extension courses. People in rural areas were to undergo training to enable them to be competent artisanal fishers. Each of the trainees attending the RFTP was provided with a Fiji Development Bank loan to buy a subsidised FAO-designed 28-foot fishing boat. In many cases, the fishers were also given fishing gear and equipment. For instance, diesel engines, winches, fish finders, nets and other equipment were supplied free to the fishers through Japanese aid (Shepard and Clark 1984). The expectation was that the villagers would become fishers to repay their loans and to improve their living conditions.

Under the Rural Aquaculture Extension Program, the Fisheries Division promoted the cultivation of prawns, carp and other suitable species and seaweed in many coastal communities throughout the country. It was hoped that aquaculture, which has been proven to be technically feasible, would provide food, employment and income to the people involved. The Raviravi fish farm was initiated as a joint Lands Department–Fisheries Division project to determine the potential of fish farming on reclaimed marshes. Dense low-cropped mangroves were cleared to make way for the ponds. Until 1978, various species such as rabbit fish, mullet and milkfish were tested. The project was abandoned due to the failure to establish commercial viability.

In 1981, the fish farming in Raviravi was resumed by the Fiji government and France Aquaculture, a French government-funded organisation. The joint venture was to investigate the feasibility of saltwater prawn (*Penaeus/*

Monodon) farming and to establish its potential for commercial production. The development was to be in three phases, each depending on the success of the previous one. Although the production results from phase one were encouraging, all the goals for the phase were not met due to unforeseen problems. Nonetheless, it was proposed that the project progress to phase two to make the project operational. However, despite the involvement of local private sector interests, FDB Nominees Limited, the project stalled there because of unforeseen problems.

As a result of the problems faced in the implementation of these DP7 and DP8 fisheries development programs, the Fisheries Division revised its position towards the end of the DP9 period. It decided to channel fisheries development away from inshore to offshore exploitation, adding value to products and moving capture fisheries towards cultivation methods.

The priorities of the 1990s placed more emphasis on management and control of resources, acknowledging the need to encourage fishermen to move offshore to preserve the inshore fisheries. The broad objectives in the development of Fiji's fisheries sector were to further develop fisheries of the Exclusive Economic Zone (EEZ) and territorial waters; improve the quality of, and increase value added to, exports; regulate and control all fisheries on the principles of optimum utilisation and long term sustainability and encourage the implementation of sound business management methods by cooperation between local fishermen and, to devolve, as far as possible, government activities to the private sector.

Some of the initiatives underpinning these policies have included the establishment of a bêche-de-mer producers' association (now defunct), the development of a Fish Aggregation Device (FAD) program, strengthening of the rural aquaculture extension program, and the redeployment of the commercial seaweed program. In addition, the Fiji Trade and Investment Board (FTIB) administers a series of incentives for potential investors interested in the development of resources outside the customary fishing areas; those that involve collection, processing and marketing of resources currently exploited, and fish farming (Richards et al. 1994).

The Fiji government's *National Environment Strategy* (Government of Fiji 1993) emphasised resource management, posing questions such as whether it was necessary for the country to pay the price of a degraded environment in order to attain material improvement; whether there was basic incompatibility between sound environmental and development policies; and whether sustainable economic growth required the conservation of natural resources as the fundamental base for productive activity.

The government's position in relation to these questions was contained in its 1993 paper *Opportunities for Growth: policies and strategies for Fiji in the medium term* (Government of the Republic of Fiji 1993). The policies and strategies for fisheries were to: expand and consolidate tuna fisheries within

Fiji's EEZ under the industrial fisheries program; encourage greater efficiency and improve the quality of fish available to consumers in the small-scale commercial fisheries sector; assist rural fishermen in their transition from subsistence to small-scale commercial fishing; develop aquaculture through continued research into appropriate production technologies and extension programs; extend the EEZ and the territorial water fisheries; improve the quality and increase the value-added components of exports; regulate and control all fisheries on the principles of optimum utilisation and long-term sustainability; encourage the implementation of sound business management methods by local fishers; and to improve the handling and processing of domestic fisheries.

To implement these policies, it is important for the government to provide the social and economic environment in which the private sector can flourish and develop the fisheries resources. The government's intervention, therefore, should only be in areas where the private sector should not or cannot invest (Nichols and Moore 1985) and the private sector should be encouraged to be involved in the processing and distribution of fish. In addition, these policies require an integrated planning approach to project formulation, design and implementation and a comprehensive strategy for the development of the inshore fisheries. For this, there is a need to have quality databases and information systems to provide the basis for good decision making. The government has to improve its capacity for data collecting and analysis.

Human resources development is required to ease the transition to commercial fisheries and the proper management of the inshore fisheries. It is also required to ease the transition to the consistent production of high-quality fish products. Training is therefore required in the post-harvest handling of fish, the proper management of fisheries operations and ventures, and the control of fishing effort to ensure the sustainability of the sector. There is need to review the procedures regarding the granting of fishing permits to externals by the owners of customary fishing rights areas.

The thrust of the *Policies and Strategies for Fiji in the Medium Term* was reiterated in Part xiv of the draft Sustainable Development Bill relating to fisheries conservation and management. The Bill aims to: conserve and manage Fiji's fisheries in the interests of present and future generations; promote the broad application of a cautionary approach to the conservation, management and exploitation of marine resources in order to protect and preserve the marine environment, protect fish habitats and prevent the pollution of waters frequented by fish; encourage management of fisheries on a sustainable basis, protecting their economic viability for persons engaged in fishing and fish processing and for the wellbeing of the communities that are dependent on these resources; and encourage the participation of persons engaged in fishing at the domestic, subsistence or commercial levels in decisions regarding the conservation and management of fisheries (Government of the Republic of Fiji 1993, 1997a, 1997b).

In addressing the above concerns at the end of 1997 the Ministry of Agriculture initiated the controversial Commodity Development Framework (CDF). A total of F$69 million was earmarked to revamp the agricultural sector. The CDF reflects the policy change from intervention to deregulation, private sector development and export-led growth. It emphasises diversification as the basis of agricultural development in Fiji and considers the need to commercialise agricultural products for export (Leweniqila 1999).

Although the aims of the CDF are laudable, its specific targets are ambitious and its delivery inefficient. There is no proper control. Indeed, there are allegations that the CDF is misconceived, misguided and mismanaged. Although the government wanted partnership with the private sector, it did not consult it. Instead, the CDF was used to bail out ailing industries such as PAFCO and the copra mills and to fund the purchase of vehicles and overseas travel. The control of the fund is such that even government does not know how much of the money has been spent and on what. Claims have also been made that the government's aim to increase annual income from commodities by more than F$745 million through the CDF is excessive (*Fiji Times* 25 November 1997 editorial). It is not surprising then, that one of the first things the Chaudhry government did was to review and subsequently suspend the CDF.

Inshore fisheries development issues

In spite of the changing strategies reflecting the shift in policies, inshore fisheries development in Fiji has been indecisive, problematic and expensive. The high number of failed inshore fisheries developments have been costly, resulting in the wastage of already scarce resources. In addition, such failures demoralise and demotivate the people involved and impede fisheries development initiatives (Liew 1990:77–86).

Although fish production has increased considerably, the bulk of the fishing is still conducted in the inshore areas, raising concern about the health of the fisheries stock. Fish handling and distribution has improved but these are still restricted to areas around the main centres. The changes have not significantly affected the price of value-added products. The short life spans of artisanal fisheries development projects illustrate the problem and the need to revise fisheries development policies and strategies. The problems in each of the projects were varied but related to the pursuit of the government's rural development objectives, poor planning, inaccessible markets, lack of attention to negative environmental changes, lack of understanding of the complex sociocultural conditions, inappropriate human resource development, and lack of evaluation.

Rural development

Inshore fisheries development projects constitute an important rural development activity. Unfortunately, they often do not perform well and are mostly short-lived. The problem lies with the somewhat contradictory nature of rural development and fisheries development projects. While rural development projects promote the involvement and participation of rural communities in commercial activities such as artisanal fishing, fisheries development projects demand more cautious planning and implementation that take into account the nature of the resource and the related activities crucial to the operation of the fishing project. Thus, it is important to consider the size of the resource and post-harvest handling and marketing arrangements as part of the fisheries development initiative. Often, inshore fisheries development projects are set up under rural development initiatives. These projects do not last because the resources are quickly exploited to the point of extinction or, alternatively, the people involved disagree because they do not know how to effectively run their operation or differ on the project's management.

The combining of fisheries development projects with rural development initiatives means that the cautious approach needed for better-planned fisheries development is more difficult. Rural development initiatives are quickly adopted by people, making it hard to control the growth of development projects. Such high enthusiasm resulted in the over-exploitation of the inshore fisheries and subsequently the failure of projects. This was evident in the majority of the Rural Fisheries Development Program and the Commercial Artisanal Fisheries Development Program projects. The RFTP was attended by people who wanted to have the fishing boats offered to all the trainees. Many of these trainees later lost their boats because they were ill-prepared to operate such ventures. In the end the fisheries resources were depleted and the boat repayments were not met because of insufficient income.

The seaweed-farming project introduced in Fiji in the late 1980s is another failed initiative, although the project was initially well received by the rural communities because of its flexible nature and low skills requirement. The low production by the Fijian farmers and their periodic withdrawal from the project resulted in constant low production and poor quality products, which in the end led to the failure of the project. So, following the initial boom, production stabilised at a low level. The recently introduced seaweed-farming scheme under the CDF is facing a similar fate although it has been claimed as a possible replacement for sugar cane farming. In this case however, the villagers are the mainstays of the industry after having taken up the activity as part of the rural development initiative.

Operation Veivueti, a collection scheme, was another rural development initiative. The people in rural areas were at first enthusiastic about fishing and selling their catch to the Fiji Army's Auxiliary Unit. However, the initial enthusiasm waned, the people returned to their subsistence schedules and there was little preparation for the return of the collection vessels. Productivity consequently decreased until it was not economical to operate the scheme. By this time, the operation had run into serious financial difficulties that led to accusations of mismanagement and abuse of government resources. In spite of all these failures, Government even as late as 1992 was still trying to organise a collection scheme, this time through the National Trading Corporation (NATCO), the corporate company that replaced the NMA.

Poor project planning

Although most of the projects were directly related to government development policies, the planning was often poor, hampering successful project implementation. The prawn culture project in Raviravi was a case in point. Despite substantial financial and technical input, production was continually low due to problems that were not foreseen during the planning stages.

The collection schemes were based on the laudable desire to bring the markets closer to people in rural areas, but it was a nightmare to work out an economically viable venture given the nature of transport links and people's complicated dispositions. Further, more recent attempts have been organised despite advice against the viability of such schemes. After conducting studies throughout the Pacific, Carleton (1983), observed that the basic structure of the subsistence sector was not conducive to the regular supply of fish to the urban markets. He then recommended that such schemes be offered only as a social service and only if there is proper planning on how the schemes should operate. In addition, Carleton observed that government officials were ill-equipped to conduct the operations and therefore should not run them. Furthermore, it was important to remember that both the people and the resources were unlikely to support regular intensive collection, and the accumulation of catch over a period of time impossible without proper storage facilities (Evening 1983).

Seaweed farming in Fiji is technically feasible but its cultivation on a commercial basis has not been recommended (McHugh and Philipson 1988). Despite warnings, commercial seaweed farming was undertaken. The project was earmarked for Fijian villagers whose lifestyle was not suited to the requirements of a highly competitive and unstable export-oriented industry. The laid-back attitude and approach of the farmers led to the failure of the industry.

Inaccessible markets

Nichols and Moore (1985) argue that the overriding constraint hindering the development of commercial fisheries is the problem of inaccessible markets. Markets are important and are not easily accessible to the people who live in areas far away from the main centres. Markets in rural areas are poor because people have no regular income and live subsistence lifestyles.

There is a need to improve the basic marketing infrastructure. In their report published in 1984, Szabo and Herman described fish handling facilities as running from moderate to poor. Nichols and Moore (1985), in another report a year later, described how developments instituted by the Fisheries Division with the support of Japanese aid were made with the appreciation of the need to get ice supplied to the commercial fisheries in order for it to realise its full potential. Training is needed on post-harvest treatment of the catch and the processing for the production of value-added commodities.

In all the attempts to bring the markets closer to the people, the results have been disappointing because either the resources are over-exploited very quickly or these people just lose interest after a while. All the fish collection schemes to address these problems have not worked well (Adams 1989). The advent of the 'roll-on-roll-off' inter-island ferries has improved the situation for the islands with this service and those close to them. The islands not served by the ferries are still facing the same marketing difficulties as before.

The relative isolation of the export markets from the fishers in rural areas is also a problem. Isolation from markets, the high cost of transportation and the uncertainty of selling products harvested by artisanal fishers makes the likelihood of operating such a market highly unlikely. Furthermore, a great deal of work is needed to improve the quality of locally produced fish if it is to meet the rigorous quality standards that are required in the export markets.

Lack of attention to negative environmental changes

Prior to the end of the DP9 years (1986–90), the emphasis was on increasing productivity through the use of better fishing techniques, better facilities and better support services. There was no mention of the need for resource management or the sustainable development of the fisheries resource (Fairbairn 1990:259–66).

The main incidences of collapsed fisheries however, brought to the fore the need to ensure that fisheries development was in line with the capacity of the stock to support it. Numerous fisheries reports have alluded to the deteriorating state of the inshore fisheries (Joint Fisheries Strategies Mission 1988; Kailola 1995; Pita 1996; and Preston 1997), but because of poor data, it has not been possible to realistically address the problem.

It is important, however, that measures are taken to ensure that the ecological carrying capacities of the fisheries resources are used as the basis for development. For instance, now that the customary fishing rights areas have been surveyed and registered, it is time to work out guidelines for their sustainable use. Each of the customary fishing ground-owning units should have some idea of the maximum number of licenses that they can offer. This determination should be based on scientific and economic research and data.

More concerted efforts should be made to promote offshore fisheries. The placement of FADs and the offer of better fishing equipment including boats would be necessary. In addition, more attractive incentives such as better prices and subsidised fuel would enhance the movement offshore. At the moment, the result of the effort to promote offshore fishing has not been satisfactory, resulting in the increased use of inshore resources. The end result has been the depletion of these resources and the subsequent collapse of the fisheries operation.

Complex sociocultural conditions

The experience with many development projects has illustrated the complex sociocultural predicament of indigenous Fijians. These conditions need to be understood if development projects earmarked for them are to be more successful. The questions of motivation, consistency and the relationship between entrepreneurial skill and Fijian tradition are still to be well understood. With most of the communal fishing boat ventures, the fishing eases off after the boat loan has been repaid. Thus, the outright profits that are to be realised once the boat loan has been cleared are not attained.

Similarly, with seaweed farming, the people rarely maximised production, because the majority of the farmers were content with whatever income they received. The farming was not consistent as some of the farmers left their seaweed farms unattended until harvesting time or only returned to seaweed farming when they needed money.

The same problems were noticeable in the rural fisheries schemes and the fisheries cooperatives. Fishing often eases off after about a year and it becomes unstructured and sporadic. It was normal to find a few active members and a lot of inactive ones. In such schemes only the active members fish regularly and do all the work for the group (Veitayaki et al. 1996). The others are involved only occasionally as they consider themselves part-time fishers.

Inappropriate human resource development

Human resources development is an important component of fisheries development. For instance, the RFTP has been an essential part of both the Rural Fisheries Development Program and the Commercial Artisanal

Fisheries Development Program. However, in order for training to be effective it must be appropriate to what the trainees will need to undertake after the courses. First, selection of trainees should be based on some objective criteria. In the past the selection was based solely on proposals from the local communities that were to do the fishing and the endorsement of the *tikina* (a traditional district) and/or provincial council. In some cases, people ingratiated themselves with their friends and relatives in positions of authority to get them included in the RFTP. Second, during the project, there has been no consideration of the suitability of each candidate to successfully complete the course or carry out their trainee duties. Third, the training must inspire the trainees, since they are expected to lead the fishing operation, train others, and assist in managing the project upon returning to their villages.

The poor selection of trainees in most cases made the trainers' work more complicated given the many skills that have to be transferred. With the limited training period, the trainees were to help build their boat and learn the finer skills of being a fisher, a boat operator and captain, a businessman and a leader. Many of the trainees, for obvious reasons, failed as a result. It is also difficult to imagine how a young trainee, selected to attend the course because of academic skill, could train village members who were older and more experienced fishers. The problem was worse in the villages because the fishers knew each other's competencies and shortcomings.

With seaweed farming, training was not made available to everybody. Although a number of the farmers who did not receive training were fairly successful, the majority had to rely on information from their colleagues and, as such, were only marginally successful, if at all. This was a problem because some of the farmers did not appreciate the care that the seaweed requires and the conditions that would allow for the production of high-quality seaweed. As a result there was low productivity of low-grade seaweed resulting in low incomes.

Lack of evaluation

Evaluation is an important part of a project because it is the stage where the benefits and costs of the project are discussed. Evaluation is also important because it allows the people involved the chance to measure and then improve their performances. Unfortunately, this procedure is often not taken seriously. The result is that problems that affected the performance of the earlier projects are not analysed and therefore people do not learn from their experiences—a precondition for repeating mistakes.

The fisheries collection schemes have been tried on many occasions in Fiji and yet the results have been disappointing. The cultivation of seaweed has again been promoted but already there are signs that the same problems of low and inconsistent production and the withdrawal of farmers are still prevalent. Thus the continued use of Fijian farmers despite their poor reputation is a cause for concern.

Proposed policy changes

Based on my past experiences with specific, failed projects and my understanding of commonly mentioned problems affecting fisheries development projects in Fiji, the following policy changes are recommended.

There is a need for a carefully coordinated and integrated plan and program for the development of inshore resources. The Fisheries Division should be responsible for all fisheries development initiatives, keeping in mind the importance of exerting effective control for the purpose of preventing resource depletion. However, the Fisheries Division should work closely with other government ministries, non government organisations and international development agencies.

The combining of fisheries development with rural development should be carefully planned and monitored. Rural development should concentrate on providing necessary infrastructure and support system, while fisheries development must be cautiously introduced after careful planning and trials that take into consideration the need to keep fisheries development within the carrying capacity of the fisheries resources.

The people selected to be involved in fisheries development projects should be provided with thorough training and should be offered follow-up courses. The participants at these training sessions should be selected properly using objective selection criteria. There should be understanding of what the project entails and how that relates to the need to manage the fisheries resources. Funding assistance must be offered only to those people who have been adequately trained or have had experience in the fisheries development activity they want to be involved in.

Government should establish reliable and up-to-date databases and information systems to assist in the making of decisions. Therefore, the number of fisheries development permits granted by the owners of customary fishing areas should be based on scientific and economic research and data.

Research should constitute an important area of work for the Fisheries Division. The reliance on estimation based on surveys conducted in the 1970s is no longer acceptable. The current rate of use and the need for effective management require that future decision making be based on the best available information.

The procedure for granting of permits by the owners of customary fishing areas should be formalised and made more transparent. Fees should be paid to the owners of the customary fishing areas as well as to the government. These fees which should be standardised, to ensure the proper management of fisheries resources within the fishing areas.

Government intervention should be selective and must recognise as its ultimate objective the handing over of all commercial functions to the private sector. The private sector must be encouraged to be involved in the development of the fisheries and the marketing of fish and fish products.

A new system of development funding must be formulated to avoid the introduction of unilateral projects and the emphasis on funding periods. The new system must also reduce the number of defaulters and the amount of unpaid debt. In addition, the funding agencies must have the capacity to conduct technical, managerial and financial evaluation of commercial fishing ventures. The project funding period should be abolished and funding agencies should be allowed more flexibility to decide on the use of their funds. Thus, instead of making project funds available for only a defined period of time, the funding agencies could provide the funds whenever appropriate people who are prepared to be involved in a project seek them out.

The earmarking of particular fisheries development projects for special groups, such as indigenous Fijians, should no longer be entertained because most of the people in the villages are not ready to be involved in fisheries development. Instead, only the people that prove they can help themselves should be given the assistance they require.

Conclusion

Inshore fisheries constitutes an important component of the development sector in Fiji. The government has devised policies and strategies for the development of inshore fisheries resources. Yet, inshore fisheries development up to now has been problematic and expensive. The achievement of the aims and objectives of fisheries development has not been satisfactory. The number of initiatives that have failed are a testimony to the need to adopt a new approach—one that is more appropriate to the socioeconomic conditions in the country and is conducive to the requirements for more successful development. The main issues for inshore fisheries development issues are related to being linked with the pursuit of rural development objectives, poor project planning, lack of attention to negative environmental changes, complex sociocultural conditions, inappropriate human resource development, and lack of proper evaluation procedures.

The proposed policy changes should better address the need to have fisheries development projects that are successful in terms of the benefits to the people involved and the fisheries resources that support the development projects.

chapter nine

Women and politics in Fiji

Chandra Reddy

Women had a low status in Fiji in the pre-independence era. They suffered from many customs and conventions which discriminated against them. Not many women were in paid employment, although most worked on cane farms, rice farms and copra plantations, making a valuable contribution to the economy as unrenumerated workers. The existing laws disadvantaged women, most seriously in the field of employment. Banks and other employers paid unequal wages for the same work to male and female employees. The civil service also had many discriminatory laws against women which deprived them of the rights and privileges enjoyed by their male counterparts. One such regulation required all female permanent civil servants to resign their positions upon marriage and to rejoin on a temporary basis without entitlement to the privileges of a permanent employee, such as long service leave! Under such circumstances, there was no question of women having any say in politics although it is true that towards the end of the colonial period in 1963, women were finally enfranchised. It was no wonder, then, that there were no women of any ethnicity in the Legislative Council of Fiji until the country became self-governing in 1966.

After independence in 1970, many of the discriminatory laws against women were slowly changed, leading to an improvement in the status of women. It was a slow process mainly because women themselves did not agitate for their rights until the 1980s. Women had also not been very active in politics although there were one or two outstanding exceptions in both the ruling Alliance Party and the opposition National Federation Party. Adi Loslini Dovi was the Government Whip in the first parliament of Fiji and the opposition had Mrs Irene Jai Narayan. However, it is significant that Mrs Narayan was not Fiji-born, while Adi Losalini Dovi was no common Fijian woman, but one who belonged to an important chiefly family, being the wife of Ratu Dovi, brother of Ratu Sukuna who is still regarded as the most outstanding Fijian leader of the twentieth century. There were gradual changes for women in the field of education over the years and the gap between men and women has narrowed considerably.

There has been a tremendous increase in the percentage of girls attaining higher educational levels in the last twenty years. The 1996 national census results show that school attendance for boys and girls of all ethnic groups has increased over the past decade to a high level by international standards.

However, at the post-secondary level, boys outnumber girls, particularly in the science and technical fields and in vocational education. It is believed that one of the reasons for fewer women at higher levels is that fewer women enter vocational and training programs (CEDAW 1999).

The older Indo-Fijian women have been the most disadvantaged group in that 14 per cent of older women have had no formal education. This is followed by Indian male adults of whom 6 per cent have had no formal education. By contrast, the figures for Fijian females and males are 2.5 per cent and 1.8 per cent respectively (CEDAW 1999).

Impediments to women's political progress

The deeply entrenched notion that politics is a man's domain created a political culture that excluded women from leadership positions in society. There are many reasons for women being left out of the political arena, including the very distinct and different social responsibilities assigned to men and women; the deeply rooted patriarchal systems in Fiji in which women are always relegated to the background; and the religious and cultural attitudes that restricted and discouraged the potential contribution that women could make in positions of leadership. But slowly, as women started proving themselves in the economic field, in spite of the many barriers in the form of gender discrimination, they began to wonder whether creating a place for themselves in the decision-making bodies of the nation might not remove these barriers and hurdles and help to achieve equality and equity for themselves and their daughters in this male-dominated society.

A global problem

Women have come to realise that active participation at all levels of informal and formal decision making is the only way forward for them. They have often found themselves overshadowed and sidelined by men. Even the woman-to-woman support has been glaringly absent most of the time. These problems are not only common to the women in the Pacific but are experienced in other developing countries and even in the developed nations in spite of the presence of women's movements for a long period of time. But the need for women to participate in politics has been established, and is irreversible. The transition from traditional to modern lifestyles has left an impact on women who have had to cope with all the social changes and demands made on them as wives, mothers, nurturers and community workers. They have also very strongly felt the need to articulate their interests and concerns at the different decision-making levels, such as the local municipal governments, statutory boards and institutions and, most of all, parliament. They have found that their concerns are listed last in men's order of priority. This has led to their realisation that if they want to bring about changes in the conditions of their lives, then they must be involved in politics.

Major changes in the world are occurring through globalisation, improved communications, and science and technology. Whilst women have no control over these changes, the consequences do affect them and their families. So the only way open to women to have some say in the global trends, or the processes of change, is active participation in politics at all levels. Through political action women hope to have some influence in future directions of development. Women have come to realise that, in politics, nothing will change unless women participate and create a niche for themselves; otherwise, they will continue to be the marginalised segment of society. Throughout the world very few women have been successful in ascending to top positions in politics. In Asia in the last few decades, there have been only five women as heads of governments, all of whom came into power through their families' long history of political involvement. Although Asia is the fastest growing region of the world in economic terms, there has not been any matching improvement in the status of women. In India and China, there are some very strong non-government organisations which are acting as catalysts in bringing about gender equality.

In India the National Commission for Women, a non-government organisation headed by Mohini Giri, is involved in promoting gender justice, apart from launching specific initiatives to amend laws to protect women's interests in different areas. In 1994 by an amendment to the Indian Constitution, the women were given a one-third representation in the *panchayat* institutions. Since this, a political revolution has taken place whereby about one million women have entered local self government. Although the majority of them are illiterate, they are beginning to grasp the new opportunities offered them and have shouldered their responsibilities with enthusiasm. They are beginning to exercise and enjoy the power vested in them, with the assistance of their husbands. Almost all have vowed to tackle gender inequality as a first priority. One consequence of this was the commitment, spearheaded by the Women's Political Watch, and supported by almost all political parties and the government, to provide 33.3 per cent representation to women in state legislatures and in national parliament. There was almost a national consensus on the proposal, but the untimely fall of the Gujral government pushed this amendment into the background.

In China, the All China Women's Federation has played a key role in the overall development of women in that country. The largest non-government organisation in China, founded in April 1949, is made up of women from all walks of life and all ethnic groups. In the 17 years since the inception of the open-and-reform policy and through the efforts of the All China Women's Federation, there has been some measure of improvement in the status of Chinese women. They have made tremendous contributions to economic growth and social progress, emerging as leaders and helping to transform the political landscape of the country.

Under-representation of women in legislature in the Pacific

According to Jean Drage, the international decade for women acted as a catalyst for change for Pacific women's organisations as their focus shifted from concentration on family concerns to broader issues of the status and safety of women and the need for their greater involvement in formal decision making. She points out that it would be a mistake to assume that the under-representation of women in national legislatures means that women are not politically active as it would be denying their participation in non-government and community-initiated activities, saying that 'It would be a disservice to Pacific Islands women to accept the national election results as a complete portrait of women's political activity' (Drage 1994).

The under-representation of women in political power is a worldwide trend. Explanations for this range from the degree of industrialisation of a country, political ideology, the type of electoral system and the length of time in which women have enjoyed the right to vote. Table 9.1 shows women's political representation in national legislatures in Pacific Island countries around 1994.

In Guam, where women gained franchise in 1934, 29 per cent of parliament were women in 1994 whereas Vanuatu, where women gained franchise in 1975, had only 2 per cent women in parliament. Fiji, where women gained franchise in 1963, had only 3 women in Parliament in 1994 constituting 4 per cent of the total elected representation.

Fiji women

Marjorie Crocombe (1994) wrote that 'The lack of women's representation in parliaments in the Pacific is of great concern to women who understand its implications for development', and that most women in the Pacific were not aware of and not interested in the issue of under-representation. While by and large accurate, Crocombe's observation is not quite true of Fiji. Fiji women had representation in the legislative council ever since the country became self-governing. Although women representatives had been few in number until 1992, they had enjoyed some degree of prominence. Until

Table 9.1   Women's political representation in national legislatures in Pacific
             Island countries, 1994

Country	The year all women were eligible to vote and stand for parliament	No. of Parl. seats available*	No. of women elected to parl. seats	Per cent of women in parl. seats	Year of last election
Micronesia					
Northern Marianas	1965	23	2	9	1993
Palau	1965	32	0	-	1992
Guam	1931	21	6	29	1994
FSM	1965	14	0	-	1991
Marshall Islands	1965	33	1	3	1991
Kiribati	1967	39	0	-	1994
Nauru	1951	18	0	-	1992
Polynesia					
Tuvalu	1967	12	1	8	1993
Western Samoa	1991#	47	2	4	1991
Wallis/Futuna	1961	20	2	10	1991
American Samoa	1957	40	1	3	1992
French Polynesia	1953	41	0	-	1993
Niue	1960	20	1	5	1993
Cook Islands	1957	25	0	-	1994
Tonga	1960	30	1	3	1993
Melanesia					
Fiji	1963	71	3	4	1994
New Caledonia	1957	36	0	-	1989
Vanuatu	1975	46	1	2	1991
Solomon Islands	1967	47	1	2	1993
Papua New Guinea	1964	109	0	-	1992

Note: Tokelau, a territory of New Zealand is not included in this Table. Nevertheless, discussion of developments in Tokelau forms part of the analysis of women's political activity.
* In most instances all available seats are included, and whether elected or appointed, and whether in unicameral or bicameral houses.
# Prior to universal suffrage there were two seats for which some women (that is, those on the Individual Voters roll) could vote and stand for Parliament.
Source: Alaima, F. and vom Busch, W., 1994. *New Politics in the South Pacific*, Institute of Pacific Studies, University of the South Pacific, Suva.

the 1980s, Fiji women, like women elsewhere in the Pacific, were not very much concerned about their political rights. But in 1984, with the opening of Women's Crisis Centre, women's issues started taking centre stage, at least occasionally. Shamima Ali, who was (and still is) the major force behind the Centre, is a bold and vocal exponent of women's rights. Following her lead, other like-minded women (mainly professionals) started coming forward openly in support of women's rights. In 1986, they formally established the Fiji Women's Rights Movement. Imrana Jalal has made a noteworthy contribution in promoting the work of the movement. Initially, there was a lot of opposition to the movement, especially from men, who tried to warn their families against these women leaders who were portrayed as troublemakers. But the women persisted, and slowly gained a firm foothold in society.

Until 1987, Fijian women kept a low profile in politics but this changed drastically after the coups with Fijian women coming forward to assume leadership roles in politics. One Fijian woman to come forward was Adi Kuini Bavadra, who became leader of the Fiji Labour Party (FLP) after the death of her husband, the ousted Prime Minister, Dr Timoci Bavadra. The Labour Party's president is a woman, Jokepaci Koroi, while Adi Kuini rose to the position of deputy prime minister. Meanwhile, other women elected to parliament in the 1992 and 1994 elections have also played significant roles in the government. They include Taufa Vakatale, Adi Samanunu Cakobau and Seruwaia Hong Tiy. All three were ministers in the Soqosoqo ni Vakavulewa ni Taukei (SVT) government.

Vakatale, who was minister for education and acted as prime minister on many occasions, was well aware of the difficulties of encouraging women to enter politics.

> Women clamour for equality with the men, and will lobby for their
> rights and fight instances of discrimination against women. Yet when
> the crunch comes and women are required to take up active political
> roles, very few have the courage to offer themselves (in Drage 1994).

Whilst generally this is true because of the insecurity associated with elective political positions, there were also some very able women who resigned from top civil service positions to contest the 1999 general elections. These included Dr Mridula Sainath, a medical practitioner/HIV specialist and a women's activist; Savitri Chauhan, a principal of a high school; and Manju Verma who was the deputy director of social welfare. None of them got elected.

There has been only one Indo-Fijian woman in parliament since the 1987 coups; she was elected in the 1999 general elections. This disparity between Fijian and Indo-Fijian women could be attributed to several factors. Whilst both were constrained by the same kind of customary and traditional practices during the colonial era and in the period leading up to 1987, the post-coup period witnessed the opening up of greater avenues in the economic and political arena for Fijian women. More Fijian women moved up in the civil service, and most non-government organisations promoting women in politics and donor-funded political-education bodies comprised mostly indigenous women. Coinciding with this was a mass exodus of skilled and professional Indo-Fijian women after the 1987 coups. Why Indo-Fijian women remain in subordinate positions is well described by Imrana

Jalal and Dr Wadan Narsey who have labelled this a 'culture of silence' that condemns women's assertiveness as disrespectful to those with traditional power. They stress that

> why women remain silent is neither about being inferior, being less knowledgeable, nor economically disadvantaged. It is a combination of many factors such as religion, culture, upbringing, the fear of retaliation, the lack of protection—dynamics which attributed to people's expectations of an ideal female in a patriarchal society such as Fiji (*Balance* September–October 1997:8–9).

Women's contribution to the economy

Women's contribution to the economy has always been significant although most of it has not been recognised as paid work or entered in any statistical data. Women's work on sugar farms, rice farms, copra plantations, in fishing and horticultural activities, although unremunerated, was essential for the economic survival of families. After Independence, women's entry into the paid workforce expanded; their other work was largely unremunerated and only 14 per cent of women workers were in paid employment. However by 1992 this figure rose to 30.5 per cent (Fiji Bureau of Statistics 1996) which represented 55 per cent of Fiji's economically active female workforce.

After the coups when Fiji, under special arrangements like SPARTECA, began to export locally made garments overseas, the manufacturing industry began to boom. At the present time, the industry employs about 18,000 to 20,000 women. Although poorly paid and often working in intolerable conditions, the only consolation is that these women are at least able to bring home a pay packet at the end of the week, when some husbands become unemployed at the close of the sugar cane harvesting seasons and for other reasons.

Concern has also been raised about the gender imbalance in the civil service. Although women comprised 45.3 per cent of the total civil service in 1996, only 11 per cent were in the senior management level; 27.9 per cent in the middle and 50.5 per cent in the lower level. Table 9.2 shows the percentage and number of females in the three broad civil service categories (Ministry of Women and Culture 1998).

It is significant that while the numbers of those in lower and middle management remained virtually the same from 1990 to 1996, the number of women at senior management level actually declined by 1.5 per cent.

This disparity in the economic arena, not only in the civil service but also in the private sector, could be partly addressed if the stereotyping of roles for boys and girls in the education system was discouraged and girls were actively encouraged to choose professions dominated by men. In many

Table 9.2   Percentage and number of females in the three broad civil service
               categories, 1990–96

	1990	1991	1992	1993	1994	1995	1996
Senior management %	12.5	12.0	11.4	11.4	11.1	10.5	11.0
(number)	(184)	(192)	(202)	(210)	(217)	(228)	(246)
Middle management %	27.1	27.1	27.4	27.8	27.8	30.0	27.9
(number)	(3119)	(3190)	(3281)	(3397)	(3491)	(3596)	(3716)
Lower level %	50.6	50.0	50.0	50.0	50.6	50.9	50.5
(number)	(8336)	(9039)	(10037)	(10797)	(11470)	(12596)	(14153)

Source: Ministry of Women and Culture, 1998. *Women's Plan of Action, 1999–2008*, Ministry of
Women and Culture, Suva, Vol. 2:90.

instances, women have felt pressurised by the traditional norms that force
women to choose family over a career, maintaining the economic differences
between themselves and men.

Launch of the Fiji women's plan of action

The SVT government, particularly former prime minister Sitiveni Rabuka,
were very sympathetic towards women and their development. The
Convention on the Elimination of Discrimination Against Women, was
ratified by the Rabuka government in 1994, with reservation on some issues
(Articles 5(a) and 9). The Fiji government and the non-government
organisations were well represented at the United Nations fourth World
Conference for Women held in Beijing in September 1995 in which 12 critical
areas of concern were identified for women's overall development. To give
effect to the commitments that Fiji made at the Beijing Conference, a
Women's Plan of Action was launched in 1998 by the Ministry of Women
and Culture, focusing on five issues
  • mainstreaming women and gender concerns
  • review of laws that are disadvantageous to women
  • micro-enterprise development for women
  • violence against women and children
  • gender-balanced partnership in decision making.
The Plan of Action called for a coordinated approach by the government,
civil societies, academic institutions and private sector to fulfil Fiji's
obligations.

Whilst consideration was given to previous efforts to address the
inequality between men and women through special programs and projects
for women, mainstreaming aims to integrate women's concerns into the
whole system of government whilst at the same time recognising and
affirming equal rights for men and women.

The second commitment in the Plan is a review of laws that are
disadvantageous to women. Although the 1997 Constitution guaranteed

non-discrimination on the basis of gender, this in itself cannot change overnight the ingrained customary practices that regulate the roles of men and women in society. The Family Law, Employment Act, Evidence and Criminal Act were to be reviewed with special focus on gender concerns.

The third commitment is the allocation of additional resources to develop women's micro-enterprises. In the informal sector, women are encouraged to develop small-scale enterprises. Although the number of women employed in the formal sector rose during the 1990s, it only accounts for 35 per cent of total paid employment today. Women are generally employed in the lower income occupations or industries and more often hold junior positions. The development of the informal sector is seen as a contribution to the economy and also a means of alleviating poverty.

Reducing violence against women and children is a major challenge. Statistics show that reported cases of violence against women are increasing, but this is believed to represent only a small percentage of the total number of crimes committed. A large number are never reported, and there are families where violence is accepted as normal behaviour. The Rabuka government had introduced the 'no drop' policy but whether this is implemented by the Fiji Police to the maximum is another matter. Women in Fiji have been, through the Fiji Crisis Centre and other sister organisations, lobbying for changes in legislation that will lessen domestic violence in Fiji. The Regional Human Rights Education Resource Team (RRRT), funded by British Aid, is an advocacy group working together with other civil society organisations to educate women on their human rights and legal rights.

The final and the most important commitment that the government made was for

> gender balance partnership at all levels of decision-making and assigning fifty per cent of representation, participation, training, appointments and promotions at all levels of government to women on merit and as appropriate and to encourage the same in the private sector (Ministry of Women and Culture 1998).

We all agree that increasing women's participation at all levels of decision-making plays a pivotal role in the advancement of women. As a result of the SVT government's decision, a lot more women have been appointed to statutory boards and other institutions where previously they were absent, the overall representation now being at 14 per cent.

Fiji Women in Politics project

In addition to the role played by the Fiji Women's Rights Movement, the Women's Crisis Centre and similar organisations in changing the attitudes of both men and women towards women's role in society, a need was felt for an organisation to motivate, educate and train women for leadership roles in the political structures of the country. Consequently, the Fiji Women in Politics Project, an initiative of the Fiji National Council of Women, was launched in 1994 with the objective of, amongst other things, encouraging women to participate in party politics and be elected to parliament and local government offices. During the last five years, along with the women's wings of various political parties, the project has been vigorously engaged in political awareness, education and training programs both for women voters and potential candidates.

During the 1997 municipal elections, 28 women candidates contested. Out of a total of 127 positions, 14 women became councillors. One woman councillor was elected a mayor and another a deputy mayor (Ministry of Women and Culture 1998). Table 9.3 shows the number of women candidates, the gender ratio of candidates and the actual councillors in the 1997 municipal elections.

'The low number of women was almost entirely due to their very low participation as candidates' said the Fiji Women's Plan of Action (1998). Whilst this is partly true, women face discrimination in the selection process itself, apart from other factors that weigh against them. The selection of candidates by all political parties has always been in favour of men as they have better financial resources and are better able to lobby for support around the 'grog bowl' and at the 'drinking parties'—where the real politicking takes place and where women in general are expected not to be present.

A major highlight and achievement through cooperation and coordination of the various women's political groups and the Women in Politics Project was the formation of a Fiji Women's Caucus which will collectively voice the concerns of women in the legislature, irrespective of political affiliations, and ensure these are translated into legislation to lift the overall status of women.

Women and the 1997 Constitution

Fiji's Constitution Review exercise (1995–96) took place in an atmosphere of dialogue, compromise and widespread consultation. The women of Fiji participated fully in making their views known to the Constitution Review Commission. For the first time, Fiji had a Constitution that reflected the wishes of the vast majority of its people, including women. The Constitution was based on principles of representative democracy and removed all discrimination based on race, religion, age, and most importantly, gender.

As I mentioned earlier, the Fiji Government when ratifying CEDAW in 1995 noted its reservation over Article 5(a) dealing with Fiji Islands' customary traditions and practices and Article 9 which deals with the citizenship rights. The previous Constitution treated men and women who married foreign citizens differently. Whereas the foreign wives of Fiji men

Table 9.3   Numbers and gender ratios—candidates and elected members of
             municipal councils, 1997

Municipality	Candidates gender ratio women:men	Elected members gender ratio women:men	Actual numbers of elected women:men	Number if voters gender women:men	Gender neutral - N Gender biased - B
Suva	1:15	1:19	1:19	1:19	N
Lautoka	1:4	1:6	3:17	4:16	B
Nadi	1:9	1:14	1:14	1:14 or 2:13	N
Ba	1:5	1:5	2:10	2:10	N
Sigatoka	1:21	1:9	1:9	1:9	N
Nausori	0:22	0:12	0:12	all males	
Lami	1:9	0:12	0:12	all males	
Labasa	1:9	0:12	0:12	1:11	B
Savusavu	1:22	0:9	0:9	0:9	N

Source: Ministry of Women and Culture, 1998. *The Women's Plan of Action*, Ministry of Women and Culture, Suva, Vol. 2:79.

were eligible for citizenship rights of Fiji as written in Section 26 of the Constitution, the foreign husbands of Fiji women were not. As a result, there was a lot of scepticism over whether the Constitution Review Commission would recommend equal citizenship rights bearing in mind the government's stand on this issue. The Commission did not disappoint the women of Fiji. Now under the new Constitution both the husband and the wife enjoy equal privileges in applying for citizenship rights. Equally importantly, the child or children of both the mother as well as the father born overseas are entitled to Fiji citizenship whereas before the male descent was the only privileged one.

Another highlight of the new Constitution has been the establishment of the Human Rights Commission under the Bill of Rights which incorporates principles and values enshrined in all the major international human rights conventions and instruments. The Constitution's affirmative and social justice provisions oblige the government to enact affirmative action policies in an open and transparent way, not only for the various ethnic groups but also for men and women. In the area of parliamentary politics, women were disappointed that their demand for a quota system for female representation in parliament was rejected especially in view of the many social and cultural obstacles faced by women who want to get into decision-making positions in public life.

But any constitutional provisions, however worthy or noble, cannot achieve much by themselves. Women in Fiji, as elsewhere, suffer disadvantages in the public and private sector because of their gender. However, our experience has shown that whilst laws are unquestionably necessary, they are not sufficient by themselves to achieve the end. Although the new 1997 Constitution that was promulgated in July last year specifically prohibits discrimination of any kind, this only remains so on paper at least at this stage. What is required is proper and quick implementation through action and if necessary, through legislative measures.

The 1999 general elections in Fiji

During the elections of May 1999, the efforts of the women's organisations were rewarded by an increase in women representatives in parliament. Twenty-seven women contested out of a total of 251 candidates. Of these, eight were elected, five of whom were appointed ministers—three as cabinet ministers and two as assistant ministers. In the upper house, five women were sworn in as senators, and one was elected its vice-president. So there was a definite improvement in terms of the percentage of women in representation at the highest level of decision making; that is, the parliament. It remains to be seen if they become an effective voice on women's issues in parliament or become drowned amongst the heavy male voices that dominate the floor.

Conclusion

The government, the civil society organisations and the non-government organisations all have to play their rightful roles in lifting the status of women in all stratas of society. The women's non-government organisations have been instrumental in raising public awareness on women's issues and in lobbying for law reform on these issues. Noteworthy among these are the Fiji Women's Rights Movement, which is involved in raising public awareness on women's human and legal rights and economic empowerment for women; the Fiji Crisis Centre which addresses the sexual assault and violence against women and children; the National Council of Women which coordinates special programs for its affiliate organisations throughout the country; the Fiji *Girmit* Council of Women which concentrates on programs for development of rural women and disadvantaged girls; and the Women's Action for Change, to name a few.

The Rabuka government started the process by launching the Women's Plan of Action which focuses on these issues, and enacting various legislative measures to ensure equality and equity for women. It established the Fiji Law Reform Commission to review many existing laws. The most recent was the review of the Family Law in Fiji which has definitely, amongst other things, improved the position of women as far as the division of matrimonial property and child maintenance is concerned.

In conclusion, it is the hope and aspiration of all women globally that, through legislative changes, networking with government and non-government organisations, fully implementing international covenants like CEDAW and other laws pertaining to women, gender parity will one day be realised.

chapter ten

Economic challenges facing Fiji before the storm

Biman C. Prasad

Fiji entered into a new era with the May 1999 general election under a Constitution which guaranteed equality to all its citizens. The real challenge for Fiji and its new government was to deliver the promised economic goods and services to its people. Economic prosperity and equality are the keys to creating a truly multiracial Fiji.

Current economic policy environment

Fiji seemed to be on its way out of the economic gloom of the last two years. The drought of 1998 leading to a 40 per cent reduction in sugar production and the 20 per cent devaluation of the Fiji dollar to enhance competitiveness due to the Asian financial crisis were some of the difficult situations to deal with. The positive factors are the expected rise in sugar production after the drought of 1998, low real interest rates, expansionary fiscal policies and the competitive exchange rate after the devaluation.

The Reserve Bank had forecast favourable conditions for sugar production, revising its estimate of 400,000 tonnes upwards to about 420,000 tonnes. It also forecast a strong performance in other sectors such as tourism, garment exports, forestry and fishing. Interest rates were continuing to decline, with the weighted average lending rate of commercial banks at 8.8 per cent in May 1999.

The Chaudhry government's 2000 budget forecast a growth rate of GDP of 7.8 per cent in 1999 up from the previous forecast of 7.4 per cent. The Reserve Bank of Fiji attributed this performance to strong growth in the forestry, building and mining industries. While these are positive factors, the negatives include the impending controversy regarding land leases and the performance of the sugar industry. The Reserve Bank, for example, points out that that the weather conditions have affected the cane quality and the total cane to sugar ratio has averaged 9.7 compared to 8.2 in 1998 (Reserve Bank of Fiji 1999).

Table 10.1   Commercial banks' lending rates in selected sectors

Sectors	April 1998 (%)	April 1999 (%)
Agriculture	10.45	9.59
Manufacturing	9.35	7.64
Building and Construction	9.75	8.85
Real Estate	10.17	9.03
Private Individuals	10.47	9.74
Housing	9.84	9.12
All sectors	9.93	8.89

Source: Reserve Bank of Fiji, 1999. *News Review*, 16(6), Suva.

Was the Chaudhry government setting a different economic policy agenda for Fiji?

It was generally expected that the Chaudhry government would substantially change the economic policy direction of Fiji. The expectation arose largely from the criticisms leveled at the previous government's economic policy by the Fiji Labour Party (FLP). Before we analyse the budget, it is appropriate to briefly state the main thrust of the People's Coalition Manifesto.

The People's Coalition, comprising four political parties in government, had indicated a strong socialist agenda and the policies to be adopted by the government were clearly spelt out in the election manifesto. Some of the broad promises and statements were
- the government is committed to promoting strong economic growth to deliver its promises
- promotion of the rural and agricultural development and redevelopment of the rice industry
- enhancing tourism development by encouraging large scale foreign investment
- reverse privatisation of public enterprises
- reduce housing interest rates from 11 per cent to 6 per cent
- implementation of minimum wages of F$120 per week
- removal of VAT from basic food items, medical charges and supplies, public transport; and essential educational materials
- increased public expenditure on health, education and social services, crime and other social ills.

The government's tax agenda was summarised in the People's Coalition Manifesto.

The People's Coalition recognises that taxation plays an important part in revenue collection and the distribution of wealth. However, the tax burden on ordinary people has been allowed to grow too large under the SVT government. We must provide incentives to reward individual effort, encourage people to save, invest, create employment and so generate growth in the economy (1999:14).

2000 Chaudhry government budget

National budgets provide two things, first they are an indication of what the people can expect in the short term and what is to come in future. Second they are supposed to lay the foundation for the country's long term economic policy agenda. For the Chaudhry government, the 2000 budget was expected to do both, deliver the promises made and at the same time lay the agenda for long-term economic policy direction.

Fiji's budgets over the last decade have emphasised private sector-led development, and government policies were designed to pursue that. For example, in the 1999 budget the SVT government provided for the sale of public enterprises, further relaxed exchange controls and twenty year tax holidays for hotels with investments of more than F$40 million, eliminated double taxation on company profits and provided a range of other benefits to potential investors. The 2000 budget did not reverse these concessions or policies, supporting the concessions provided by the SVT government. There was no change in the trade policies. This would have relieved private sector investors. The government included funding for research and development of new products for export which would have been welcomed by potential investors. However, the government should have realised that concessions to investors in the last 2–3 years have not produced the expected results and investment has remained sluggish. Since 1988 private sector investment has continued to decline; it has remained at less than 5 per cent of gross domestic product (GDP) since 1990. New initiatives and changes to policies were not considered to attract private investment. There were no statements on new projects like the Namosi Copper mine and other private sector initiatives to attract new investment into the natural resources-based sector.

The 1999 budget had a number of measures that benefited low-income earners. These included increases in the income tax threshold from F$5,000 to F$6,500, increases in dependent child allowance, widowed persons allowance and increases in Fiji National Provident Fund (FNPF) and insurance allowance. What did the Coalition's 2000 budget have? It continued in the same direction by increasing spouse tax allowance from F$1,000 to F$1,200, child tax allowance and FNPF allowance. But these increases will not help those on lower incomes, they will largely benefit middle and high-income earners. Those earning below F$6,500 are not paying taxes anyway. The positives of the budget and its implication for the poor are not surprising. Judging by the People's Coalition manifesto, the provisions in the budget fell far short of what was promised. The government answered critics wanting to know where the money would come from, by not delivering too much and thereby containing the deficit. However, it could be excused for not delivering all its promises in this budget—in fact it never intended to do so when the promises were made. After all they thought they had at least another four budgets to deliver on their promises. The increases in the budget allocation to the Health, Education and Social Welfare ministries are welcomed. These are positive moves that would benefit the poor and the economy in the long-run. However, on the expenditure side and reallocation, government has continued with the allocation of unproductive expenditure—it makes little sense to increase expenditure for the army by F$6 million dollars while the police department receives only an extra F$1 million. Is this enough given the importance of reducing crime, corruption and having good governance? The Social Welfare department, on the other hand received an increase of only F$3.3 million.

On the revenue side there seems to be an assumption that tax compliance will make up for the shortfall in income tax revenue from the collection of value-added tax (VAT). For example the estimates show that VAT revenue is estimated to only decline by F$7.6 million, and that income tax revenue will increase by about F$15 million dollars. Furthermore, there were hopes to raise an extra F$9.6 million from dividends on government capital investment. These are strong assumptions in an area of revenue collection and one has to be wary of these.

The Chaudhry government continued with a policy of financial liberalisation and the progressive relaxation of the exchange controls, building on the significant relaxation announced by the Soqosoqo ni Vakavulewa ni Taukei (SVT) government. With regard to the financial services reform, the government announced the establishment of the Banking Commission and the Banking Ombudsman. This was a healthy development which should have been welcomed by the consumers.

Low wages and lack of employment is the biggest cause of poverty in Fiji. The government's decision to remove VAT from essential services was laudable, but it did not go far enough towards addressing the problem of real poverty. The interim government led by Ratu Sir Kamisese Mara implemented a VAT of 10 per cent in 1991. This was seen by many as a regressive tax as indeed many indirect taxes are. The VAT was implemented in the absence of parliament and without much debate—one of the reasons why it was seen as politically irresponsible. The concern that the poor would be most affected was to some extent mitigated by the allocation of funds for poverty alleviation. While it cannot be denied that the VAT had an initial adverse impact on the poor, its revenue potential and contribution to government finances has been very significant. After an initial decline, government revenue remained above 25 per cent of total GDP, and increased slightly in 1996 and 1997.

After the general elections in 1992, the Fiji Labour Party (FLP) supported the coup leader becoming Prime Minister. One of the conditions for such support was the total removal of VAT. However, that position changed with the coalition government announcing the removal of VAT from basic food items, medical charges and supplies, public transport and essential educational materials.

A VAT was introduced largely to increase the tax base and provide some administrative ease in collecting them. It was designed to bring a larger number of people into the tax net. From the income distribution point of view, the VAT has been a regressive tax which is why the Chaudhry government reduced it on essential items. When VAT zero-rates a number of essential goods and services, and taxes luxury goods the tax may become progressive. However, the administrative cost of doing this could be enormous, and could create further distortions from an economic efficiency point of view. In Fiji, where there is already a problem of proper compliance, exemption of some goods could create further compliance problems. In some developed countries social security adjustments have been considered to take into account those at lower income levels. The government was also considering reducing the across-the-board VAT of 10 per cent to a lower level to reduce administrative and compliance problems, which may also be economically efficient.

Over 70 per cent of the people in Fiji earn less than F$6,000 dollars—on a weekly basis this is less than the minimum wage of F$120 dollars per week. The majority of people in the lower income bracket earn less than F$100 dollars a week. The Chaudhry government missed a golden opportunity to announce definite measures to bring about a national minimum wage which would have helped thousands of lower paid workers. Instead only small benefits are being derived through the reduction in prices brought about by the removal of VAT on essential items.

The situation with regards to employment in Fiji is serious. Official estimates point out that there are 15,000 school leavers who enter the market every year in search for jobs. Of these, 5,100 are females and 9,900 males. The minimum qualification of the majority of these school leavers is the Fiji School Leaving Certificate which does not equip the person with the appropriate skills to enter the job market easily. Apart from school leavers, there are another 2,000 persons entering the job market every year. These include about 500 females and 300 youths who have no formal qualifications, and about 1,200 who are the victims of downsizing in the government sector and the laying-off of workers by commercial enterprises.

A total of 17,000 unemployed persons per year are looking for employment. The Chaudhry government's claim it would create 9,000 jobs was an overly optimistic projection.

In terms of changes to taxation policies, the opportunity went begging. The Chaudhry government didn't make any statements on reviewing or changing income tax, which is not as progressive as it should be. There was no statement on company taxes, capital gains tax, nor on estate and gift duties. It was expected that rather than political procrastination the government would at least consider these aspects of the taxation system— they are the ones that would ultimately provide the incentives and mechanism for redistribution of wealth.

The People's Coalition had indicated that a capital gains tax might be implemented. From the equity and social point of view this tax may be desirable. In the case of Fiji this may bring popular accolade from some sections of the electorate, at a potentially inappropriate time and it could be inimical to economic growth. What Fiji needs is investment from the private sector, and a capital gains tax may not provide the right incentives. I believe that anticipation of the tax itself led to the consumption and flight of capital. Tax revenue amounts to about 82 per cent of the total revenue for the Fijian government (see Table 10.2). Tax policies are sensitive economic issues and the review of the existing tax policies, if not done carefully, can provide the wrong signals for potential investors.

An increase of F$10 million in the Agriculture budget was a step in the right direction, and efforts to support diversification and marketing of agricultural products should be the key agricultural policy for the future.

Table 10.2   Sources of Fiji government revenue, 1991–98

Year	Customs excise	Inland revenue	Non-tax revenue	Capital revenue	Grants	Total revenue and grants
1991	220.1	229.2	114.5	5.4	7.3	576.5
1992	198.3	284.4	106.3	6.3	7.2	602.5
1993	179.0	340.6	126.2	4.2	4.1	654.1
1994	190.3	375.5	123.2	4.3	4.5	697.8
1995	207.3	395.1	103.6	6.7	6.3	719.0
1996	203.8	417.9	108.0	6.3	7.3	743.3
1997	219.6	445.2	129.3	4.4	4.9	803.4
1998						
March	49.8	87.8	19.8	0.7	0.6	158.7
June	51.8	111.0	40.1	26.4	0.9	230.2
September	59.6	144.9	27.3	0.4	0.5	232.7

Source: Reserve Bank of Fiji, 1999. *Quarterly Bulletin*, March, Reserve Bank of Fiji, Suva:Table 23.

The SVT government managed to reduce the deficit to as low as 1.6 and 0.5 per cent of the GDP through strong revenue from tax. However, unexpected commitments such as the bailing out of the National Bank of Fiji, led to an increase in the deficit in 1996 and 1997 and a projected decrease in 1998 and 1999. The Coalition's 2000 budget maintained that trend, recognising that a small deficit is an important impetus for economic growth.

Trade and investment policies

Trade and investment policies will be the key to Fiji's economic growth. The Coalition government's position was to encourage trade and investment. However, it is important to point out that Fiji's economic reform agenda for the last ten years has been to move away from a largely import-substitution policy direction to a export-oriented market economy. The economic reform agenda for the last ten years has included

- trade deregulation
- taxation reforms
- labour market reforms
- reduction in the size and management role of government
- public enterprises reform and
- moblisation of all sectors of the community in support of economic expansion.

Trade deregulation was designed to increase competition and encourage investment in sectors where Fiji had a competitive edge; for example, the garment industries. As part of these policies barriers to trade such as tariffs were reduced gradually. The labour market also underwent reforms. The expectation that the overall direction of economic policies would change substantially was not delivered in the Coalition's 2000 budget. The overall policy direction was maintained. The challenge for a new government is to balance these policies with both the changing world market conditions and its promises to the electorate. Fiji's exports increased between 1995 and 1996, but declined dramatically in 1997 and 1998, while imports continued to increase (Figure 10.1).

Private investment seems to be the key factor in the economic growth in Fiji in the long run. However, the level of private investment has remained weak at below 5 per cent of the GDP since 1992. Public sector investment, while strong between 1993 and 1995, has declined since 1996. Therefore, the total level of investment in the country has declined over the last few years. Figure 10.2 provides the trend in investment levels in Fiji since 1970.

The construction sector has also been relatively weak. This can also be attributed to low private sector investment. There is however, potential for growth in the construction sector if work on some of the up-market hotel facilities continues.

Role and size of government

The basic philosophy of the coalition government was that the role of the government in managing the economy must also include the provision of essential services. It also believed that the government must actively pursue policies for the redistribution of wealth in the country through deliberate fiscal policies. One of the platforms on which the Chaudhry government was elected included the reduction in waste and proper management of the state's resources. This was not realised.

In Fiji, the relative size of government to GDP has been a major issue. The Rabuka government relied heavily on borrowing and ran a deficit budget of more than 5 per cent of the GDP. The rationale behind the reduction in the size of government has been to free up resources for growth in the private sector. Whilst the SVT government's stated objective was to reduce the size of government, its progress towards that goal was less promising. The composition of the total expenditure has been moving towards more consumption-related operating expenditure (see Figure 10.3). Productive capital investment expenditure has remained relatively weak in the last 8 years.

Table 10.3   Fiji's net budget deficit as a percentage of GDP

Year	1996	1997	1998	1999	2000
% of GDP	5.2	9.2	2.8	2.3	1.9

Source: Ministry of Finance, 2000. *Supplementary to the 2000 Budget: Fiji Government budget 2000,* Ministry of Finance, Suva.

Figure 10.1   Fiji's merchandise exports and imports, 1991–97

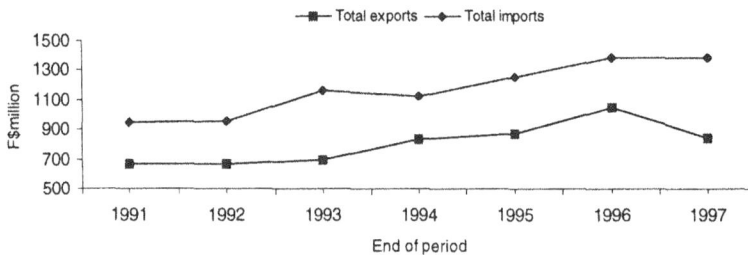

Source: Reserve Bank of Fiji, 1999. *Quarterly Bulletin,* March, Suva: Tables 31and 32.

Total expenditure as a percentage of GDP has declined from 35.5 per cent in 1991 to 30.9 per cent in 1995. This trend has continued. While total revenue has continued to increase the total debt has also increased. The breakdown of the total debt shows that while external debt has not increased too much, domestic debt has continued to increase in the last few years (Table 10.4).

The SVT government had undertaken deliberate policies to do away with losses of F$11 million dollars per year through its public enterprises, undertaking major reform of public enterprises. These reforms included the corporatisation and privatisation. The Labour Party and the trade union movement in Fiji opposed many of these reforms. One the main issues in the opposition to these reforms was the subsequent job losses and the increase in the cost of services. The government owns 31 commercially oriented public enterprises with a total equity exceeding F$600 million (Government of Fiji 1997). A previous government policy was to slowly privatise these enterprises, for example selling shares in Fiji's national airline

The Chaudhry government had a platform intended to reverse the process of privatisation and corporatisation. It believed that public utilities such as water, electricity, telecommunications and civil aviation facilities must remain in public hands. As a matter of priority it reversed the reforms instituted in the Civil Aviation Authority and Fiji Electricity, but continued to sell government shares, hoping to raise revenue and selectively pursuing the process of privatisation. The issue with regards to corporatisation and privatisation is that there are enterprises which have not been profitable for many years, draining the public purse, but there are others which have been very profitable and could contribute to government revenue. However, the SVT government did not make that distinction and sold shares in

Figure 10.2   **Investment level in Fiji, 1970–98**

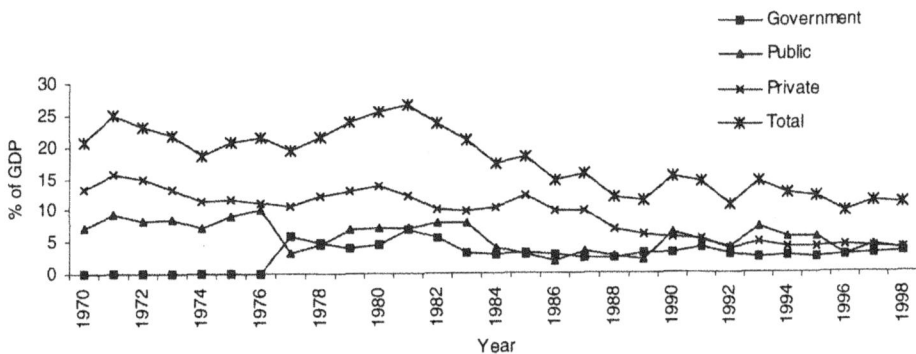

Source: Reserve Bank of Fiji, 1999. *Quarterly Bulletin*, March, Suva: Table 21.

enterprises which were making profits. The new government will have to strike the right balance in its approach to the management of public enterprises.

Other challenges

One of the key obstacles to the performance of the Fijian economy has been the uncertainty of property rights to land in Fiji. There is no doubt that this uncertainty has affected production and efficiency in both the agriculture and the tourism sectors (Prasad and Tisdell 1996). Under the Agricultural Landlord and Tenant Act (ALTA), native land leases had been granted to tenants for 30 years. The legislation provided the mechanisms through which rent was determined and the relationship between tenants and landlords have been regulated. However since 1997 the land leases have begun to expire. Over the last few years a lot of uncertainty has been created in the minds of the tenants, causing a decline in productivity and efficiency. Landowners have been demanding compensation for public

Figure 10.3   **Fiji government's expenditure, 1991–97**

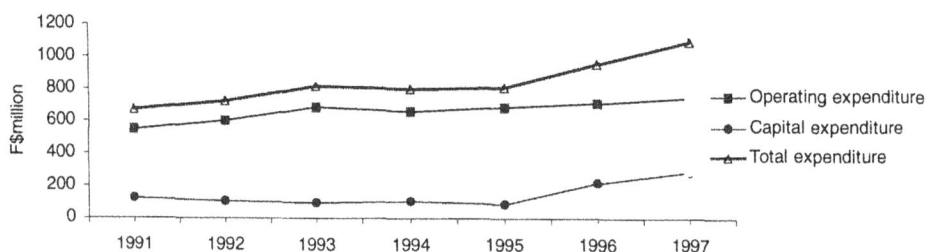

Source: Reserve Bank of Fiji, 1999. *Quarterly Bulletin*, March, Suva.

Table 10.4   **Fiji's total external and domestic debt (F$million)**

Year	External debt	Domestic debt
1992	499.07	638.2
1993	449.98	733.5
1994	399.17	792.3
1995	384.70	807.3
1996	353.64	942.8
1997	352.11	1,156.0
1998	394.29	1,060.6

Source: Reserve Bank of Fiji, 1999. *Quarterly Bulletin*, March, Suva: Tables 25 and 26.

infrastructure on native land and government will have to deal with more of this in the future.

The resolution of the ALTA legislation and the provision for the renewal of the leases is now an immediate priority for the government. Apart from the uncertainty in the farming sector, other sectors such as investment in fisheries development, forestry and tourism are also waiting for a satisfactory resolution to this issue.

The allocation for the ALTA tenant's resettlement and compensation of F$20 million is inadequate in view of the number of leases that are expiring. In 2000 about 1,828 farm leases will expire, of which 1,215 are sugar cane farm leases. If we take all the farm leases and multiply that by the planned F$28,000 compensation, or cost of resettlement, then government would have to budget for about F$51.184 million for 2000 alone. However, if government were to provide F$28,000 to just the cane farmers, it would still cost F$34.2 million. One can reduce this further by taking away 25 per cent of the leases occupied by indigenous Fijian tenants, but still it would cost F$25.536 million in 2000 to provide compensation to the cane farmers that would have lost their leases. Furthermore, the amount of F$28,000 is the cost of resettlement of the tenants, it does not compensate the tenants for the improvements, building and other farm implements which may attract very low market prices.

Fiji's sugar industry is passing through a critical period. First, there is insecurity of land tenure and the threat of non-renewal of leases after 1997. Second is the exposure of the industry to the changing global economic conditions. Currently the bulk of Fiji's sugar is sold under the Lomé Convention. This provides preferential arrangements for Fiji's sugar to be sold at more than the world market price in the European Union (EU). With the increasing globalisation of the world economy and the successful conclusion of the GATT, prices received for Fiji's sugar may not be sustainable in the long-run.

These circumstances have called for reforms within the sugar industry. With the increasing surge towards freer trade worldwide, the EU preferential price for Fiji sugar may end sooner rather than later. Reforms in the industry cannot proceed without a solution to the property rights structure in land. Reforms to increase efficiency and productivity without corresponding reforms in the system of land tenure are unlikely to yield the desired results.

Productivity in the sugar industry depends on many factors such as production cost, milling efficiency, availability of labour and fertiliser input. Increasing farmer indebtedness is also affecting investments in productivity. While these factors are an important consideration, the overwhelming concern of the farmers is about the tenure of their leases. So long as the lease question hangs in the balance any reform process designed to increase productivity could be counterproductive. The major concern of the tenants is the insecurity of their tenure and that the renewal of the leases will involve much higher rents. Table 10.5 shows the number of leases that expire in each year from 1997 to 2005.

After the adoption of the 1997 Constitution, the then prime minister and the leader of the Opposition worked towards setting up a committee which was in the process of working out the best possible arrangement to resolve the native land lease problems. The SVT government, in consultation with the Native Land Trust Board (NLTB), had agreed to renew about 90 per cent of the leases and out of 134 expiring leases, 104 had already been renewed.

The Chaudhry government opened up another controversial debate on the issue of converting state lands to native land. This issue is not new, but it did not have public support, nor has it had support in parliament since the 1950s. The state only owns 10 per cent of the land in Fiji, so it was considered that in the interest of good governance this land should remain under government control. The Chaudhry government tabled a Bill in parliament seeking the conversion of Crown schedule A and B land. It is yet to be debated. This in my view created more uncertainty in the minds of the tenant community and could potentially open up native title claims for the freehold land. The attempt to convert state land is not a new move, but when it was tried before it was found that there were no compelling reasons to do so. For example, the Burns Commission said '[t]here is no moral or legal reason why government should give up control of schedule A and B land which should be held in trust for the benefit of the colony as a whole for leasing or otherwise' (Legislative Council: Paper No.1).

Table 10.5   **Expiration of agricultural farm and cane leases in Fiji, 1997–2005**

Year	No. of farm leases	No. of cane leases
1997	45	26
1998	189	129
1999	231	168
2000	1,828	1,215
2001	1,808	1,536
2002	479	325
2003	645	466
2004	332	231
2005	288	244

Source: World Bank, 1995. *Fiji: restoring growth in a changing global environment*, The World Bank, Washington, DC.

The situation in Fiji is not comparable to Australia and New Zealand where the majority of the land is freehold. In Fiji 83 per cent of land is owned under native title.

The challenge for a new government will be to create a climate conducive to continuing the negotiations for a satisfactory resolution of the land lease problem. The Chaudhry government proposed to establish a land use commission to identify unused land. Inevitably, government has to allocate extra resources if the majority of the land leases are not renewed. This will put further strain on the budget.

Conclusions

The Chaudhry government's orientation towards a strong social agenda was laudable. However, its 2000 budget pointed to the fact that its economic policy direction did not change too radically after all. This may have been realistic given the world economic policy environment and the dependence of the Fijian economy on its main trading partners, Australia, New Zealand and the United States. The Chaudhry government may just have been a capitalist government in a socialist garb, like many Labour governments in other parts of the world.

Economic growth is the key to the delivery of promised social services. And for economic growth to occur the Fiji's government will have to promote the private sector as the engine of growth, since public sector expenditure will be limited given the country's current financial position. However, government should not shy away from some fundamental changes that may put Fiji in a better position as a small island country to endure the forces of global capitalism.

The issues that would need to be considered carefully for sustained levels of growth include the following

- consistent investment policy with appropriate incentives for the private sector
- competitive and productive labour force
- development of appropriate public infrastructure
- satisfactory resolution of the property rights in land generally and the more specifically the resolution of expiring native land leases under ALTA
- sound monetary and exchange rate policy to ensure that Fiji's exports are competitive in the world market
- competitive and productive labour market
- stability in government and a reduction in the crime rate.

Those who believed that Fiji's economic policy direction would change remarkably will be disappointed with the Chaudhry government's missed opportunity to implement policies that would have sent the right signals to the world economic community, the World Trade Organization and international organisations such as the International Monetary Fund and the World Bank—that countries can steer their own economic agenda and not fall into the global trap of world trade. In this sense the Chaudhry government's 2000 budget was no different; it continued with the policies of deregulation, financial liberalisation, free trade policy and disguised privatisation. For example, it continued to support limited privatisation hoping to make F$70 million from the sale of government shares, it suggested contracting out public services to private companies, it continued the policy of deregulation and it failed to consider changes in the taxation system which would have further led to the redistribution of wealth. There was hardly any change in overall economic policy direction, which is regrettable. It was the same old song, with a slightly different tune.

Note

An earlier version of this paper was presented at the Samoa and Fiji Focus, in association with the Centre for the Contemporary Pacific, The Australian National University and Economic Insights, Brisbane, 9 July 1999.

chapter eleven

Madness in May
George Speight and the unmaking of modern Fiji

Brij V. Lal

I would like to begin, if I may, with the month of May. It is an ill-fated month of some moment in the modern history of Fiji. It was on the 14th of May 1879 that the first group of 60,000 Indian indentured labourers arrived in Fiji, where their descendants now comprise about 43 per cent of the population. It was the election of a government headed by one of them that ostensibly precipitated the present crisis. Exactly 108 years later, on 14 May 1987, the Fijian military, acting on behalf of other social interests and institutions, attempted to close the parenthesis opened by the earlier voyage by overthrowing a duly elected government in which Indo-Fijians had finally found a measure of equitable representation. Thirteen years and five days later, on 19 May 2000, George Speight and six other gunmen once again interrupted democracy by hijacking the parliament, holding the prime minister and his government political prisoners and tearing up a constitution, once so widely praised, which had brought to power a multiracial People's Coalition. The forces unleashed by that cataclysmic event, still unfolding and gathering momentum, could potentially re-shape Fijian social and political life and re-structure traditional power relations in novel and significant ways, beyond what the makers of the May 19th mayhem may have imagined or wanted. The madness of May is likely to be with us for sometime yet.

Nonetheless, it possible to make some tentative assessments about what has happened and why, and to identify some possible future trends, mindful of the fact that historians are much better at predicting the past than divining the future. The present crisis has left in its wake an impressive list of casualties. The process of political reconciliation, symbolised by the 1997 constitution which was approved unanimously by a parliament dominated by indigenous Fijians, blessed by the Great Council of Chiefs and warmly welcomed by the international community, is among them.[1] The road of reconciliation had never been easy and yet political leaders of different communities and political persuasions had, over years of intense and open-hearted discussion, managed to forge a common national agenda. That paved the way for the appointment of a constitution commission whose widespread consultation throughout the country over some 12 months had not only reviewed the contested 1990 constitution but suggested a way forward and, in the process contributed significantly to national healing. 'The primary goal of Fiji's constitutional arrangements should be to encourage the emergence of multi-ethnic governments,' the Commission recommended. 'Power-sharing should be achieved through voluntary cooperation of political parties, or increased support for a genuinely multi-ethnic party. The people of Fiji should move gradually but decisively away from the communal system of representation. They should adopt electoral arrangements which encourage parties to seek the support of other communities as well as their own.' Those words hark back to an era now almost vanished beyond recall.

Ratu Sir Kamisese Mara, president of the republic, a central figure in contemporary Fijian public life and a paramount chief in his own right, was asked by the army to step aside, while the Republic of Fiji Military Forces assumed executive control of the country, sending him, after the presentation of a customary forgiveness-seeking *tabua* (whales tooth), under the cover of darkness, guarded by soldiers, on a patrol boat heading towards the Lau sea. It was a sad end to a distinguished though not uncontroversial career. Mara sought to play the role of the saviour as he had done so often in the past. He abandoned his democratically elected government and promised to review the constitution to enhance and further entrench Fijian rights in the hope of appeasing the rebels. But they saw him as a part of the problem, not a part of the solution, an imperious man, Speight said, who haboured dynastic ambitions. He, too, had to go, and he did reluctantly. His departure marked the final eclipse of the long reign in Fiji politics of powerful paramount chiefs with overarching authority and wide personal influence who were tutored for national leadership by the colonial government in the years following the Second World War.[2] No chiefs with even remotely close national influence are on the horizon. Many are embroiled in local, provincial and regional machinations to command national loyalty and support. And Rabuka's example shows that capable or ambitious commoners can rule just as well as those of chiefly blood. The old assumption that the business of national leadership is the business of chiefs no longer holds.

The crisis also ruined the reputation of once sacred institutions of Fijian society in previously unthinkable ways. Among them is the military, with a proud record of service in the jungles of Solomon Islands in World War II, in Malaya against the Chinese communist insurgents in the 1950s, and as peacekeepers in the Middle East in the 1970s. In the face of the coup, the army stood divided and confused, unable or, worse still, unwilling to uphold the constitution or protect the security of the state. The security forces were shown to be infected by the virus of provincialism and regionalism, insubordination and indiscipline.[3] Had martial law not been declared when it was, and the rebels gone further than they had, the army might well have fragmented into factions defending their own *vanua* (land, province) and chiefs. Once the bastion of indigenous Fijian power, the army is now a captive of indigenous vested interests.

The Great Council of Chiefs (GCC), seeking in recent years to enlarge its role and status as the guardian of national, and not only indigenous Fijian interests, failed the test of national leadership. 1997 gave constitutional recognition to this body for the first time in Fijian history. The Commission recommended that the GCC be set up as an independent body with its own secretariat and chairperson rather than coming under the ambit of the Fijian Affairs Act. The GCC would nominate the president and the vice president to be voted, without debate, by both houses of parliament though the Constitution dispensed with this and left the matter entirely in the hands of chiefs. The expectation was that with their independence guaranteed, the GCC would exercise a greater national role besides its traditional functions, as the guardian of the national interest. Sadly, the Chiefs failed the test of national leadership. They vacillated while the country awaited their wise counsel, which never came. Their deliberations got embroiled in traditional confederacy and provincial politics, their proceedings dominated by younger, more assertive chiefs wanting their own place in the Fijian sun, leading to further division and fragmentation. They backed Speight but then asked Ratu Mara to lead the country. Wittingly or unwittingly, they allowed themselves to be pressured by rebels to accede to their wishes, which kept escalating as the crisis dragged on. As army spokesman Col. Filipo Tarakinikini put it, the chiefs 'are riddled with personal agendas'[4] and incapable of impartial, decisive action.

However it is looked at, the hostage crisis-cum-coup is a disaster for Fiji. The economy, which was just beginning to recover from the downturn of the 1990s, is once again poised at the precipice.[5] The current crisis has cost the government millions in lost revenue, and the government's Microfinance Unit (in a paper prepared for the military) predicts a trade deficit of F$400 million. If the economy continues to decline, as it will, GDP would suffer a reversal of 13 per cent, exports decline by 22 per cent and imports by 20 per cent. Already, hundreds of workers, often those at the bottom of the economic ladder and, therefore the most vulnerable, have been laid off, especially in the handicraft, garment and tourism industries, and more will follow. Even if no trade bans were imposed, unemployment was expected to rise by 6 per cent, and some 7,000 workers are likely to be retrenched. Many local investors have already fled the country in the wake of riots which ravaged the commercial district of Suva, and their foreign counterparts will be equally hesitant to invest in a country wrecked by continuing civil unrest and breakdown of principles of good governance.

Some costs, though, are less easily measured. Within the indigenous Fijian society, for instance, old assumptions about the traditional structure of power have been questioned in novel and potentially significant ways. It is almost a truism now to say that this crisis, as it unfolded, became more about intra-Fijian rivalries than about race. Even George Speight himself admitted that 'the race issue between Fijians and Indians is just one piece of the jigsaw puzzle that has many pieces' (interview, *Fiji Sun* 10 June 2000). In this respect, it is unlike the crisis of 1987 which was seen largely as an ethnic conflict between Fijians and Indo-Fijians. It can be argued that the 1987 coups were about protecting the foundations of the Fijian establishment. Then, there was much sympathy for the Fijian 'cause' across the Pacific whereas now there is condemnation.[6] But this crisis is a coup against the Fijian establishment and traditional power arrangements. Some have argued convincingly that George Speight represents the interests of the Kubuna confederacy against the long ascendancy of the traditional hierarchies of the Koro Sea. His demand that Adi Samanunu should be appointed prime minister supports that contention. Tailevu chief Ratu Jope Seniloli is already one of two vice presidents. Fijian political analyst Jone Dakuvula's claim to this effect brought upon the local television station broadcasting his remarks the wrath of the Fijian mob allied to George Speight.[7]

As the crisis dragged on, the western chiefs, long aggrieved about their absence from the national centre of power threatened to secede from the state of Fiji, failing which they promised to settle for a much-cherished and long-demanded fourth confederacy, the *Yasayasa Vaka Ra*.[8] The west, they say, drives the engine of the national economy. Sugar, pine, gold and tourism are produced from its soil, and they want representation in national councils proportionate to their contribution to the national economy. The demand for a western confederacy is longstanding, and criticism of step-brotherly treatment of the west has been aired in various ways and in different fora for much of the twentieth century, beginning with Apolosi R. Nawaii and articulated by Apisai Tora and Ratu Osea Gavidi and other chiefs in the 1960s and since. The east-west divide exists, but it is not a sharp, clear line, extensively crisscrossed now by marriage and kinship ties that blur the distinctions of old (see *The Fiji Times* 10 June 2000). It is also important to emphasise that those Fijians who champion the cause of the fourth confederacy do not necessarily support democracy or espouse multiracialism. Tora is a classic example of one who champions one and rejects the other. The threatened secession of Western Viti Levu was followed by a declaration of partial autonomy by the province of Cakaudrove proposing to set up a separate Tovata state, but the declaration lacked conviction or authority (*Sunday Times* 11 June 2000). What it did indicate, however, was the willingness of the Fijian people to consider options unthinkable in the twentieth century. We may be witnessing the first fumbling efforts to dismantle the structure of power set in place in the latter half of the nineteenth century and blessed and nurtured by the colonial government. Fijian politics in future may be comprehensible only in terms of its pre-colonial, pre-cession past.

Race relations have been severely strained just when things looked to be on the mend following the successful review of the constitution; the scars of the present crisis—reflected in the images of looting and violence on the streets of Suva, the fleeing of terrorised Indo-Fijians from parts of the Rewa delta to safe havens in western Viti Levu, the destruction of schools and desecration of places of worship, the unruly Fijian mob roaming the neighbourhoods around the parliamentary complex—those scars will take a generation to heal. There are also deeper questions here than I can deal with, questions about culture and history and identity. The Fijian, the *taukei*, the indigenous owner of the land, who has lived side by side with his/her Indo-Fijian neighbour, still regards him/her as a *vulagi*, a foreigner, welcome to stay and enjoy the hospitality of the host but knowing fully well whose house it is.[9] Even the chiefs of western Fiji, who have—or should have—a better understanding of Indo-Fijian fears and aspirations and who oppose Speight, want Fiji to be declared a Christian state so that Hindus, Muslims and Christians can all solve their problems in the proper Christian way.

It is hugely ironic that many—not all—Fijians regard Indo-Fijians as the cause of their difficulties: noisy, insensitive, self-seeking, ungenerous, grubby, ungrateful, alien in their religion, social relationships and world view, altogether a most undesirable people. It is ironic because Indians were brought to Fiji to work on CSR sugar cane plantations in conditions often akin to slavery so that the indigenous population could be spared the fate of other similarly situated communities whose interests and aspirations were subjugated to those of the settler community. So Fijians continued to live in their subsistence villages, under the leadership of their chiefs, their lifestyle closely regulated by 'Native Regulations' and carefully formulated programs of work. The Indo-Fijians, on the other hand, laboured on plantations and when indenture ended in 1920, they established themselves through thrift and self-reliance on leased lands in scattered settlements in the sugar cane belts of Fiji. To escape the shadow of indenture and the petty humiliations and poverty that was their lot, Indo-Fijian parents struggled to provide their children education secure in the knowledge that while they could earn their livelihood from the farm, their children and grandchildren would not be able to. No affirmative action, no helping hand for them. It has been said often, and lost some of its force in reiteration, but it is true that Indo-Fijian labour contributed crucially to Fiji's economic and commercial development. Indo-Fijians, now fourth or fifth generation, are hurt to be still regarded as outsiders in the land of their birth, threatened with the denial of equal citizenship and equal protection of the law. Sometimes, those who applaud the indigenous Fijians for maintaining their culture and tradition ask the Indo-Fijians to subjugate theirs in the cause of assimilation. Salman Rushdie, writing about the Fiji crisis makes a telling point. 'Migrant people do not remain visitors forever,' he has written. 'In the end, their new land owns them as their old land did, and they have a right to own it in their turn' (*New York Times* 8 June 2000).

This crisis is far worse than its 1987 counterpart in terms of violence and damage to property. In 1987, the army was held responsible for the maintenance of law and order. To its credit, it did manage to contain the mobs. This time around, the mobs had a free hand, directed, if they were directed at all, by invisible hands in the parliamentary complex, armed and energized by Speight's racial rhetoric, terrorising the rural Indian countryside for food and fun, as they did in the hinterland of Nausori. The main targets were Indo-Fijians in outlying rural areas, their cattle slaughtered and root crops stolen. After 1987, some 70,000–80,000 migrated from Fiji, most of them Indo-Fijians. They now live in Australia, New Zealand, Canada and the United States. It is often said that there is hardly an Indo-Fijian family in Fiji which does not have at least one member outside. Kinship has become a multinational or transnational corporation, sustaining those left behind on money remitted from abroad. Now, many more would leave—the doctors, the computer technicians, mechanics, the accountants. In short, virtually anyone who is accepted outside will go, draining the country of skills it can ill-afford. 'I would rather be a dog in America than an Indian in Fiji,' said a man whose house had been demolished and his possessions taken by Fijian mobs. He was not alone in holding that thought. Indo-Fijians will leave, in larger numbers than ever before. Perhaps, in a hundred years time, some future historian may see the Indian presence in Fiji as a temporary stopover in a long and fateful millenarian journey.

The public face, though not perhaps the principal instigator, of this crisis was George Speight. A businessman with a career littered with failures in Australia and Fiji (and possibly elsewhere as well), the 45 year old Speight was wandering on the fringes of the local commercial circles on the eve of the coup.[10] He had been sacked by Agriculture Minister Poseci Bune as Chairman of the Fiji Pine Commission and the Hardwood Corporation. Shortly before he stormed parliament, he had been negotiating on behalf of the American company Trans Resources Management (TRM) to win a tender for harvesting the country's massive mahogany forests valued at over $F300 (see *Sunday Times* 11 June 2000). The government chose the

Commonwealth Development Corporation, with a proven record in the exploitation of natural resources. Speight was declared an undischarged bankrupt and was about to face court proceedings when he launched his assault on parliament. Clearly, Speight had his own private grievances, which he carefully hid behind a fiercely nationalist rhetoric. Like Sitiveni Rabuka in 1987, Speight portrayed himself as a faithful servant of the Fijian cause, an anointed saviour of the Fijian 'race.' Speight, however, is no Rabuka, as even his most ardent supporters admit. Indeed, an important reason why the international community—as seen in Australian Foreign Minister Alexander Downer's and New Zealand's Phil Goff's reaction— has been so severe in its condemnation of Fiji is because of George Speight as the face of indigenous Fijian nationalism. A part-European of Fijian descent, head shaved, Speight was articulate, engaging, bantering with the international media; still, for all that, he was an unconvincing Fijian hero. And as time has gone on, his facade has been exposed. He is no champion of Fijian interests: he is a champion of his own interests. He has threatened and ridiculed the chiefs, insisted, indeed, demanded that chiefs do his bidding. Having had an ill and aging Ratu Josefa Iloilo installed as president, and agreeing to abide by the president's decision, he reneges on his undertaking and demands that his own candidate, Adi Samanunu Cakobau, a high chief of Bau, be installed as prime minister.

But it would be a grave mistake to see George Speight acting all on his own. If he were, the crisis would have had a limited and inconsequential life. Behind him, in the shadows, were individuals and groups, writing his speeches, devising position papers, building up the mass support base, and orchestrating the crowds, people who had little to lose but everything to gain from the overthrow of the Chaudhry government. Among them were politicians defeated at the last elections or otherwise excluded from power, and seeking redress and probably revenge. Apisai Tora and Berenado Vunibobo come readily to mind. The Fijian opposition leader Ratu Inoke Kubuabola was there as well, and so, strangely enough, were factional leaders of Fijian political parties in coalition with Chaudhry's Labour Party. Fijian Association Party's Adi Kuini Vuikaba Speed is the Deputy Prime Minister, but Ratu Cokanauto Tua'akitau was with Speight's group. Apisai Tora, the founder of the spectacularly mis-named Party of National Unity, wanted Chaudhry's head, but three members of his party were in the cabinet.

Speight was also supported by people like himself, young businessmen on the make, who rode the gravy train of the 1990s, benefited from opportunistic access to power, secured large, unsecured loans from the National Bank of Fiji, but then found their prospects for continued prosperity dimming upon the election of a new government. Prominent local businessmen-cum politicians in the previous SVT government supported the destabilisation campaign.[11] For them, the Chaudhry government had to go before it managed to entrench itself. In this group of the ambitious, upwardly mobile, I would also include what one might call the 'Children of 1987'. This group includes those who benefited from the post-coup racially-based affirmative action programs—sanctioned by the 1990 constitution—in the award of scholarships, promotions in the civil service, and training opportunities. They were the children of privilege, sons and daughters of the well connected. Many of them had come of age in the mid-1990s, at the height of SVT government's reign.[12] This new generation of fast-tracked Fijian middle class had a narrow, limited experience of multiculturalism, and little taste or patience for it. They contrast starkly with an earlier post-independence generation of the 1970s, which grew up working in a multicultural environment, dedicated to professionalism and the principles of good governance, under governments publicly committed to a unifying vision.[13] The 'Children of 1987' did not understand nor approve of the spirit of the 1997 constitution.

While the indigenous Fijian middle class, or at least sections of it, provided the brains for Speight's agenda, the Fijian social underclass provided the brawn. The bedraggled unemployed, unskilled Fijian youth armed with sticks, knives, bamboo spears, stones and some with guns who looted, burned and trashed Suva, terrorised the countryside, and acted as human shield for Speight and his men, had little understanding of the larger, hidden personal agendas and complex forces at work. They were in some sense the human casualties of globalisation and economic rationalism and, more immediately, the victims of the structural reform policies pursued by the Rabuka government in the 1990s. They could not understand why they remained behind, mired in poverty and destitution, unemployed and unemployable, while others had moved on. Without hope and without a future, they fell easy prey to George Speight's mesmeric rhetoric and easy solutions: get rid of the Indians, revert to tradition, put Fijians in political control, and all would be well. Speight gave them a purpose, an explanation, a mission and a brief spot in the Fijian sun. They in turn responded enthusiastically to his clarion call of racial solidarity.

How did this crisis come to a head? To understand this, it is necessary to look at events over the previous 12 months, beginning with the 1999 general elections which took place under the revised 1997 constitution.[14] Chaudhry's Labour Party won 37 of the 71 seats in its own right. Together with his other coalition partners, Party of National Unity (PANU), Fijian Association Party (FAP) and Veitokani ni Levenivanua Vakaristo (VLV), the People's Coalition won 58 seats. The unexpectedly large victory was due to two factors: an effective campaign against the outrages and excesses of the Rabuka government, of which there were many, and a sharp, carefully calibrated focus on the bread and butter issues affecting ordinary working and middle class people. Labour promised to roll back the unemployment-causing structural reform programs of the Rabuka government, introduce minimum wages, lower interests on housing rates, provide social security for the elderly, resolve the long-festering issue of expiring agricultural leases. These un-costed but electorally appealing policies were effective on the hustings, but they came to haunt the party when it came to power. The opposition National Federation Party (NFP), Fiji's oldest political party long the champion of Indo-Fijian interests, which did not win a single seat, opportunistically kept the government's heel close to the fire. To counteract criticism and keep its support base from fragmenting, the Chaudhry government embarked on a hectic program of legislative reform, setting up commissions (Education and Human Rights), instituting inquiries (into corruption), and staffing statutory organisations with competent staff (Housing Authority).

The appearance of movement and change was impressive, but it also embroiled the government in a hugely counterproductive tussle with the media. Small things were magnified in an atmosphere already rife with suspicion and distrust about the government's motives.[15] Why did Chaudhry appoint his own son, not a civil servant, as his personal assistant on the public pay roll? Here was a man who, as long term secretary of the Fiji Public Service Association, had been scathing of nepotism and corruption in previous governments, but once in power, had begun to ignore his own wise counsel about transparent governance and public accountability. There was nothing illegal in the appointment: a prime minister can, of course, appoint anybody he or she wants. But the perception of the government favouring its own was created, which stuck despite repeated denial. Fijian civil servants, appointed under the Rabuka government when ethnicity and loyalty were privileged over merit and seniority, complained about being marginalised and not consulted in important decision making.

Faced with intensifying opposition, the governed battened down the hatches. To every question and all opposition, it chanted—to its opponents with constant, arrogant regularity—the mantra of having a mandate to do what it had promised in its election manifesto. The government did have a mandate, but its mandate was one among many in Fiji. The parliament is not the sole source of all power in Fiji: the Native Land Trust Board has its mandate to look after native land, the Great Council of Chiefs has its own mandate under the constitution, the Army its own. It was the failure, or perhaps the unwillingness, to balance the complex equation of competing mandates that compounded the government's problems. Chaudhry's own forceful personality, forged in the long years spent in the trade union movement, also played its part in galvanising the opposition. Chaudhry is highly intelligent and resourceful, tenacious and uncompromising (confrontational to his opponents), a born fighter who was a painful thorn in the side of the Rabuka government for years. He was feared by Fijians, but not trusted. He was a strong and decisive leader of a generally weak cabinet, and his opponents, rightly or wrongly, saw his unmistakable imprint on every policy decision of the government.

Another problem facing the government was the fractious nature of the People's Coalition itself. As mentioned, the Coalition was a loose structure made up of four parties: Labour, PANU, FAP and VLV. Some of these parties espoused philosophies directly contradictory to Labour's. The VLV, for example, wanted to make Fiji a Christian State and have an urgent review of the 1997 constitution to address the concerns of the Fijian people, both of which Labour repudiated (see Lal 1999:14–15). Indeed, soon after the elections, Bune of the VLV had threatened to lead a coalition of Fijian parties against Chaudhry—until he was inducted into cabinet reportedly at Ratu Sir Kamisese Mara's behest. PANU had its own agenda for western Fiji, as did the FAP for southeastern Viti Levu, its stronghold. But what they all had in common was their adamant opposition to Sitiveni Rabuka, both for who he was and what he had done. He was not forgiven for the coups of 1987 by one side, and punished by another for breaching the traditional protocol regarding the appropriate place for commoners in the traditional Fijian social hierarchy dominated by chiefs. Opposition to a common enemy, then, rather than commitment to a common agenda, brought the disparate groups together. And when that enemy (Rabuka) was defeated, the difficulties of internal cohesion came to the fore, almost immediately after the election. Chaudhry rightly took steps to become prime minister: his party had an outright majority in parliament. The FAP cried foul, accusing Labour of reneging on a deal that a Fijian, one of its own members, would be chosen prime minister by the Coalition. Chaudhry was helped unobtrusively and opportunistically by Ratu Mara who urged the Fijian parties to rally behind Chaudhry, but Chaudhry's ascension also split the coalition. A faction of the FAP disregarded Adi Kuini's leadership and informally aligned itself with other Fijian opposition parties, eventually going so far as to back George Speight. Tora became a fierce rabble rousing critic of the government, expressing his disgruntlement by leading a revived Taukei Movement. So the Chaudhry government was buffeted by its opponents and hobbled by internal divisions, speaking on crucial issues with discordant voices.

The issue which united the Fijians was land. Land has always been a sensitive issue in Fijian politics (see Lal 1992:224–7). The question always has been the use rather than the ownership of land. Now, 83 per cent of all land in Fiji—3,714,990 acres—is held in inalienable rights by indigenous Fijians, 8.2 per cent is freehold, state freehold is 3.6 per cent and Crown or State land 5 per cent.[16] Much of the country's agricultural activity—in particular sugar cultivation—is carried out on land leased from Fijian landowners. The country's 22,000 cane growers, the overwhelming majority of whom are Indo-Fijians, lease native land under the Agricultural Landlord and Tenant Act. This Act, which came into existence in 1969, provides for 30 year leases, whose renewal is negotiated between the tenants and landlords upon the expiry of the leases. These leases are beginning to expire and some, but by no means all, landlords want their land back either to cultivate the land themselves, re-zone it for commercial or residential purposes, or use the threat of non-renewal to extract more rent. They are led by the head of the Native Land Trust Board, Marika Qarikau. He is by all accounts, a hard-line, abrasive nationalist who has used every means available, from addressing the provincial councils to using the network of the Methodist Church, to rally Fijian landowners behind him and against the government. The NLTB is Qarikau's power base, and he, too, claims a mandate: to protect native Fijian land. Three weeks after the coup, Qarikau circulated a 20 page 'Deed of Sovereignty' which demands, among other things, the return of all state and freehold land to native ownership.

Chaudhry did not contest the land owners' desire to reclaim their land. Nor, on other hand, could he—or any government for that matter—ignore the human plight of the tenants, unskilled, uneducated, poor, evicted from land their families had cultivated for four our five generations. The government offered the displaced tenants F$28,000 to start afresh in some other occupation, and about F$8,000 to landlords who repossessed their former leasees' land to become cultivators themselves. Meanwhile, it also resuscitated the idea of a Land Use Commission (LUC), mentioned in his party's manifesto but with a history going back nearly forty years, to work with landowners to identify idle land and to put it to productive use, including, if possible, for resettlement of the displaced tenants. With the NLTB on a war path, the government went directly to the Fijian landlords. Early in 2000, it sent a delegation of Fijian landowning chiefs to Malaysia to familiarise themselves with the work of a similar commission there. The chiefs returned impressed but by then, Qarikau had already orchestrated a move among the provincial councils to reject the concept outright. Poseci Bune, the Agriculture Minister, recalled the malicious misinformation spread among the people. In one province, he was told, the LUC was a ploy by Chaudhry to bring Indians to Fiji. Apparently Air India had expressed an interest in opening an office in Suva. But this was a false front. The main aim behind setting up an Air India office was to bring Indians from India to settle on land identified for development by the LUC. Faced with this malicious propaganda, the government then did what it should have done earlier: it took the proposal to the Great Council of Chiefs, which approved it in principle but asked the government and the NLTB to develop it further cooperatively. It was a hard fought victory for the government.

Just when the government seemed to be gaining an upper hand as shown in generally approving polls, Tora's Taukei Movement re-surfaced in western Viti Levu, fuelling and galvanising extreme Fijian opinion against the government. The Cakaudrove Provincial Council passed a vote of no confidence in the government, and others followed. Ratu Tevita Bolobolo, Tui Navitilevu, formed a landowners' council, Matabose ni Taukei ni Vanua, attacking the government and threatening non-renewal of leases. Ratu Tevita had lost to Labour in the 1999 general election. Taniela Tabu, former Taukei Movement stalwart and a trade unionist with a chequered career, formed the Viti National Union of Taukei Workers and attacked the Chaudhry government for 'Indianising the public service.' The charge was baseless—the upper echelons of the public service, and nearly 90 per cent of the permanent heads of government departments, were dominated by indigenous Fijians—but effective among many Fijians already distrusting of the government. The Christian Democrats labelled the government—in which it was partner—anti-Fijian over its hesitation to renew the work visa of expatriate Fiji TV head Kenneth Clark, because the Fijian provinces held the majority shares in the company headed by Clark.

The protest movement, small and disorganised at first, gained momentum and focus as May drew near. The government continued to chant the mantra of mandate and refused to acknowledge that trouble was in the offing, dismissing the marches as the work of a few miscreants and misguided people. The police commissioner Isekia Savua's public warning to the government to raise its political antenna to catch the grumbling on the ground was ignored, and Savua chastised for daring, as a public servant, to advise the government on questions of policy. Convinced that its policies were beginning to bear fruit and were popular with the electorate, which had learned the hard lessons of 1987, the government adopted a business-as-usual approach as tension mounted around the countryside. Ignoring all the warning signals, the government sent the Commander of the Military Forces, Commodore Frank Bainimarama to Norway on an official trip. The Police Commissioner was on holidays, and the President was away in Lau celebrating his 80th birthday. When the parliament met on 19th May, marking the first anniversary in government, no special security precautions were taken, no special police forces were deployed around the parliamentary complex. While the police force focused on the 5,000 protest marchers downtown heading towards the Government House to present a petition to the president, Speight and his men stormed parliament around 10 am, led by 20 year SAS veteran Major Ilisoni Ligairi and members of the Counter Revolutionary Warfare Unit he had set up at the request of the 1987 coup leader Sitiveni Rabuka.

How the crisis the unfolded since the early days is a subject that requires separate treatment. But that account would include a discussion of the violence and terror unleashed upon an unsuspecting population by Speight's gang, the struggle for power among important sections of indigenous Fijian society, the muddled, and as it turned out unconstitutional, attempts to maintain a semblance of constitutional normalcy amidst a grave and rapidly deepening crisis, the tense stand off between the army and the rebels, the takeover of police and army barracks throughout the country, the roadblocks designed to immobilise the country, the disabling of utilities, the international condemnation and the imposition of sanctions. Within a fortnight after he had staged his coup, Speight had achieved virtually all his goals. Mahendra Chaudhry's Peoples' Coalition government was out. Ratu Mara was also forced to vacate his office. The 1997 constitution was abrogated with promise made by the Great Council of Chiefs to install a new one entrenching Fijian political paramountcy. And Speight and his co-conspirators had received pardon for their deeds with full and unconditional amnesty to follow upon the release of all the hostages and return of illegally seized arms. But I want to turn now to the basic question: what do George Speight and his supporters want?

Of course, they want power for themselves and their 'cause' but that cause is explained to the world in various ways. One, emotionally appealing in nations of dispossessed and disadvantaged indigenous minorities is 'indigenous rights'. To gain sympathy, Speight has often equated the supposed fate of the indigenous Fijians with that of the Maori and the Aborigine, and judging by media reports, not altogether unsuccessfully. And he has invoked various international conventions on indigenous and civil rights to bolster his claims. Speight is not the first to play the indigenous card. Ratu Mara had sent a similar message to the Lau Provincial Council in 1988, when he had said: 'The Fijian people are all too aware of the destiny of the indigenous Aztecs of Mexico, the Incas of Peru, the Mayans of Central America, the Caribs of Trinidad and Tobago, the Inuits of Canada, the Maori of New Zealand and the Aborigines of Australia, to a name a few' (*Fiji Times* 11 May 1989). But Fijians are not Maori or Aborigines or Hawaiians or Kanaks. The majority of Fiji's population now, they own nearly all the land in Fiji as well as fisheries and forests, and receive substantial royalties from the extraction of mineral resources. The army is theirs, as well as 75 per cent of the permanent heads of departments and the police force, to name only a few. They have their own separate system of administration and parliamentary power of veto over all legislation affecting Fijian rights and interests.

Speight and his nationalist supporters have frequently invoked international conventions on indigenous rights in support of their claims or their 'cause.' In particular, they have cited *ILO Convention no 169 on Indigenous and Tribal Peoples* and the *Draft Declaration on the Rights of Indigenous Peoples.*[17] I admit that these instruments are susceptible to multiple readings, but as we (the Constitution Review Commission) read them, it was clear that neither instrument assumes that tribal and indigenous peoples will necessarily be a minority in the country where they live. In the main, they are concerned with situations in which the land, culture and separate identity of indigenous peoples may be at risk, as, for example, in Hawaii, New Zealand and Australia. That being the case, the relevance of these instruments to indigenous Fijians is remote. As already noted, Fijian land and distinct cultural identity have always been protected through the Native Land Act and the Fijian Affairs Act. The two instruments focus on the special rights of indigenous peoples as a distinct community, but make it clear that indigenous people equal citizenship rights with other communities in society. Article 2 of *Convention 169* requires governments to ensure that

> Members of these peoples benefit on equal footing from the rights and opportunities which national laws and regulations grant to other members of the population.

Article 3 (1) provides

> Indigenous and tribal peoples shall enjoy the full measure of human rights and fundamental freedoms without hindrance or discrimination.

The *Draft Declaration* makes similar provisions. Article 1 provides that

> Indigenous peoples have the right to the full and effective enjoyment of all human rights and fundamental freedoms recognised in the Charter of the United Nations, the Universal Declaration of Human Rights and international human rights law.

Article 4 provides

> Indigenous peoples have the right to maintain and strengthen their distinct political, economic, social and cultural characteristics, as well as their legal systems, while retaining their rights to participate fully, if they so choose, in the political, social and cultural life of the State.

The Commission concluded from these documents that 'at the national level, the political and other rights of indigenous peoples are on exactly the same footing as those of other members of the national society. Both instruments see the special rights of indigenous peoples as distinct communities as supplementing the fundamental human rights and freedoms they already share with all other citizens. Nothing in either instrument gives an indigenous people superior or paramount rights in taking part in the government of their country.'[18] As far as self-determination is concerned, the *Draft Declaration* (Article 3) provides that

Indigenous peoples have the right of self determination. By virtue of that right they freely determine their political status and freely pursue their economic, social and cultural development.

The Commission advised that the phrase 'freely determine their political status' should be read in context. The phrase refers to indigenous peoples 'taking control of their own affairs, not their political status as it affects their participation in the national government.' The indigenous Fijians already, and still, exercise complete self-determination over their land and social and cultural affairs. The point the Commission sought to emphasise was that no political community, by reference to either 'self-determination' or 'sovereignty', can legitimately claim that it has political rights which entitle it to a position of dominance over other groups forming part of the same national society'.[19]

Speight has also frequently invoked the emotionally charged phrase 'paramountcy of Fijian interests' in support of his claim. The phrase has a long and contested history in Fiji politics. Many who invoke it assume its origins in the Deed of Cession. That assumption is factually incorrect. These words do not occur once in the document. The chiefs, the Deed noted, had 'determined to tender unconditionally' the sovereignty of the islands to Queen Victoria and her successors 'relying upon the justice and generosity' of Her Majesty in dealing with her subject peoples. Cession, the Chiefs hoped would promote 'Civilisation' and 'Christianity'—their words—in the islands and secure good and stable government for all its residents, native and while, putting an end to the turbulence of the preceding decades. Towards these ends, the Crown promised that the 'rights and interests of the said Tui Viti and other high chiefs of the ceding parties hereto shall be recognised so far as it is and shall be consistent with British Sovereignty and Colonial form of government.' Nonetheless, from the early years of the twentieth century, the colonial government, and even some of the very same planter community which coveted Fijian land, used the phrase.

The government did so partly out of genuine concern for the welfare of the indigenous community so that it could boast of at least one colony in the world where the protection of indigenous interests, over and above the interests of settler and other immigrant communities, formed the cornerstone of colonial policy. But, of course, the principle also served the interests of the colonisers for by invoking it, the government was able to blunt the Indo-Fijian demand for political change which accorded them power in a compartmentalised colonial society roughly commensurate with their numbers and contribution to society. 'Paramountcy of Fijian interests,' in its original usage referred to protecting indigenous Fijian institutions and social and cultural practices which were then placed above and beyond the purview of ordinary public debate. Other communities accepted this arrangement, which was given watertight legislative and later constitutional protection. But to extend this to demand political paramountcy at the expense of the fundamental democratic rights of other citizens makes a mockery, and is in breach, of virtually every international instrument on civil, political and human rights.

Moreover, the ideal of permanent Fijian political unity. The Fijians, like other people in Fiji and elsewhere, have a diversity of interests across occupations, regions and social and economic interests. In the past, many Fijians lived a subsistence lifestyle in villages united by a common purpose and aspirations, but today nearly 40 per cent of them live in urban and peri-urban areas, facing a variety of conflicting challenges and opportunities. That makes it difficult, if not impossible, for one political party to cater for a huge multiplicity of interests. As the Commission pointed out, the 'emphasis on Fijian unity also means that Fijians are not free to vote out a Fijian government if it does not deliver what they expect.' The idea that 'a Fijian government must be maintained in office at all costs has grave consequences for political accountability. It requires setting aside the normal democratic controls on a government's performance in office. That is bad for the Fijian community as well as for the country as a whole.'[20] In any case, indigenous Fijians, under the 1990 constitution, had an outright majority in parliament, but they fragmented politically to such an extent that they could form government only with the support of non-Fijian parties and independents. No constitution can keep a Fijian government in office permanently unless, of course, it jettisons all pretence to democratic rule altogether.

Speight and his supporters want affirmative action for the indigenous Fijian and Rotuman people. The 1997 constitution already provides for affirmative action in its Compact: 'Affirmative action and social justice programs to secure effective equality of access to opportunities, amenities or services for the Fijian and Rotuman people, as well as for other communities, for women as well as men, and for all disadvantaged citizens or groups, are based on an allocation of resources broadly acceptable to all communities.' Broadly acceptable could be interpreted in the context of the previous section which enjoins the government to continue applying the principle of the paramountcy of Fijian interests as a protective principle 'so as to ensure that the interests of the Fijian community are not subordinated to the interests of other communities.' Fijians could reasonably expect to receive more than 50 per cent of public assistance on the strength of their population size, as, indeed, they were. But the assumption that only Fijians are in need of assistance is misleading. Study after study of income levels and poverty has shown that, among Fijian and Indo-Fijian households, each group has a roughly comparable percentage living in poverty, though there are some differences, depending on what measure of poverty is used and whether the household is urban, or in a village or settlement.

It is also important to stress that indigenous Fijians are not as disadvantaged in the public sector as is often claimed. In 1985, Fijians made up 46.4 per cent of established public servants, Indo-Fijians 48 per cent and General Voters and expatriates 5.6 per cent. The figures by October 1995 were Fijians 57. 3 per cent, Indo-Fijians 38.6 percent and General Voters and expatriates 4.1 percent. In 1995, of the 31 permanent secretaries, 22 were Fijians, 6 were Indo-Fijians and 3 were General Voters.[21] The pattern of disproportionate Fijian representation in the upper echelons of the public service, the police and some other sectors has continued. It is, of course, true that in the commercial sector, indigenous Fijian participation has been disappointing, but affirmative action for them in this area has been in place since the 1970s. The Fiji Development Bank, established in 1967, has for many years provided loans for a range of economic activities to Fijians through the Commercial and Industrial Loans and the Joint Venture Loans schemes. In 1974, the Project Evaluation Unit was created in the Ministry of Fijian Affairs to 'assist Fijians both individually and in groups to understand, cope and operate within the modern business world' (Lal 1992:232–3). The name of the Unit was changed to the Fijian Business Opportunity and Management Advisory Services (BOMAS). Between May 1975 and December 1984, Fijians received, without parliamentary debate, soft loans to the sum of $F6,721,553, not an insignificant sum for a small island nation like Fiji. And these and other schemes have continued since then. If they have not been attended by a reasonable level of success, Fijian leaders need to ask why. Merely enacting more affirmative action plans will not achieve the desired results.[22] Cultural as well as institutional factors would need to be thoroughly examined to identify the causes of commercial failure among Fijians.

George Speight laments the 'gradual erosion of things that are important to Fijians in their own country' (see *Fiji Sun* 10 June 2000). This erosion has been taking place for many decades. In the early 1980s, Fijian geographer and administrator Isireli Lasaqa had sounded similar warnings about the gradual disintegration of rural Fijian society: 'the weakening of Fijian social organisation and kinship ties as a means of providing some measure of social welfare to its members,' 'the encouragement of an enquiring mind and a willingness to question tradition, rather than a passive acceptance of fate.' The social system, Lasaqa said,

> has become increasingly coarse so that more and more elderly Fijians pass through the net and cannot derive much support and benefit from the system. In other words the kinship links have weakened and

the younger generation, with their increased commercial sense, greater individual needs, and commitment to their nuclear family, are either unwilling or unable to look after their aged relatives (in Lal 1992b:111).

Other Fijian leaders and intellectuals have echoed similar sentiments, expressing deep doubts about the efficacy of traditional institutions and practices in the modern arena.

Sitiveni Rabuka

I believe that the dominance of customary chiefs in government is coming to an end and that the role of merit chiefs will eventually overcome those of traditional chiefs: the replacement of traditional aristocracy with meritocracy (*Fiji Times* 29 August 1991).

Ropate Qalo

[Traditional authority] is a farce, because Fijians want the new God, not the old traditional Dakuwaqa or Degei. The new God is money and the new chapel is the World Bank. Like all the rest of the world, traditional authority has to go or be marginalised (*Islands Business*, January 1991).

Asesela Ravuvu

Most Fijians have taken the opportunity of being freed from the yoke of subservience to traditional authority and obeisance then supported by statutory sanctions. They have continued to assert their individual rights and freedom and made new social links and political alignments. This has posed a threat to the long established Fijian traditional order and its hierarchical structure of chiefly authority (Ravuvu 1988:189).

Jale Moala

[The Fijian people] are now facing so many issues that challenge the very fabric of traditional and customary life. Things they thought were sacred have become political topics, publicly debated, scrutinised and ridiculed. The Fijians are threatened and this time the threat is coming from within their own communities where the politics of numbers are changing loyalties and alliances. For the first time in modern history, the Fijian community is in danger of fragmentation; democracy is taking its toll. The chiefs are losing their mana and politicians enjoy increasing control (*Fiji Times* 21 March 1992).

Simione Durutalo

> If the average Fijian worker doesn't see the bus fare coming down and his son has graduated from USP and doesn't have a job, he's not going to be very amused. No matter how much you talk about tradition and the GCC (Great Council of Chiefs), you can't eat them (*The Review* December 1993).

Two decades later, the problems remain. They will not disappear. The solution? Army spokesman Col. Filipe Tarakinikini

> The social problems facing our country cannot be solved by putting in place a constitution that guarantees 100 per cent the rights and paramountcy of indigenous Fijians in this country. It will not safeguard, it will not ensure, that indigenous Fijians will succeed. The only way we indigenous Fijians will succeed is to make sure that we make sacrifices today for the sake of our prosperity tomorrow (Talk on Radio FM 96, 4 June 2000).

He is echoing a point Ratu William Toganivalu made several years ago: 'We, the indigenous people of this country, should not be tempted into the notion that by suppressing the Indian people, it would enhance our lot. If you do that, we are all suppressed' (*Hansard* 30 June 1992).

Forces of social and economic change cannot be arrested by the barrel of the gun. The ultimate, inescapable truth is that Fiji is an island, but an island in the physical sense alone. There is no alternative to co-existence.

Notes

This chapter is based on a Paper given at the Stout Research Centre, Victoria University of Wellington in July 2000.

1   The making of the 1997 constitution is covered in Lal 1998.
2   The four great chiefs of the latter half of the twentieth century groomed for leadership by the British were Ratu George Cakobau, Ratu Edward Cakobau, Ratu Penaia Ganilau and Ratu Kamisese Mara.
3   See Army spokesman Col. Filipe Tarakinikini's statement on *fijilive*, 14 June 2000: 'The army is just a reflection of society, so what is happening there [fragmentation] is happening in the army as well; you can't deny that.'
4   Interview in *The Australian* 14 June 2000. See also *Daily Post*, 9 June 2000 for a similar view from Marika Qarikau, manager of the Native Land Trust Board.

5   See *Pacnews* 9 June 2000 and *Sunday Sun* 4 June 2000 for more discussion.

6   There are some notable exceptions, though, including Cook Island's Geoffrey Henry (*Cook Island News* 27 May 2000), and New Zealand Maori lawyer Anthony Sinclair (*fijilive* 3 June 2000) who declared, without irony: 'We believe that revolution is a legitimate part of the democratic process.'

7   Information such as this is a part of the public record, broadcast by *fijilive*, hence it is not necessary to provide documentation. A copy of the transcript is at the Centre for the Contemporary Pacific, The Australian National University.

8   This is discussed at length in Simione Durutalo, 1985.

9   For more discussion of this concept, see Asesela Ravuvvu, 1991.

10 For a profile of Speight, see *Fiji Times* 23 May 2000.

11 In the papers, Fiji businessmen Kanti Punja and Jim Ah Koy, among others, have been identified, but both have denied involvement.

12 Good representatives of this cohort would include Speight's legal advisor Ratu Raquita Vakalalabure, Ro Filipe Tuisawau, Saimone Kaitani, Ratu Timoci Silatolu among others.

13 Among them would be names such as Josefata Kamikamica, Mosese Qionabaravi, Savenaca Siwatibau, among others.

14 I have discussed the elections in Lal 1999.

15 See, for example, Bingham 2000.

16 For more discussion, see Josefata Kamikamica 1997.

17 I base my comments here on the Report of the Fiji Constitution Review Commission, 43ff.

18 Ibid:44.

19 Ibid:46.

20 Ibid:15.

21 Ibid:228.

22 The latest example is Laisenia Qarase's 'Blueprint for the protection of Fijian and Rotuman rights and interests, and the advancement of their development,' a Paper presented to the Great Council of Chiefs on 13 July 2000.

References

Adams, T., 1989. *Fiji Fisheries Aid, 1979–1989*, Fisheries Division, Suva.

Aidney, C.D., Ratuvuki, L. and Teaiwa, T., 1994. *Report of the Committee of Inquiry into the Rabi Council Affairs*, Fiji Government Printing Office, Suva.

Alailima, F. and vom Busch, W., 1994. *New Politics in the South Pacific*, Institute of Pacific Studies, University of the South Pacific, Suva.

Anderson, J. and Neary, J.P., 1994. 'Measuring the restrictiveness of trade policy', *World Bank Economic Review*, May 8(2):151–69.

Bellamy, J.A., Lowes, D., Ash, A.J., McIvor, J.G. and MacLeod, N.D., 1996. 'A decision support approach to sustainable grazing management for spatially heterogeneous rangeland paddocks', *The Rangeland Journal*, 18(2):370–91.

Bingham, Eugene, 2000. 'Fiji tragedy woven from many strands', *New Zealand*, 3–4 June.

Carleton, C., 1983. *Guidelines for Establishment and Management of Collection, Handling, Processing and Marketing Facilities for the Artisanal Fisheries Sector in the South Pacific Commission Area*, SPC/Fisheries 15/WP.6, Noumea.

Chand, S. and Abello, R., 1997. The emerging challenges for the Fiji sugar industry, National Centre for Development Studies, The Australian National University, Canberra (unpublished).

Clapham, C., 1985. *Third World Politics: an introduction*, Croom Helm, London.

Collinson, M., 1987. 'Farming systems research: procedures for technology development', *Experimental Agriculture*, 23:365–86.

Convention on the Elimination of Discrimination Against Women (CEDAW), 1999. *Draft Initial Reports for the Fiji Islands*, CEDAW.

Crocombe, M., 1994. 'Women and politics in Polynesia', in F. Alailima and W. vom Busch (eds), *New Politics in the South Pacific*, Institute of Pacific Studies, University of the South Pacific, Suva.

Davidson, A.P., 1987. 'Does farming systems research have a future?', *Agricultural Administration and Extension*, (24):69–77.

Davies, J., 1997. *An Analysis of the Efficiency of Fiji's Sugar Cane Rail System*, University of the South Pacific, Suva.

Dean, E. and Ritova, S., 1988. *Rabuka: no other way*, The Marketing Team International, Suva.

Devaki, J., 1997. *A Study on Legal and Political Impediments to Gender Equality in Governance*, United Nations Development Programme.

Drage, J., 1994. 'The exception, not the rule—women's political activity in Pacific Island countries', in F. Alailima and W. vom Busch (eds), *New Politics in the South Pacific*, Institute of Pacific Studies, University of the South Pacific, Suva.

Durutalo, A.L., 1996. 'Social consequences of economic policy', in R. Grynberg (ed.), *Economic Prospects for the Pacific Islands in the 21st Century*, School of Social and Economic Development, University of the South Pacific, Suva.

——, 1997. Provincialism and the crisis of indigenous Fijian political unity, MA thesis, Centre for Development Studies, School of Social and Economic Development, University of the South Pacific, Suva (unpublished).

Durutalo, S., 1995. Internal colonialism and unequal regional development: the case of Western Viti Levu, MA thesis, University of the South Pacific, Suva (unpublished).

Easter, K., Dixon, J. and Hufschmidt, M., 1986. *Watershed Resource Management Integrated Framework with Studies from Asia and the Pacific Studies in Water Policy and Management*, No. 10, Westview Press, London.

Electoral Commission Report for 1 January, 1994 to 31 December, 1996. Parliamentary Paper No. 49, 1997, Parliament of Fiji, Suva.

Evening, C.S. 1983. *The 'West' Hurricane Oscar Fisheries Rehabilitation Program Report*, Fisheries Division, Lautoka.

Ewing, S.A., Grayson, R.B. and Argent, R.M. 1997. *Research Integration in ICM: review and discussion document*, CEAH Report No. 1, Centre for Environmental Applied Hydrology (CEAH), Melbourne.

Eyzaguirre, P., 1996. *Agriculture and Environmental Research in Small Countries—innovative approaches to strategic planning*, John Wiley & Sons, Brisbane.

Fairbairn, T.I.J., 1990. 'The environment and development planning in small Pacific Island countries', in W. Beller, P. d'Ayala and P. Hein (eds), *Sustainable Development and Environmental Management of Small Islands*, UNESCO and Parthenon Publishing Group, Paris.

Feder, G., 1987. 'Land ownership security and farm productivity: evidence from Thailand', *Journal of Development Studies*, 24:16–29.

Fiji, Central Planning Office, 1975. *DP7: Fiji's Seventh Development Plan, 1976–1980, Policies and Programs for Social and Economic Progress*, Suva.

——, 1980. *Fiji's Eighth Development Plan, 1981–1985: DP8 policies and plans for regional development*, Central Planning Office, Suva.

——, 1985. *Fiji's Ninth Development Plan, 1986–1990: DP9 policies, strategies and programs for national development*, Central Planning Office, Suva.

Fiji Bureau of Statistics, 1996. Statistical information, Fiji Bureau of Statistics, Suva.

Fiji Constitution Review Commission, 1996. *The Fiji Islands: towards a united future*, Parliamentary Paper 34, Government Printing Office, Suva.

France, P., 1969. *The Charter of the Land: custom and colonisation in Fiji*, Oxford University Press, London.

Fiji Sugar Commission (FSC), 1996. *Annual Report*, FSC, Lautoka.

——, 1998. *Annual Report*, FSC, Lautoka.

Government of Fiji, 1993. The national environment strategy, Government of Fiji, Suva (unpublished).

Government of the Republic of Fiji, 1993. *Opportunities for Growth: policies and strategies for Fiji in the medium term*, Parliamentary Paper No.2, Parliament of Fiji, Suva.

——, 1997a. *Development Strategy for Fiji: policies and programs for sustainable development*, Parliamentary Paper No.58, Parliament of Fiji, Suva.

——, 1997b. *Sustainable Development Bill*, Suva.

——, 1999a. *Economic and Fiscal Update: supplement to the 2000 Budget Address*, November, Suva.

——, 1999b. *Budget Estimates*, Suva.

——, 1999c. A strategic plan for the new century: policies and strategies for the sustainable development of Fiji, Suva (unpublished).

Grimble, R. and Wellard, K., 1997. 'Stakeholder methodologies in natural resource management: a review of principles, contexts, experiences and opportunities', *Agricultural Systems*, 55(2):173–93.

Hermann. R. and Weiss, D., 1995. 'A welfare analysis of EC-ACP Sugar Protocol', *The Journal of Development Studies*, 31(6):918–41.

Holling, C.S., 1995. 'What barriers? What bridges?', in L.H. Gunderson, C.S. Holling and S.S. Light (eds), *Barriers and Bridges to the Renewal of Ecosystems and Institutions*, Columbia University Press, New York:3–34.

Howard, M., 1991. *Fiji: race and politics in an Island state*, University of British Columbia Press, Vancouver.

Howard, M.C., 1989. State power and political change in Fiji, Paper presented to the Journal of Contemporary Asia Conference, Manila, 10–12 November.

Jakeman, A.J., Chaithawat, S., Attachi, J., Karn, T., Evans, J.P. and Wong, F., 1997. 'Biophysical component of an Integrated Water Resources Assessment Project in the Upper Chao Phraya Headwaters, Northern Thailand', *International Congress on Modelling and Simulation*, *(MODSIM 97)*, 2:687–91.

Joint Fisheries Strategy Mission, 1988. *Opportunity for Fisheries Development Assistance in the South Pacific*, a regional mission undertaken by FFA, SPC, UNDP, FAO, USAID and BDDP, Volumes 1 and 2.

Kailola, P.J., 1995. *Fisheries Development Fiji Review of Policies and Initiatives to Enhance Fisheries Management and Development in Fiji*, FAO, Rome.

Kamikamica, Josefata, 1997. 'Fijian native land: issues and challenges', in Brij V. Lal and Tomasi Vakatora (eds), *Fiji In Transition: research papers of the Fiji Constitution Review Commission*, School of Social and Economic Development, University of the South Pacific, Suva, Vol. 1:259–90.

King, G., Keohane, R.O. and Verba, S., 1994. *Designing Social Inquiry*, Princeton University Press, Princeton.

Lal, B.V., 1988. 'Before the storm: an analysis of the Fiji general election of 1987', *Pacific Studies*, 12(1):71–96.

——, 1992a. *Broken Waves: a history of Fiji in the twentieth century*, University of Hawaii Press, Honolulu.

——, 1992b. 'Rhetoric and reality: the dilemmas of contemporary Fijian politics', in Ron Crocombe Unetebo Neemia, Asesela Ravuvu and Werner vom Busch (eds), *Culture and Democracy in the South Pacific*, Institute of Pacific Studies, University of the South Pacific, Suva.

——, 1993. 'Chiefs and indians: elections and politics in contemporary Fiji', *The Contemporary Pacific: a journal of Island affairs*, 5(2):275–301.

——1997. 'Towards a united future: report of the Fiji Constitution Review Commission', *Journal of Pacific History*, 32(1):71–84.

——, 1998. *Another Way: the politics of constitutional review in post-coup Fiji*, Asia Pacific Press, Canberra.

Landell Mills Commodity Studies, 1991. *A Review of the Sugar Industry in Fiji*, Report prepared for the Sugar Commission of Fiji, Landell Mills Commodities Studies Inc., Time, Oxford.

——, 1998. The efficiency and competitiveness of the ACP sugar production, Paper presented at the Fifth Special Ministerial Conference on Sugar, Yanuca Island, Fiji, 15–19 June.

Lawson, S., 1991. *The Failure of Democratic Politics in Fiji*, Clarendon Press and Oxford University Press, New York and Oxford.

——, 1992. 'Constitutional change in Fiji: the apparatus of justification', *Ethnic and Racial Studies*, 15(1):61–83.

Leckie, J., n.d. Women in post-coup Fiji: negotiating old and new realities, unpublished manuscript.

Leweniqila, M., 1999. 'The purpose of CDF', *Fiji's Daily Post*, 20 April.

Liew, J., 1990. 'Sustainable development and environmental management of atolls', in W. Beller, P. d'Ayala and P. Hein (eds), *Sustainable Development and Environmental Management of Small Islands*, UNESCO and Parthenon Publishing Group, Paris.

Lundqvist, J., Lohm, U. and Falkenmark, M. (eds), 1985. *Strategies for River Basin Management: environmental integration of land and water in a river basin*, D. Reidel Publishing Co., Dordrecht.

MacAulay, G. and Owen, 1999. A spatial equilibrium model of the Australian dairy industry, Report prepared for the Dairy Research and Development Corporation, Department of Agricultural Economics, The University of Sydney, Sydney.

MacDonald, D., 1994. The Lomé Convention and the Sugar Protocol, Paper presented to the ESRC Development Economics Study Group 18 November, quoted in Prasad, Satendra and Akram-Lodhi, A.H., 1997. Towards 2010: the impacts of the sugar protocol on Fiji sugar industry, Paper prepared on behalf of the Fiji Sugar industry, Suva.

McHugh, D. and Philipson, P., 1988. *Post-Harvest Technology and Marketing of Cultured Eucheuma Seaweeds*, FFA Report, 88/2.

Mallawaarachchi, T., Lal, P., Janekarnkij, P., Punyawadee, V. and Wong, F., 1997. Economic analysis framework for integrated water resources assessment and management: case study of the upper Chao Phraya headwaters, Northern Thailand, MODSIM 97, International Congress on Modelling and Simulation, Hobart, Tasmania.

Mallawaarachchi, T. and Quiggin, J., 1999. Determining public welfare values in land allocation: a case study of the sugar industry in northern Australia, Paper presented to the 43rd Annual Conference of the Australian Agricultural and Resource Economics Society, Christchurch, 20–22 January.

Margerum, R., 1996. *Catchment Management in Australia: achievements and challenges*, Resource Policy, Centre for Water Policy Research, University of New England, Maine.

Maude, H.E. (ed.), 1989. *Tungaru Traditions: writings on the atoll culture of the Gilbert Islands/Arthur Francis Grimble*, University of Hawaii Press, Honolulu.

Ministry of Agriculture, Fisheries and Forests, 1995. *Fisheries Division Annual Report*, Ministry of Agriculture, Fisheries and Forests, Suva.

——, 1996. *Fisheries Division Annual Report*, Ministry of Agriculture, Fisheries and Forests, Suva.

——, 1996b. *Community Development Framework (CDF), Year 1997–Year 2000; Detail Commodity Annexes*, Ministry of Agriculture, Fisheries and Forests, Suva.

——, 1997. *Fisheries Division Annual Report*, Ministry of Agriculture, Fisheries and Forests, Suva.

Ministry of Finance, 2000. *Supplementary to the 2000 Budget: Fiji Government budget 2000*, Ministry of Finance, Suva.

Ministry of Women and Culture, 1998. *The Women's Plan of Action, 1999–2008*, Ministry of Women and Culture, Suva, 2 Volumes.

Muchow, R.C., Wood, A.W., Robertson, M.J. and Keating, B.A., 1997. 'Scope for vertical expansion in the Australian sugar industry', in A.K.L. Johnson, I.B. Robinson and M.K. Wegner (eds), *Coastal Queensland and the Sugar Industry—land use problems and opportunities*, Proceedings of a workshop, 41st Annual Conference of the Australian Agricultural and Resources Economics Society:26–32.

Murphy C., 1992. *Macroeconomic Model of Fiji*, Research School of Pacific Studies, The Australian National University, Canberra.

Nichols, E.H. and Moore, G.K.F., 1985. *Report of the Review of International Arrangements of the Commercial Fisheries Sector, Fiji 12 July–14 September*, FAO, Rome.

Norton, R., 1990. *Race and Politics in Fiji*, University of Queensland Press, St. Lucia.

——— , 1994. 'Ethnic conflict and accommodation in post-coup Fiji', *Communal/Plural*, 3:43–64.

———, 1998. 'Politics in Fiji', in R. Chandra (ed.), *Atlas of Fiji*, School of Social and Economic Development, University of the South Pacific, Suva.

———, 1999. 'Chiefs for the nation: containing ethnonationalism and bridging the ethnic divide in Fiji', *Pacific Studies*, 22(1):21–50.

———, 2000. 'Reconciling ethnicity and nation: contending discourses in the Fiji constitutional reform', *The Contemporary Pacific*, 12(1).

People's Coalition, 1999. *1999 General Elections Manifesto*, People's Coalition, Suva.

Pita, E., 1996. *Development of a Multidisciplinary Masterplan for the Sustainable Management and Development of Fiji's Inshore Fisheries Resources*, FAO, Rome.

Prasad, B.C and Tisdell, C., 1996. 'Getting property rights "right": land tenure in Fiji', *Pacific Economic Bulletin*, 11(1):31–46.

Prasad, S. and Akram-Lodhi, A.H., 1997. Towards 2010: the impacts of the Sugar Protocol on Fiji Sugar industry, Paper prepared on behalf of the Fiji Sugar industry, Suva.

Preston, G.L., 1997. *Review of Fishery Management Issues and Regimes in the Pacific Islands Region*, SPREP, SPC, FFA, Noumea.

RAC, 1993. *Resource Assessment Commission Coastal Zone Inquiry Information*, Paper No.6, Resource Assessment Commission, AGPS, Canberra.

Ravuvu, A., 1988. *Development or Dependence: the pattern of change in a Fijian village*, University of the South Pacific, Suva.

———, 1991. *The Facade of Democracy: Fijian struggles for political control, 1830–1987*, Reader Publishing Service, Suva.

Rawlinson, N.J.F., Milton, D.A., Blaber, S.J.M., Sesewa, A. and Sharma, S.P., 1995. *A Survey of the Subsistence and Artisanal Fisheries in the Rural Area of Viti Levu*, Fisheries Division, Ministry of Agriculture, Forests and Fisheries, Cleveland, CSIRO, Suva.

Reddy, M., 1998. Production economics analysis of Fiji's sugar industry, PhD dissertation, University of Hawaii, Honolulu (unpublished).

Reeves, P., Vakatora, T. and Lal, B., 1996. *The Fiji Islands: towards a united future*, Report of the Fiji Constitution Review Commission, Parliamentary Paper of Suva, No.34 of 1996, Parliament of Fiji, Suva.

Reserve Bank of Fiji, 1999. *Quarterly Bulletin*, Reserve Bank of Fiji, Suva.

Richards, A., Lagibalavu, M., Sharma, S. and Swamy, K., 1994. *Fiji Fisheries Resources Profiles*, FFA Report No.94/4.

Rigamoto, W.G., 1999. The 1999 general elections—assessment and reflections, Paper presented to the Citizen's Constitutional Forum seminar, Elections Watch: citizens review of the 1999 general elections, The University of the South Pacific, Suva, 17 July.

Roberts, I., 1997. *Australia and the Next Multilateral Trade Negotiations for Agriculture*, ABARE Research Report, 97.6, Canberra.

Robertson, R.T., 1998. *Multiculturalism and Reconciliation in an Indulgent Republic: Fiji after the coups, 1987–1998*, Fiji Institute of Applied Sciences, Suva.

Roth, G.K. (ed.), 1953. *Fijian Way of Life*, Oxford University Press, Melbourne.

Routledge, D., 1975. *Matanitu: the struggle for power in early Fiji*, Institute of Pacific Studies, The University of the South Pacific, Suva.

SCOF (Sugar Commission of Fiji), 1997a. *Industry Strategic Plan—Changing Attitudes: implementing best practice for a new world trade*, SCOF, Lautoka.

——, 1997b. *Industry Strategic Plan—Action Plans, 1997–2000*, SCOF, Lautoka.

Shepard, M. and Clark, L.G., 1984. South Pacific Fisheries Development Assistance Needs: opportunities for participation by UNDP, FAO, and other donors interested in supporting South Pacific fisheries development, Vol. 1, (unpublished).

South Pacific Commission, 1994. *Twenty-fifth Regional Technical Meeting on Fisheries, The Present Status of Coastal Fisheries Production in the South Pacific Islands*, Working Paper at the 25th Regional Technical Meeting on Fisheries, SPC Fisheries, 28 February.

Sturton, M., 1989. *Modelling the Fiji Economy*, Research Report Series No 12, Pacific Islands Development Program, East–West Centre, Honolulu.

Sugar Cane Research Centre, 1995. *Annual Report*, FSC, Lautoka.

——, 1996. *Annual Report*, FSC, Lautoka.

——, 1998. *Annual Report*, FSC, Lautoka.

Sutherland, W., 1992. *Beyond the Politics of Race*, Political and Social Change Monograph 15, Department of Political and Social Change, Research School of Pacific Studies, The Australian National University, Canberra.

Szabo, A. and Herman, T., 1984. *Proposal for the Development of the Small-Scale Fisheries Cooperative Sector*, Report on a Consultancy Mission, April 18–May 18.

Tabor, S.R. and Faber, D.C., 1998. *Closing the Look: from research on natural resources to policy change*, International Service for National Agricultural Research (ISNAR), Policy Management Report No. 8.

Teaiwa, K., (forthcoming). 'Banaban history and postcolonial realities', *Indigenous Affairs*, International Working Group for Indigenous Affairs, Copenhagen.

Vakatora, T., 1999. *From the Mangrove Swamps*, Suva (privately published, revised ed.)

Veitayaki, J., Ram-Bidesi, V., Matthews, E. and Ballou, A., 1996. *Preliminary Baseline Survey of Marine Resources of Kaba Point, Fiji*, Marine Studies Technical Report, 96/1.

Walker, A., Scoccimarro, M., Dietrich, C., Schreider, S., Jakeman, T. and Ross, H., 1999. 'A framework for integrated catchment assessment in northern Thailand', *Environmental Modelling and Software Journal*, 14(6):567–77.

Wallace, M.G., Cortner, H.J., Moote, M.A. and Sabrina, B. 1996. 'Moving toward ecosystem management: examining a change in philosophy for resource management', *Journal of Political Ecology*, (3):1–36.

World Bank, 1995. *Fiji: restoring growth in a changing global environment*, The World Bank, Washington, DC.

Index

www.ingramcontent.com/pod-product-compliance
Lightning Source LLC
Chambersburg PA
CBHW041120280326
41928CB00061B/3462